Intellectual Privacy

INTELLECTUAL PRIVACY

RETHINKING CIVIL LIBERTIES IN THE DIGITAL AGE

NEIL RICHARDS

OXFORD
UNIVERSITY PRESS

OXFORD
UNIVERSITY PRESS

Oxford University Press is a department of the University of
Oxford. It furthers the University's objective of excellence in research,
scholarship, and education by publishing worldwide.

Oxford   New York
Auckland   Cape Town   Dar es Salaam   Hong Kong   Karachi
Kuala Lumpur   Madrid   Melbourne   Mexico City   Nairobi
New Delhi   Shanghai   Taipei   Toronto

With offices in
Argentina   Austria   Brazil   Chile   Czech Republic   France   Greece
Guatemala   Hungary   Italy   Japan   Poland   Portugal   Singapore
South Korea   Switzerland   Thailand   Turkey   Ukraine   Vietnam

Oxford is a registered trademark of Oxford University Press
in the UK and certain other countries.

Published in the United States of America by
Oxford University Press
198 Madison Avenue, New York, NY 10016

Library of Congress Cataloging-in-Publication Data
Richards, Neil.
Intellectual privacy : rethinking civil liberties in the digital age / Neil Richards.
pages cm
ISBN 978-0-19-994614-3 (hardback)
1. Privacy, Right of.   2. Freedom of speech.   3. Intellectual freedom.   I. Title.
K3263.R53 2015
342.08'58—dc23
2014021682

1 3 5 7 9 8 6 4 2
Printed in the United States of America
on acid-free paper

For Wendy

CONTENTS

PART III. Information Policy and Civil Liberties

ACKNOWLEDGMENTS

THIS BOOK IS the product of my thinking, writing, and teaching about privacy, free speech, technology, and the history of civil liberties for the past decade. It has only been possible to write thanks to the generosity of many colleagues, friends, and family.

That I ever came to be a law professor in the first place is a debt I owe to many former teachers and professors of law and history, some of whom I am now lucky enough to count as friends. They taught me, first and foremost, the importance of critical thinking and clear writing, values of special importance to the exercise of the civil liberties this book is about. I am indebted to too many of them to mention, but especially to Richard McAdams, Lillian BeVier, Beth Garrett, Jack Goldsmith, Dick Howard, John Harrison, Mike Klarman, Chuck McCurdy, and Peter Onuf.

I was also fortunate to work early in my career for two truly eminent jurists, Judge Paul Niemeyer and the late Chief Justice William Rehnquist. They were role models of what lawyers and judges should be in every sense, and their intelligence and deep-rooted professionalism made a deep impression on me early in my career. We may not always have agreed on the answers to the legal questions before their courts (in fact, we frequently didn't!), but it was a true honor to have served each of them as their law clerk.

I am incredibly grateful that I have been able to work with current and former colleagues at Washington University, a university with a vibrant interdisciplinary community of generous and brilliant scholars. At the risk of omission, for repeated support and engagement with the ideas in this book, I must especially thank Sam Buell, Deborah Dinner, John Inazu, Pauline Kim, Frank Lovett, Ian MacMullen, Greg Magarian, Andrew Rehfeld, Kent Syverud, and Brian Tamanaha.

Beyond my home institution, the past decade has seen the birth of a generous, thoughtful, and fun community of privacy, technology, and First Amendment law scholars in the United States and Britain. I could not begin to count the number of times conversations with colleagues and friends at workshops, conferences, or just over a beer have improved my understanding of the complex problems of civil liberties in our digital age. Many, many thanks to Anita Allen, Jack Balkin, the late Ed Baker, Vince Blasi, Marc Blitz, danah boyd, Ryan Calo, Danielle Citron, Julie Cohen, Deven Desai, Amy Gajda, Mark Graber, Woody Hartzog, Kirsty Hughes, Leslie Kendrick, Paul Ohm, Gavin Phillipson, Joel Reidenberg, Paul Schwartz, Dan Solove, Lior Strahilevitz, Peter Winn, and Tim Zick. The book also benefited greatly from the input of these and other scholars at workshops at the University of Cambridge, Durham University, the University of Edinburgh, Fordham Law School's Center on Law and Information Policy, Duke Law School, Washington University School of Law, the Washington University Political Theory Workshop, Amherst College, Berkeley Law School, Harvard Law School, the University of Maryland School of Law, a "tech talk" at Google, Inc., and the annual Privacy Law Scholars Conference at Berkeley and George Washington University. I am also grateful for many conversations about how privacy law and technology really work with Jonathan King and Chris Wolf, professionals who combine the curiosity of academics with the skills and attention to detail of practitioners, and who encouraged me to write for a broader audience.

A large group of Washington University law students have helped me with my research over the years. Special thanks to Aaron Block, Matthew Cin, Joanna Cornwell, Megan Dredla, Ananth Iyengar, Bryan Lammon, Jay Lee, Andrew Nash, Chini Bose, and Matt Venezia. Special thanks must also go to Jim Stanley, who worked with me for many years as an undergraduate and law student, and who I am now delighted to call my friend, even though he supports Arsenal.

I must also thank my editor Dave McBride at Oxford University Press, who believed in this project from the beginning and whose advice and counsel have made this a much better book than it otherwise would have been. Sarah Rosenthal at OUP was also very helpful in shepherding it through the editorial and production process.

I owe a great debt to family on both sides of the Atlantic. My grandfather George Richards nurtured my love of history when I was a very little boy by pushing me around the park in Widnes in my pram and telling me stories of his service in the British Army during the Second World War. My extended family in England and Wales have always welcomed me home with open arms, love, and good food and drink. Don and Peggie Niece have welcomed me into their American family as a second set of parents, and have been spectacular grandparents to our children. My parents, Peter and Pauline Richards, taught me to love reading and learning, and always to question. The greatest regret that I have about this book is that my Mum is no longer alive to read it.

Without the support of my immediate family, this book would have remained merely a good intention. My children put work in perspective, and they continually remind me of the importance of the future, and the magic and wonder of learning to read. Declan has always been eager to distract me from my work with a "quick game of footy" in the back garden or in the house. Fiona's greatest contribution to this book was her comment that intellectual privacy was important "so me and Declan can read inappropriate books." I hope you both will read inappropriate books (including this one), but not until you are older.

Wendy has been my biggest supporter, smartest and most constructive critic, first reader and last proofreader throughout this project. She put up with the various moods and neuroses this project created, and she has loved and helped me in incalculable ways for over twenty years. She is my best friend and the love of my life. It is to her that this book is dedicated.

Intellectual Privacy

Introduction

IT WAS ONE part James Bond and one part Benny Hill, and the spies called it "Operation Optic Nerve." A pilot project of British Intelligence, Optic Nerve captured and stored millions of still images of the webcams of ordinary people using Yahoo Messenger. The images were stored in bulk and archived in agency computers for future use. The scale of Optic Nerve's capture was breathtaking—in one month in 2008 the program collected webcam images from 1.8 million users across the globe, one image taken from each active webcam every five minutes. These would have included a wide variety of activities from people's offices, living rooms, and bedrooms—grandparents adoring new baby grandchildren, business videoconferencing, academics or journalists in different countries talking with colleagues or sources, and traveling parents calling home from business trips to say goodnight to their children. Optic Nerve's window into our lives also captured lots and lots of sex. As one internal document put it in a characteristically British way, "unfortunately... it would appear that a surprising number of people use webcam conversations to show intimate parts of their body to the other person."[1] This included professional "cam girls" performing digital peep shows and more graphic sex acts, as well as intimacies between separated lovers and spouses.

We don't know exactly why Optic Nerve pried into our personal and professional lives. It may have had something to do with terrorism, though the bulk capture of everyone's images means that only a miniscule fraction—if any—of the images had anything to do with that. It may also have been a study of facial recognition technology, as these tools work best when presented with a face, from the front, of the sort common in webcam conversations. All we know is what the documents said: "Yahoo webcam is known to be used by GCHQ targets."[2] By that logic, of course, so is everything else in the world—telephones, planes, iPads, and shoes. So the next time you use a device with a camera—whether it's your laptop, your tablet, your iPhone, or your Xbox-equipped TV—be sure to smile, because you never know who might be watching.

Optic Nerve is hardly the only recent example of webcam surveillance. In 2010 a Pennsylvania school district installed remote monitoring software on 2,300 MacBooks issued to students, which was used to capture images of the children at home, often sleeping or partially dressed, along with transcripts of their web-surfing and online chats.[3] The software also contained a security hole that would have allowed others to remotely control the computer, monitoring, or photographing of the students.[4] The school district eventually settled lawsuits brought by victims of the monitoring,[5] but webcam hacking is also regrettably common. YouTube is full of videos recorded by "ratters," hackers who use software techniques like the Remote Administration Tool (RAT) to hijack the computers of remote users and record the mayhem they create. The victims of such hacks are known as "slaves," and the videos depict their stunned reactions overlaid on video of their desktop as shocking, pornographic, or just plain weird images get displayed on their computers.[6]

How did we get to a place where our communications and reading behavior are so visible to others? The answer in part is that we are living through an intellectual revolution. For hundreds of years, the technologies we've used to communicate have been based on paper—the letter, the newspaper, and the book. But in our lifetimes, these technologies have been supplemented and increasingly supplanted by electronic versions—the email, the web page, and the e-book. Computers now mediate the ways we read, write, and think. The embrace of digital platforms has been an undeniable force for good, enabling almost anyone with a networked computer or mobile phone to read widely and speak to the world instantaneously. Yet even as these technologies enable new forms of learning and expression, they have been designed to create a data trail for each of us of what we think, read, and say privately.

Consider the records that Google has of your web searches: records of your wonderings, musings, and fantasies. Or the records your email provider has of your communications, or a cloud company has of your documents. Or consider Facebook or other social networks, which allow us to gossip and post photos and videos of other people. Searching and sharing are undeniably cool, but they have a potential dark side. In 2006 most of the major search engines turned over millions of user search requests to a government agency investigating online obscenity. In 2010 Rutgers University student Tyler Clementi killed himself after a secretly captured video of his sexual activities was shared online. And in 2011, during the "Arab Spring," social media technologies and the intellectual records they created were the source of vibrant political dissent; they thus became a new target for political censorship and surveillance by oppressive states. How should we think about these new technologies and forms of information? What should we do with them? And what must we not do with them?

While we're being dazzled by the latest gadgets and digital toys of the intellectual revolution, something important is being lost. The novelist Zadie Smith has warned that "in the Anglo-American world we race ahead with technology and hope the ideas will look after themselves."[7] Our ideas and values must keep pace with our technological revolution. Today our intellectual technologies are in flux, but soon they will stabilize. When that happens, we will start to view the haphazard world they have created as normal and natural. We need to think through the values our technologies encode before it is too late.

So what are those values? We typically think of questions of monitoring and personal information as involving our right to privacy. Questions of speaking, sharing, and spreading of information involve our right to free speech. But we're often confused about how to think about these concepts and how to apply them. We also tend to see them as naturally in conflict, forcing us into a difficult decision to choose just one. In the digital age, both our confusion about these ideas and their conflict seem to have increased. Must we choose between privacy and speech? Must we have one or the other? Is privacy dead?

Put simply, no. But we need to be clearer by what we mean by both "privacy" and "speech." We need to think more deeply about the complexity of these two values, what they mean, what they do for us, and the surprising, mutually reinforcing relationships between them.

This is a book about law, and about big ideas in legal theory. It's about different ways of thinking about privacy, freedom of speech, and other civil liberties. And it's about how we can fit them together to make our society better (or worse). These are serious and important topics, but it's precisely because they matter that I have tried to set them out as clearly as possible. When it comes to the future of our digital civil liberties, we can't just leave the solutions to experts. We all need to understand what is at stake and why it matters, and we all need to be part of the solution.

For over a century, the law in the United States and in Britain has treated speech and privacy as conflicting values. This was the case when legal scholars Louis Brandeis and Samuel Warren called for a "right to be let alone" by the press in 1890, and it is true in some of the most recent cases involving databases, blogs, and new social media. The rise of the Internet—in which anyone with a networked device can speak to the world—has unsettled many traditional norms, including how we think about privacy and free speech. But these issues are everywhere throughout our society, from questions about Facebook's privacy practices to block-buster First Amendment and surveillance cases before the Supreme Court. What does it mean to have privacy in an increasingly digital society? What kinds of rights should we have—not only to speak but also to control or participate in the communication of information about us? Who can read our diaries, our emails, and our search logs? Does privacy still have relevance, or has it gone the way of telegrams, typewriters, and vinyl records? This book is the product of my thinking and writing over the past decade, trying to come to grips with these issues and propose new solutions to these timeless and timely problems.

Despite the complexity of privacy, speech, and the Internet, my argument boils down to two simple ideas. First, I suggest that when free speech and traditional notions of privacy conflict, free speech should almost always win. Warren and Brandeis thought of privacy as a tort action against newspaper gossip causing emotional harm. Their idea that privacy and speech are in conflict has framed how we think about privacy in the legal system and in the wider world. But as I will show, the Warren and Brandeis argument for tort privacy was flawed even on its own terms in 1890. Over a century later, their argument is inconsistent with a society committed to free speech and robust public debate. Our commitment to free speech means we must reject their argument in almost all cases.

Yet we don't need to give up on privacy altogether. The First Amendment limits on privacy aren't absolute. Tort privacy is a poor vehicle for protecting against hurtful speech and disclosures of information, but other legal tools can be more effective. We just need to think more creatively. Confidentiality law, consumer protection law, anti-stalking and anti-threat laws, and more nuanced use of privacy torts can all play a role in the digital environment. Preserving both free speech and privacy requires us to define both carefully, but we can have meaningful protection of our personal data without sacrificing our commitment to free speech.

The second simple idea in this book is that privacy and free speech are not always in conflict. In fact, a specific kind of privacy is *necessary* to protect our cherished civil liberties of free speech and thought. I'll call this second kind of privacy "intellectual privacy." Intellectual privacy is protection from surveillance or interference when we are engaged in the processes of generating ideas—thinking, reading, and speaking with confidants before our ideas are ready for public consumption. Law has protected intellectual privacy indirectly in the past. But the digital revolution in the way we think and speak has raised the stakes. More and more, the acts of reading, thinking, and private communication are mediated by electronic technologies, including personal computers, tablets, e-books, and smartphones. Whenever we shop, read, speak, and think, we now do so using computers that create records of these activities.

Your ISP, for instance, has records of every website you've visited—a virtual transcript of your intellectual explorations, of your reading and thinking. And many powerful entities, from Facebook to the National Security Agency, have shown an interest in our intellectual records—our reading habits, web-surfing habits, and private communications. Surveillance or interference of our reading and thinking can drive it to the average, the mainstream, and the boring. And in a world of "multiveillance"—surveillance not just by the state but by companies, marketers, and those in our social networks—we need to reconsider the ways we allow monitoring and access.

If we are interested in the development of new ideas and new, original speech, we must safeguard the processes of intellectual explorations and belief formation by providing a meaningful guarantee of intellectual privacy. Once we jettison the old way of thinking about privacy as always in conflict with free speech, we can see the need to protect our ancient values of free minds and free speech in the modern digital age.

Intellectual privacy is an important piece of that protection, especially when it shields the freedom of thought, the freedom to read freely, and the confidentiality of communications. Taken together, such overlapping and mutually supporting protections can help incubate new ideas in their formative stages. Privacy and speech are not always opposed, and I will show how we can think more carefully and more clearly about the problems of information, to ensure meaningful protection of both vital civil liberties.

Technology and Human Values (and Brandeis)

My argument in this book is about the new and the old. It's about some of our newest technologies—the Internet, electronic readers, large databases, and hand-held smartphones. But it's also about some of our oldest values—our rights to free speech and privacy, free thought, free belief, and free association. There is a tension here that sometimes pulls us in both directions at once—forward into the digital future and backward into the mists of time. But this tension is, I believe, essential.

We are told that the Internet changes everything; that we face the end of history, or as technologist Ray Kurzweil puts it apocalyptically, a "Singularity."[8] I disagree. In this book, I'll make the case that the values we see advanced, encoded, and often threatened in our new digital future are *human values*—ones like individualism, democracy, and autonomy—that have been refined and reevaluated for centuries. They are values that matter; they are our political and philosophical heritage, and we should not put them aside without good reason. Our new technologies certainly change the terms of the debate; they are altering the ways we interact with one another and possibly even the ways that we think and speak. But I believe that there is wisdom in the past if we know where to look. The project of civil liberties in a digital age should adapt that wisdom to our new electronic horizons, instead of creating them anew. Adaptation certainly means change, but I will try to show that our old human values must continue to play an important role in how we deal with one another in the decades to come, whether our interactions are "real," "virtual," or some combination of the two.

Our civil liberties of privacy and free speech are the product of a rich humanist tradition to which many men and women have contributed over the years and across cultures. But in the pages that follow one man in particular plays a special part, because his contributions lie at the core of each of this book's two major themes. Louis Brandeis is well known as the father of American privacy law. His 1890 article with his friend Samuel Warren, *The Right to Privacy*, is the seminal text of American privacy law, the document that introduced privacy as a legal concept and gave it intellectual heft and credibility. Unsurprisingly, most accounts of privacy today still begin with Brandeis and Warren.

But Brandeis's thinking evolved over the course of his life, and he came to be deeply ambivalent about *The Right to Privacy*. He almost immediately began to embrace the somewhat contradictory idea that public disclosure of many kinds of fraud and wrongdoing is in the public interest. As he famously put it, "sunlight ... is the best of disinfectants."[9] Brandeis also changed his mind about the importance of free speech. Although he had not been a strong believer in free speech as a young lawyer, he thought deeply about the importance of free speech after the First World War. He also came to believe that a robust free press was essential for a democratic state, and that the excesses of expression had to be tolerated rather than suppressed. Although he never repudiated tort privacy, by the end of his life, Brandeis had moved to a position on publicity and free speech that was inconsistent with a broad reading of the tort theory of *The Right to Privacy*.

But Brandeis's partial rejection of tort privacy is not the most important part of the story. His later writings reveal a commitment to intellectual privacy. Late in his life, he penned a second major contribution to privacy—his dissent in *Olmstead v. United States*. This introduced modern concepts of privacy into constitutional law. It led to the "reasonable expectation of privacy" test governing Fourth Amendment law,[10] and shaped the constitutional right to privacy recognized in *Griswold v. Connecticut* and *Roe v. Wade*.[11]

In *Olmstead* and his free speech writings, Brandeis suggested subtle ways in which privacy and First Amendment values could be related. Privacy of thought and private discussion, he argued, are essential foundations for meaningful First Amendment liberties. Free speech thus requires some measure of intellectual privacy to be effective. These connections have been overlooked in the past, but they have important implications for modern civil liberties. In the Information Age, Brandeis's forgotten ideas have enormous potential to change the ways we think about information, speech, and privacy. And to change them for the better.

But let me be clear: While Brandeis' writings suggest a way forward, we must chart that path forward ourselves. We should embrace intellectual privacy because it is valuable, not merely because Brandeis suggested it. Our human values are ones we must choose, and shape, ourselves, for our own time.

A Note on "Privacy" and "Free Speech"

Before we get too deeply into the details of my argument, I want to say a word about the two big ideas of "privacy" and "free speech." When talking about online tracking, expression, and information-sharing, writers sometimes throw these words around without thinking about or explaining what they mean. I think it's important to be clear up front about what these ideas are, since confusion about what they are and what values they serve is at the root of much of our societal unease.

One of the most difficult (and frustrating) things about privacy is that it has a bewildering variety of meanings. Sometimes it seems as if privacy can mean almost anything—from information collection by Facebook, to lawsuits against the press for publishing celebrity sex gossip, to misuses of personal information leading to identity theft, to "big data" analysis, to the use of wiretaps by the police to investigate crime, to the ability to enjoy dinnertime at home without a telemarketer calling. In our everyday uses of the English language, and in the technical language of law, the word "privacy" has been used to mean each of these examples and more besides. We employ it to mean a wide variety of different things, so our use of it often lacks precision. But if "privacy" can mean almost anything, then it will mean almost nothing in practice.

Scholars of privacy across disciplines have struggled to define the term, groping around with definitions that were too narrow or too broad, or giving up hope of defining it altogether. For many years, privacy lawyers used to think of privacy as the ability to control information about yourself, which captured many, but not most, uses of the term.[12]

But privacy law scholars found the looseness of privacy as control over information limiting, and sought more precise understandings of what we mean when we say "privacy." In recent years, many scholars have settled on an understanding of privacy as an umbrella term that encompasses a variety of related meanings. Sociologist Gary Marx, for example, argues that rather than trying to define privacy, we should understand it as "a family of concepts encompassing personal information."[13] Philosopher Helen Nissenbaum has argued that we should understand privacy as "Contextual Integrity." Under this view, information is always flowing, but we take certain flows and restrictions for granted. Only when the norms governing the appropriate flows of information are violated, Nissenbaum argues, do we experience a violation of privacy in context.[14]

Other scholars have sought to pin down more specifically what we mean by "privacy." In a 2005 article, I argued that when talking about conflicts between privacy and the First Amendment, we must distinguish among four different ways privacy rules can affect information flows— the collection, use, and disclosure of data, and invasions of privacy based upon that data.[15] Law professor Daniel Solove has offered a more developed theory along these lines, taking Marx's notion of family associations, and expanding my four categories into a full-blown taxonomy of privacy with sixteen separate subcategories including surveillance, interrogation, aggregation, and disclosure.[16] Solove argues that privacy is a related group of problems that share family resemblances. Moreover, he warns that we should worry less about precise definitions of privacy and focus instead "on the specific activities that pose privacy problems."[17]

Privacy is certainly both varied and contextual. I will not attempt here to advance a definition of privacy that is good for all seasons. But "privacy law" is a requirement that people who use, collect, or disclose information must act in a certain way with it. Privacy law is the conclusion that some boundary between ourselves and others must be respected in a certain way, depending on the context. Solove and Marx are correct that we mean many distinct but related things when we talk about "privacy." But there is a danger in calling privacy varied and contextual and leaving it at that. If privacy is a general umbrella term encompassing related concepts, scholars must define the more specific concepts. This book tries to do that for two of them—tort privacy and intellectual privacy.

"Free speech" is easier to understand than privacy, but it also has ambiguous meanings. In the United States, most people associate freedom of speech with the First Amendment to the Constitution. The Supreme Court has interpreted the First Amendment broadly to prevent the government from censoring our speech, punishing us directly for its content, or creating legal rules that allow us to be sued for speaking the truth. In the United States, freedom of speech enjoys unusual protection, even when compared to other Western democracies. But beneath the surface level of protection, there is less agreement about *why* free speech should receive such special treatment. Courts and scholars have developed numerous theories about why free speech is special, but three theories have been truly influential. Most important is the idea that free speech contributes to the processes of *democratic self-government*, an idea associated with the writings of James Madison, Louis Brandeis, and Alexander Meiklejohn.[18] Under this view, self-governing citizens need to hear the information and viewpoints shared by others in order to make sensible decisions in the democratic process about how society should be governed. A second theory justifies giving free speech special protection because it contributes to the *search for truth*, a theory that was popularized by Justice Oliver Wendell Holmes Jr., but which builds on the ideas of John Milton and John Stuart Mill.[19] Finally, some scholars argue that we should protect free speech because it promotes individual *autonomy* or the self-fulfillment of individuals.[20] Although each of these theories is reflected in American First Amendment law, no single theory explains the case law. Although there is a broad consensus that courts should protect free speech, digging a little deeper makes the question of why we protect speech a much more complicated one.

My point in this analysis is to reveal the conceptual mess we face at the intersection of privacy and free speech at the dawn of the twenty-first century. We are pretty sure that privacy is important, but don't know what it means or what it does for us with any specificity. We are more sure that free speech is special, but while we can agree that we should protect it, we can't agree precisely why. At the same time, technology is revolutionizing (and undermining) both values. In situations like these, we must tread carefully. We must be clear about what we mean and why it matters. As the information revolution gains pace, these questions will take on ever-increasing importance. This is the challenge I will take up in the pages that follow—not just to argue how we should protect privacy and speech, but to show why we should protect them, and what that protection should look like.

A Roadmap

Having introduced the major themes of my argument, a roadmap is in order. This book is divided into three parts, each dealing with one of three big ideas—tort privacy, intellectual privacy, and information policy.

Part I is about the conflict between free speech and the idea of privacy that law has used in the past—Warren and Brandeis's idea of tort privacy rights against press disclosures of the truth. The basic argument of part I is that our existing framework of "tort privacy" protecting personal information against disclosure is flawed—it is limited in theory and ineffective in practice. But I argue that even though tort privacy is limited, it does not follow that regulation of information or protection of other forms of privacy is impossible. In a digital age, we must be able to collectively make a choice about what kind of information society we want.

Part II reimagines the relationship between speech and privacy in a more radical way altogether. The tort privacy model treats privacy and free speech as conflicting values, as if having more privacy always requires a tradeoff of less free speech. Part II shows that this view of the relationship between privacy and speech is incomplete and misleading. It illustrates how privacy and free speech are often related, and how a meaningful amount of privacy—what I call "intellectual privacy"—is essential to a robust culture of free expression. Intellectual privacy is different from tort privacy, because it is the privacy necessary to produce speech, rather than a privacy protecting against injury from unwanted speech. I show how intellectual privacy has three essential elements—freedom of thought, the right to read freely, and the right to communicate in confidence—and how each of these rights is being destabilized by digital technologies.

Part III takes the insights of the book's arguments about tort and intellectual privacy and sketches out some ways in which we can better promote freedom of speech and thought in the digital age, while still allowing room for government regulation of the trade in commercial information. The digital revolution is a challenge to our legal and policy imagination, and imaginative answers are needed. Drawing on parts I and II, part III suggests a few of those answers. I argue that we can protect the interests of personal privacy, but we must look beyond the disclosure tort and even tort privacy to do so. I argue that we must build protection for intellectual privacy into our law, and I suggest five ways we can do that. I also show how law will not be enough to solve the problems of our intellectual revolution. In an information age, a civil libertarian culture and information ethics will be necessary, and I suggest ways to build such a human, ethical culture into our digital networked future.

PART I

The Limits of Tort Privacy

I

Tort Privacy

Warren (and Warren) and Brandeis

The right to privacy wasn't Louis Brandeis's idea. As he told his official biographer, "[t]his, like so many of my public activities, I did not volunteer to do."[1] Brandeis's involvement in the creation of privacy law was just a favor for a friend; a favor whose deep ironies continue to limit how we think about privacy today.

The right to privacy in America began instead with Mabel Warren. Born Mabel Bayard, Mabel was a member of one of Delaware's oldest and most aristocratic families. The Bayards were a political dynasty as well— Mabel's great-grandfather, grandfather, father, and brother all served as United States senators. And in the eyes of upper-class Washington society, Mabel was one of the great family's jewels. Henry James described her as a "happy specimen of the finished American girl—the American girl who has profited by the sort of social education that Washington gives."[2] Mabel was a star of the Washington elite. She was also proud, class-conscious, and deeply anti-Semitic.[3]

On January 25, 1883, twenty-one-year-old Mabel married Samuel D. Warren, a young lawyer from a powerful Boston family. The Warrens were Brahmins, part of Boston's ruling elite, and the owners of a successful family paper business.[4] Sam was their heir. The wedding was a highly anticipated society event, held at the Church of the Ascension in Washington and attended by the ambassadors of Russia, Denmark, Argentina, Portugal, and Spain. The *Washington Post* called it the "marriage of the season," and the *New York Times* covered it with three paragraphs on its front page.[5]

Notably absent from the wedding guest list was Sam's best friend and law partner, Louis Dembitz Brandeis. Brandeis was neither a Brahmin nor a Bostonian by birth; his parents were middle-class Jewish immigrants from Germany who had settled in Louisville, Kentucky, to start a textile business. Sam and Louis met at Harvard Law School and struck up a friendship that transcended region, religion, and class. When Louis suffered from a severe eye strain that threatened to end his studies, Sam read his assignments to him to preserve his vision. By graduation, Louis was first in the class, with grades that would not be duplicated in his lifetime; Sam was ranked second behind him.[6] Louis practiced briefly in St. Louis for his uncle's law firm before accepting Sam's offer to join him in starting a firm in Boston. Today, he would be a logical wedding guest, even a best man. But in nineteenth-century genteel society, the wife's family controlled the wedding guest list. And their anti-Semitism excluded Louis because of his religion. After her wedding, the new Mrs. Mabel Warren would continue to do all she could to keep Louis out of their home.[7]

Though Louis was rarely involved, the Warrens' social activities remained a matter of press interest in the years that followed. They appeared in the papers over sixty more times in the 1880s. The society pages occasionally featured details of their dinner parties and other engagements. The Warrens may have found this distasteful, but they were even more dismayed at other stories in which they featured. The press covered (occasionally sensationally) the sudden deaths and funerals of Mabel's mother and sister in 1886. The same year, it also covered Mabel's friendship with Frances Folsom, an old family friend who married President Grover Cleveland. When the pair wed after a three-year courtship, Frances was just twenty-two. President Cleveland was fifty, a fact the papers noted with keen interest.[8]

Privacy was very much in the air in 1890, as elites like the Warrens felt the threat to their social position posed by a new generation of newspaper reporters. Writing for the newly affluent middle classes and armed with new cameras that could take pictures instantaneously, the "Yellow Press" blurred settled lines between public and private. In June, the *New York Times* reported that opera star Marion Manola had obtained an injunction after a photograph of her taken on stage wearing tights was used by a theater promoter for publicity.[9] In July, E. L. Godkin, editor of *The*

Nation, argued that the rise of the Yellow Press required greater protection for what he called "the right to privacy." This was a person's right "to decide how much knowledge of his personal thought and feeling, and how much knowledge, therefore, of his tastes and habits, of his own private doings and affairs, and those of his family living under his own roof, the public at large shall have."[10]

Godkin's essay was part of a wave of privacy anxiety sweeping the Gilded Age's upper classes. Some of their concern was technological. Innovations like the new portable Kodak camera allowed photography almost anywhere, not just in the controlled studios of professional photographers. But there was deep-seated class anxiety at work as well. Established Victorian elites felt their social status and control in doubt as literate urban lower classes challenged their authority. They saw their social control eroding, as disrespectful reporters scrutinized life inside their townhouses in pursuit of a scoop.[11]

Encouraged by Mabel, Warren sought out Brandeis to write an article about the excesses of the press and the need for a legal right to privacy.[12] Both men recalled later that it was Warren's "deep-seated abhorrence" about invasions of his "social privacy" that caused him to enlist Brandeis's help.[13] Their article on privacy law was actually their third scholarly project. As active Harvard Law alumni, the two friends had helped found the Harvard Law School Association in 1886, upon whose heels the *Harvard Law Review* was established early the next year.[14] To help the fledgling student journal get off the ground, Warren and Brandeis gave financial support and also copy for it to publish. In 1888 and again in 1889, they wrote articles on the obscure topic of "pond law." One cause for their scholarly collaborations was that they missed each other. Louis was still largely excluded from the Warren home, and Sam had reluctantly left their law firm to run the family paper business on the death of his father.

Warren and Brandeis worked on their article through the summer of 1890, and the fruits of their labors were published in the *Harvard Law Review* as *The Right to Privacy* in December.[15] The result was far more successful than their intervention in pond law. The essay argued that the common law should protect a right to privacy. It came to define not just the field of privacy law but also popular understandings of what privacy means. It was as brilliant as it was loose with the existing Anglo-American legal precedent, which did not really protect a right to privacy after all.[16]

A lot has been written about *The Right to Privacy*, but three choices Warren and Brandeis made in building their argument affected the story of tort privacy in American law. These choices matter because they brought Warren and Brandeis's privacy creation into conflict with free speech. As we will see, this conflict is not inevitable, but Warren and Brandeis created a conflict when they (1) chose to focus on emotional harm, (2) targeted the press and public debate, and (3) urged courts to police a line between what was fit for the public to know and what was not.

Emotional Harm

Mabel Warren's goal was to protect elites against *emotional harm*—specifically the publication of private facts and photographs that produced hurt feelings. This was quite a radical argument in 1890. Traditionally, the common law had rejected claims of emotional injury and had required plaintiffs to prove physical or property injuries before they could recover damages.[17]

Warren and Brandeis nevertheless argued that the "evil of the invasion of privacy" by journalists caused serious emotional and psychological damage.[18] They were particularly concerned that the new kind of press, armed with the new portable cameras, had "invaded the sacred precincts of private and domestic life; and … threaten[ed] to make good the prediction that 'what is whispered in the closet shall be proclaimed from the house-tops.' "[19] These invasions of privacy caused psychological injuries to the personality of their victims—especially when those personalities were refined and cultured ones.

The trade in gossip thus created by the press, the authors continued, included the publication of:

> details of sexual relations and idle gossip, which can only be procured
> by intrusion upon the domestic circle. The intensity and complexity of
> life, attendant upon advancing civilization, have rendered necessary
> some retreat from the world, and man, under the refining influence
> of culture, has become more sensitive to publicity, so that solitude
> and privacy have become more essential to the individual; but mod-
> ern enterprise and invention have, through invasions upon his privacy,

subjected him to mental pain and distress, far greater than could be inflicted by mere bodily injury.[20]

In other words, the core of the injury Warren and Brandeis were seeking to remedy was emotional harm—the offense felt by Mabel when she was mentioned in the press without her consent, and the embarrassment felt by Marion Manola when her theatrical performance was photographed.

The emotional injury presented by Warren and Brandeis reflected the class biases of aristocrats like the Warrens. From a social class perspective, Warren and Brandeis clearly wanted to protect the refined sensibilities of elites from the unwanted gaze of their social inferiors, as legal scholars have recognized.[21] Lower classes would suffer less injury from invasions of privacy, both philosophically, since they were thought to be less refined by culture, and practically, because their domestic affairs were less likely to be the subject of journalistic reports. This argument was a part of what legal historian Lawrence Friedman has called the "Victorian Compromise" efforts among American urban elites to protect their reputations and also allow occasional slippages from their own demanding codes of morality.[22] Friedman has shown how Warren and Brandeis were actually part of this broader cultural movement that sought to protect both the existing social structure and the ability of elites to misbehave from time to time.[23]

Targeting the Press

The second important choice that Warren and Brandeis made in defining the right to privacy was to target the press. Newspapers were the primary source of the invasions of privacy they decried, and newspapers were the intended defendants in the lawsuits they wanted courts to recognize.

Warren and Brandeis argued that although verbal gossip was harmful, gossip by journalists was much more dangerous because it was widely circulated and embodied in print. Worse still, they argued, the gossip trade by newsmen was causing "the lowering of social standards and of morality."[24] Newspaper gossip was thus a threat not just to individual feelings but also to public morality itself. Viewed in this way, even harmless printed gossip would have the effect of "inverting the

relative importance of things, thus dwarfing the thoughts and aspira-
tions of a people. When personal gossip attains the dignity of print, and
crowds the space available for matters of real interest to the community, what wonder that the ignorant and thoughtless mistake its relative
importance."[25]

By crowding out more serious and important information in the minds
of citizens, gossip journalism lowered social standards and encouraged
"the weak side of human nature" to flourish.[26] Protecting privacy was thus
essential to safeguarding not just hurt feelings but the sanctity of public
discourse itself.

But by choosing to defend the new tort in this way, Warren and
Brandeis called for holding newspapers liable for disclosing true but
private information. A right to stop newspapers from printing the truth
about elites that ordinary people wanted to read was inevitably going to
come into conflict with the constitutional values protected by the First
Amendment.

"Public" and "Private"

Warren and Brandeis recognized the tension between a right of privacy
and a free press and tried to solve this problem by relying on a distinction
between the "public" and "private" spheres. They suggested that courts
could separate "private" facts from "public" facts, with the press entitled
to publish only the latter. The proposed privacy tort would protect only
facts "concern[ing] the private life, habits, acts, and relations of an individual."[27] It would not "prohibit any publication of matter which is of
public or general interest,"[28] allowing, for example, the publication of
information with a "legitimate connection" with the fitness of a candidate
for public office or any actions taken in the public sphere.[29]

Warren and Brandeis admitted that the line between public and
private was a fuzzy one, and conceded that they had provided only a
rough sketch to guide courts. But they were confident that courts in the
future could develop a better picture of what the public had no right to
know.[30] Future courts should recognize, they suggested, that "[s]ome
things all men alike are entitled to keep from popular curiosity, whether
in public life or not, while others are only private because the persons
concerned have not assumed a position which makes their doings legitimate matters of public investigation."[31] Such "public men" could not

insist on a broad right of privacy, but they could "still demand that all the details of private life in its most limited sense shall not be laid bare for inspection."[32]

In relying on a line between public and private, *The Right to Privacy* relied on a basic idea in the Gilded Age that there were identifiable and separate public and private spheres. This reflected traditional Gilded Age notions of gender roles and the "cult of domesticity." This theory divided society into gendered separate spheres of male and female. Those in the male sphere were thought to be public, while those in the female one were deemed private.[33] Masculine activities involved things like politics and commerce, whereas feminine ones included the home, the family, religion, and morality. Warren and Brandeis's own language reveals how they embraced this view of the world. For example, they repeatedly drew a distinction between the feminine "sacred precincts of private and domestic life,"[34] such as the publication of a "woman's face, her form, her actions,"[35] and the masculine public sphere, such as a man's business or "his fitness for a public office."[36] "Public men" were thus beyond the right to privacy, but private women weren't. Mabel's social engagements and her personal grief were private. So was Marion Manola's body, even though she was photographed performing on a stage.

The Rise of Tort Privacy

The Warren and Brandeis theory of privacy thus had three important elements, each of which was problematic. It protected against emotional harm and weighed the emotions of elites as more fragile than those of ordinary workers. It targeted the press for publishing true facts that enquiring minds wanted to know, believing that courts could determine which facts the public had a right to know. Recognizing that this approach could conflict with the idea of a free press, it relied on an accepted but gendered nineteenth-century distinction between a masculine public sphere and a feminine domestic one.

At first it seemed as if the Warren and Brandeis article would, like most scholarly papers, have no effect on the law. A few early cases almost immediately toyed with the idea of protecting privacy through law, and California enacted a short-lived and ineffective privacy law in 1899, but it took over a decade for privacy to take serious root.[37] Once again, it would involve the protection of a young woman from unwanted public attention.

Abigail Roberson was a teenager in Rochester, New York, who had her picture taken in a photography studio. Someone (presumably the photographer) gave the picture without her consent to the Franklin Mills Flour Company, which used it on twenty-five thousand advertising posters that were displayed all over Rochester in 1901. The ads featured Roberson's photograph along with the pun "flour of the family."[38] Roberson was mortified when she saw her picture all over town, and sued the company under the Warren and Brandeis theory. She claimed that the "scoffs and jeers" of people who had recognized her caused her a "severe nervous shock" that confined her to bed.

The New York Court of Appeals denied her claim on the ground that it lacked the power to create a new "right of privacy."[39] However, after a popular outcry against the decision, the New York legislature passed a law allowing people to sue when, like Abigail Roberson, their "name, portrait, or picture" had been used without consent "for purposes of trade."[40]

Three years later, the Georgia Supreme Court recognized the right of privacy under almost identical facts—an advertisement for life insurance that used a photograph of artist Paolo Pavesich without permission.[41] Pavesich had sat for photographs in a professional studio, but his photographer had given the negative to the insurance company without consent. Two features of the *Pavesich* case are particularly important. First, the court recognized the inevitable tension between allowing people to keep their names and pictures out of the media and a free press, but believed that courts could police such a line. "We understand," said the court, "liberty of speech and of the press to imply not only liberty to publish, but complete immunity from legal censure and punishment for the publication, so long as it is not harmful in its character, when tested by such standards as the law affords." It considered the real possibility that "there may arise cases where the speaking or printing of the truth might be considered an abuse of the liberty of speech and of the press." But while it considered this possibility, it was confident that the common law could separate out such cases from ones in which "matters of purely private concern, wholly foreign to a legitimate expression of opinion on the subject under discussion, are injected into the discussion for no other purpose and with no other motive than to annoy and harass the individual."[42] In other words, a right to privacy might raise free press issues, but courts could and should separate out legitimate matters of press concern from those that were not fit for the public to read because they caused emotional harm to private citizens. This, of course, was Warren and Brandeis's solution.

Second, the Georgia court recognized the right to privacy under the common law, rather than deferring to the legislature as the New York courts had. This set a precedent for the high courts of other states to do the same. With *Pavesich* on the books, other state supreme courts began to follow Georgia's lead. Most of these early cases recognized a right to privacy for the use of photographs for commercial purposes without their subject's consent, just like the facts of *Roberson* and *Pavesich*.[43]

But soon other cases followed these pioneers under a bewildering array of theories. Some cases protected famous people from having their likenesses used—not because they wanted them kept private, but because their public selves had value that they alone should be able to exploit. These cases came to be known not as the right of privacy, but the "right of publicity," a kind of intellectual property monopoly on making money from one's image.[44] Others protected against intrusions into private places by peeping toms.[45] But although these cases relied on the Warren and Brandeis article, they involved different contexts from Warren and Brandeis's annoyance at the Yellow Press's coverage of society events.[46]

In fact, courts only began to protect against the disclosure of private facts in earnest in the 1920s, more than thirty years after the publication of *The Right to Privacy*. In *Brents v. Morgan* (1927), the Kentucky Supreme Court found a violation of privacy where a man had posted a sign reading "Dr. W. R. Morgan owes an account here of $49.67. And if promises would pay an account this account would have been settled long ago. This account will be advertised as long as it remains unpaid."[47] *Brents* produced a flurry of commentary noting the significance of the recognition of a new kind of privacy right in Brandeis's home state.[48] In 1931 the California Supreme Court decided the famous case of *Melvin v. Reid*, recognizing a privacy claim by a reformed prostitute against the producers of a movie that told the story of her colorful earlier life as a sex worker tried for murder.[49] Such cases, of course, were precisely what Warren and Brandeis had in mind, but the range of cases shows the malleability of their call for privacy protection.

Other courts and legislatures recognized the tort in the ensuing decades, but fifty years after publication of *The Right to Privacy*, privacy law remained a doctrinal backwater of more interest to academics than litigants.[50] Privacy was a recognized but unusual cause of action that operated as a "residual category of tort law," picking up intentional actions resulting in emotional injury that were not covered by the tort of intentional infliction of emotional distress, or injuries caused by publicity of facts that were not actionable defamation.[51] It remained unclear whether the privacy tort would survive on its own merit, or whether it would be swallowed up by the more vibrant tort of intentional infliction of emotional distress.[52]

But privacy was about to enter the mainstream of American law thanks to William Prosser. Prosser was dean of the law school at Berkeley and the leading authority on tort law of his day. If Warren and Brandeis gave tort privacy its name and guiding principles, Prosser gave it form and credibility.[53] By the time Prosser began to write about privacy in the 1940s, there were only a few hundred privacy cases from the fifty years since Warren and Brandeis.[54] Over the next three decades, Prosser worked to give the privacy torts order and form.[55] His principal contribution was to argue that the cases adopting the Warren and Brandeis formulation were not one tort but really "four distinct kinds of invasion of four different interests of the plaintiff, which are tied together by a common name, but otherwise have nothing in common except that each represents an interference with the right of the plaintiff, in the phrase coined by Judge Cooley, 'to be let alone.'"[56] Prosser described his four torts as follows:

1. Intrusion upon the plaintiff's seclusion or solitude, or into his private affairs.

2. Public disclosure of embarrassing private facts about the plaintiff.

3. Publicity which places the plaintiff in a false light in the public eye.

4. Appropriation, for the defendant's advantage, of the plaintiff's name or likeness.[57]

Courts recognized this way of organizing the law, and it has become the foundation of modern tort privacy.[58]

But Prosser's influence on tort privacy was mixed. While he gave the torts a stature they had previously lacked, by including them as recognized causes of action in his casebooks and treatises, Prosser also limited tort privacy's ability to evolve.[59] Today the four privacy torts remain on the books much as Prosser left them at his death in 1972—intrusion, disclosure, false light, and appropriation. But virtually all states now recognize some or all of the four Prosser privacy torts.[60]

Consider in this respect the case of *Lake v. Wal-Mart Stores* (1998), in which Minnesota became the forty-sixth state to recognize some or all of the privacy torts.[61] College-age Elli Lake went on vacation to Mexico with both her friend Melissa Weber and Melissa's sister. The trouble started when, perhaps after an evening of partying, Melissa's sister photographed Elli and Melissa naked in the shower together. At the end of the trip, Elli and Melissa took five rolls of film (this being 1995) to the Wal-Mart in Dilworth, Minnesota, for developing. When they picked up the prints, Elli and Melissa found a note with their photos, stating that some of the photos had not been developed due to their "nature."[62] Over the next few months they became aware that the nude photographs had in fact been developed and were circulating in the community along with hurtful speculation about the plaintiffs' sexualities. Feeling their privacy to have been invaded, they sued Wal-Mart. Invoking both the Warren and Brandeis article and Prosser, the court held that

> The right to privacy is an integral part of our humanity; one has a public persona, exposed and active, and a private persona, guarded and preserved. The heart of our liberty is choosing which parts of our lives shall become public and which parts we shall hold close. Here [plaintiffs allege] that a photograph of their nude bodies has been publicized. One's naked body is a very private part of one's person and generally known to others only by choice. This is a type of privacy interest worthy of protection.[63]

Although liability in privacy cases appears to be rare, *Lake* illustrates how the privacy torts remain alive and have an application beyond press defendants.

The case also shows how the issues that troubled Mabel Warren remain vital. The facts of *Lake v. Wal-Mart* are less than twenty years old but may seem slightly quaint, involving rolls of film and manual developing. The questions they raise, however, not only remain important today but also have taken on added importance in the digital age. What happens to the photos we take with our cameras, whether they are manual film cameras or attached to our smartphones and coded to upload all our photos to the cloud? When embarrassing photographs go out of our control, do we have the power to keep them out of the press? Off Facebook? To stop them from circulating at all?

Lake also raises the critical legal issue started by Mabel Warren's irritation with the Boston press over a century ago—the disclosure of true but embarrassing information about us that causes us emotional pain. As we will see, this interest is often in direct tension with another interest we value highly—the freedom of speech.

2

Free Speech

The Socialist Socialite (or, Whitney and Brandeis)

Anita Whitney was an unlikely revolutionary. Like Mabel Warren, Whitney was born into a privileged family in the 1860s. Her ancestors included five passengers on the Mayflower and a governor of Massachusetts Bay Colony. Her father was a successful California lawyer and future state senator, while her favorite uncle was conservative Supreme Court Justice Stephen J. Field. By birth and class, Anita was very much like Mabel Warren, but their lives turned out very differently.[1]

Whitney graduated from Wellesley College in 1889, and then toured Europe and the United States. She took up charitable and social work in Boston, New York, and finally California, where she helped victims of the 1906 San Francisco earthquake. In the parlance of the time, she was a social worker and "clubwoman," but her relief work soon took a political turn. Concerned about the effects of alcoholism on the poor, she joined the Prohibition movement, where she developed a keen interest in issues of race, class, and gender inequality.

Prohibition politics led Whitney to socialism and workers' rights. In the early twentieth century, industrialization, immigration, and widening inequalities of wealth and opportunity combined to divide labor and capital. Workers were represented by groups like the International Workers of the World, or "Wobblies." Fiercely critical of the excesses of capitalism, the Wobblies called for "one big union" of workers to counter the power of the robber barons. Whitney decided that the Wobblies had a point and that the only way to solve the problems of poverty that concerned her was by changing the structure of American industry. In

1914 she joined the American Socialist Party, rising quickly to a position of prominence and becoming increasingly radical in her politics. Her commitment was personal, as she spent most of her savings bailing out radicals she believed to be political prisoners.[2]

The foremost question facing the workers' movement was how to change the economic inequality caused by the industrial economy. Could it be fixed through democratic processes weighted in favor of the owners, or was outright revolution the only option? With the bloody Russian Revolution as a backdrop, this was no mere philosophical question. Although mainstream Progressives had initially sympathized with the Wobblies, that support waned as America entered the First World War in April 1917, and the Russian Revolution shifted in October from democratic white to violent communist red. America became gripped by the "Red Scare," fearing a communist revolution in the United States. Panicked state legislatures began to pass "criminal syndicalism laws," outlawing the teaching of revolutionary doctrines. California's law went further than most, outlawing membership in any group that taught the necessity of revolution.[3] This law was used to round up suspected radicals, and to break up peaceful political meetings of labor organizers.[4]

As peaceful reform seemed more unlikely, some workers became more radical. At a Chicago convention in the summer of 1919, the more moderate Socialist Party refused to join the Moscow-controlled Communist International. The moderates expelled the radicals, who re-formed as the Communist Party of America. Whitney believed in the more peaceful option, but her Oakland chapter of the Socialist Party tilted radical and voted to join the Communists. At the organizing convention, she pushed a moderate agenda, but when it was defeated, she remained a member of the new Communist Labor Party of California and a member of its executive committee.[5] The new group provoked outrage in Oakland; a week after the meeting, a group of veterans destroyed the hall where the meeting had occurred. It was November 11, 1919, the first anniversary of Armistice Day.

Whitney continued to speak her mind despite the charged political air. The police cancelled a speech she intended to give to the Mother's Club because she was a woman of "known political tendencies." After a contentious vote, the California Civic League decided to let her speak. Her topic that evening was "The Negro Problem." Whitney was outraged by a wave of lynchings of African-Americans that had swept the country following the Armistice, in which some of the victims had been veterans themselves. The solution, she argued, was an anti-lynching law and a vigilant electorate sympathetic to equal rights for all, regardless of race. At the end of the meeting, Whitney was arrested and charged with criminal syndicalism.[6]

Whitney's problems continued. At her trial, her lawyer fell victim to the epidemic Spanish influenza of 1919 and died. The trial continued, and Whitney was convicted. The case went to the Supreme Court in 1925, and the Court affirmed her conviction. Writing for the Court, Justice Edward Sanford declared that mere membership in a group that advocated syndicalism was enough to violate the law, and the law was constitutional because legislatures had the power to declare which ideas were dangerous.

Whitney's case is famous today not for the Court's forgettable opinion but for the impassioned separate opinion of Justice Louis Brandeis. Brandeis argued that free speech can only be punished in an emergency. Any other rule might endanger both the First Amendment and the entire project of democratic self-government it was designed to support. His most important words are contained in just one paragraph of the opinion, a paragraph bristling with insight about freedom of speech and why it is important. It reads in full as follows, though I have italicized some of its most important ideas:

Those who won our independence believed that the final end of the State was to make men free to develop their faculties, and that, in its government, the deliberative forces should prevail over the arbitrary. *They valued liberty both as an end, and as a means.* They believed liberty to be the secret of happiness, and courage to be the secret of liberty. *They believed that freedom to think as you will and to speak as you think are means indispensable to the discovery and spread of political truth; that, without free speech and assembly, discussion would be futile; that, with them, discussion affords ordinarily adequate protection against the dissemination of noxious doctrine;* that the greatest menace to freedom is an inert people; that public discussion is a political duty, and that this should be a fundamental principle of the American government. They recognized the risks to which all human institutions are subject. But they knew that order cannot be secured merely through fear of punishment for its infraction; that it is hazardous to discourage thought, hope and imagination; that fear breeds repression; that repression breeds hate; that hate menaces stable government; *that the path of safety lies in the opportunity to discuss freely supposed grievances and proposed remedies, and that the fitting remedy for evil counsels is good ones.* Believing in the power of reason as applied through public discussion, they eschewed silence coerced by law—the argument of force in its worst form. Recognizing the occasional tyrannies of governing majorities, they amended the Constitution so that free speech and assembly should be guaranteed.[7]

In relatively few words, in some of the most poetic sentences ever written about free speech, Brandeis set out its most important justification: We need free speech if we are to govern ourselves. If we're to be trusted with self-government, we must also be trusted with dangerous political ideas. We must have courage and have faith in our institutions. Discussion must occur, because coerced silence produces an inert citizenry who are incapable of self-government.

Brandeis's First Amendment in *Whitney* has become *our* First Amendment, the most important explanation for the extraordinary protection that American law gives to the freedom of speech. It is also the source of the most powerful arguments as to why the Warren and Brandeis right to privacy is unconstitutional. Unpacking the ironies of Brandeis's relationships to privacy and freedom of speech is thus essential if we want to understand how privacy and free speech fit together.

Publicity, Facts, and Sunlight

By 1925 Brandeis was no longer a young lawyer and amateur legal scholar. In the thirty-five years since the publication of *The Right to Privacy*, he had become very successful, working increasingly on matters involving industrial conditions and the public interest, and developing a national reputation as "The People's Lawyer." Appointed to the Supreme Court by Woodrow Wilson in 1916, Brandeis revealed himself to be both intellectual and fiercely opposed to the prevailing interpretation of the Constitution as primarily protecting economic rights. Along with his friend, mentor, and fellow Justice Oliver Wendell Holmes Jr., Brandeis developed an alternative reading of the Constitution, one in which legislatures had greater power to regulate economic activity in the public interest, and political rights should receive greater protection.

Though he had been busy with many public and intellectual causes since 1890, Brandeis had not worked on privacy since his *Harvard Law Review* article. He remained proud of the article, but privately reflected that on receiving the page proofs in November 1890, "the little I read did not strike me as being as good as I had thought it was."[8] Brandeis only worked on privacy twice in his life—his article with Warren when he was thirty-two and his dissent in *Olmstead v. United States* almost four decades later. (We'll see more of that case in chapter 9.)

Brandeis was more interested in a related but contrary idea—one he called the "duty of publicity." These ideas were running through his mind when he was working on *The Right to Privacy*, and he found them more compelling than the privacy argument that Warren had proposed. In a letter to his fiancée, Alice Goldmark, shortly after *The Right to Privacy* was published, Brandeis remarked:

> Lots of things which are worth doing have occurred to me as I sit calmly here. And among others to write an article on "The Duty of Publicity"—a sort of companion piece to the last one that would really interest me more. You know I have talked to you about the wickedness of people shielding wrongdoers & passing them off (or at least allowing them to pass themselves off) as honest men. Some instances of that have presented themselves within a few days which have fired my imagination. If the broad light of day could be let in upon men's actions, it would purify them as the sun disinfects. You see my idea; I leave to you to straighten out and complete that sentence.[9]

The expression of this idea—drafted hastily in a love letter—expressed one of Brandeis's most important beliefs, the idea that wrongdoing often hides behind privacy, and that publicity can have the power to correct wrongdoing and fraud.

Brandeis refined the idea over the years, and it became the centerpiece of his 1914 book, *Other People's Money*.[10] In that book, he argued that securities underwriters were charging excessive commissions and passing those on to unsuspecting investors.[11] Believing that ordinary investors could better protect themselves if they knew the size of the commissions he proposed publicity as the remedy. Underwriters should be forced to disclose their rates to give investors the knowledge (and power) they needed to protect themselves.[12] The rhetorical core of his argument was the phrase from his love letter twenty-five years before:

> Publicity is justly commended as a remedy for social and industrial diseases. Sunlight is said to be the best of disinfectants; electric light the most efficient policeman.[13]

Publicity required facts to work. True and accurate information, Brandeis believed, was essential to solving any problem, especially those involving government or the economy. As he told a congressional committee in 1911, "in all our legislation we have got to base what we do on facts and not on theories."[14] And the modern state needed the power to compel facts from individuals and businesses in order to govern effectively.[15] To produce these facts, the state needed to pry into areas of American life that had previously been thought private, such as private industry and private property.

Brandeis also believed that accurate facts were necessary for courts to do their jobs properly.[16] This approach is exemplified by the "Brandeis Brief" he filed in *Muller v. Oregon* (1908).[17] In *Muller*, Brandeis defended Oregon's statute providing a ten-hour day for female workers. Hoping to show the practical necessity of a cap on hours, his brief contained barely two pages of legal citations and more than a hundred pages of employment statistics about the effects of long hours on the health of women.[18] This belief in the power of facts continued when he became a Justice himself. As he put it in one case, even in a system of precedent, "the logic of words should yield to the logic of realities."[19]

Brandeis's love of publicity, sunlight, and facts eventually led him to free speech. In 1890 free speech had been just another value to be traded off against the right to privacy. Warren and Brandeis, you will recall, believed that judges could effectively separate out facts the public had a right to know from the private ones that were none of its business. But as the nineteenth century turned into the complex twentieth, Brandeis reconsidered this belief.

The famous 1918 case of *International News Service v. Associated Press* is still read today by most first-year law students studying property law. In it, the Supreme Court approved an injunction against a company that copied and redistributed breaking news gathered by its rival, the Associated Press.[20] In a typically fact-laden dissent, Brandeis warned that the "free use of knowledge and of ideas" could be curtailed by the majority's recognition of a kind of property right in news reports.[21] He also questioned the competence of courts to separate out the private interests in the news business from the public interest in the free dissemination of true facts. He argued that although the common law could prove useful for simple legal problems involving only private rights, "with the increasing complexity of society, the public interest tends to become omnipresent."[22] Courts, in other words, were becoming incapable of separating what was public from what was private.

It is striking from a present-day perspective that although the *Associated Press* case involved an injunction against the press for publishing true, newsworthy facts, none of the Justices understood the case to involve the First Amendment. Brandeis came the closest, but even he dissented because of the public interest in the news, rather than because of the First Amendment.

Brandeis was not alone in having thought little about the importance of free speech. Before American entry into the First World War, the Supreme Court had decided few free speech cases and had never upheld a free speech claim under the First Amendment.[23] But this was about to change, presenting Brandeis with facts that would change his mind about the importance of free speech.

Brandeis's First Amendment

Congress passed the Espionage Act of 1917 upon American entry into the First World War.[24] It criminalized draft obstruction and produced more than a thousand convictions, many of which were based solely upon speech critical of the war, the government, or conscription.[25] The Supreme Court heard many of these cases, which provided the context within which Brandeis and Holmes developed more modern ideas about the First Amendment. The cases fall into two groups—a first group decided in March 1919 and a second from late 1919 through the 1920s. In the first set of cases, a unanimous Court rejected all free speech claims under the Espionage Act. In the second, Brandeis and Holmes dissented, articulating new speech-protective theories of the First Amendment.

In the first group of cases, Brandeis and Holmes actually wrote the opinions dismissing the free speech claims. Brandeis's opinion in *Sugarman v. United States*[26] upheld a conviction for draft obstruction based solely upon a political speech and rejected the First Amendment claim without analysis.[27] The same day, he joined Holmes's majority opinion in *Schenck v. United States*,[28] upholding a conviction under the Espionage Act for printing anti-draft leaflets. The leaflets called on the targets of conscription to do no more than assert their constitutional rights and to sign an anti-conscription petition.[29] Holmes's opinion rejected Schenck's First Amendment defense on the grounds that Schenck's words could be punished because there was a "clear and present danger" they could bring about "substantive evils that Congress has a right to protect."[30] Although Holmes (and Brandeis) would later use this phrase in a speech-protective way in the 1920s, *Schenck* was not intended this way.[31] Holmes announced two other unanimous opinions a week later upholding convictions under the Espionage Act for subversive speech.[32]

Brandeis and Holmes developed free speech reservations about these decisions almost immediately and resolved to vote differently. As Brandeis told a young Felix Frankfurter:

> I have never been quite happy about my concurrence in the *Debs* and *Schenck* cases. I had not thought the issues of freedom of speech out—I thought at the subject not through it. Not until I came to write the *Schafer* and *Pierce* cases did I understand it ... [and] made up my mind that I would put it all out, let the future know what [we] weren't allowed to say in the days of the war and following.[33]g

Brandeis's papers from this period document his growing interest in free speech; he kept a number of letters from friends dealing with the growing threat to free speech and a news clippings file of articles about the persecution of pacifists and socialists.[34]

For Holmes, a chance encounter on a train with Judge Learned Hand sparked a lengthy exchange of letters about the importance of free speech. Hand eventually persuaded Holmes that speech should receive greater protection.[35] Holmes and Brandeis may also have been affected by the negative commentary that the opinions received in progressive journals like *The Nation* and *The New Republic*.[36] Another cause of their change of heart was Harvard law professor Zechariah Chafee. Chafee published *Freedom of Speech in Wartime* in the June 1919 volume of the *Harvard Law Review*, which was sharply critical of the Supreme Court's approach in the Espionage Act cases, arguing that it was ignoring important free speech issues.[37] Brandeis and Holmes both read the article and were greatly influenced by it.[38] They were also outraged when conservative Harvard alumni tried to drive Chafee from the academy because of his criticism of the Espionage Act cases, the widespread arrest of radicals, and deportations of radical immigrants initiated by Attorney General Mitchell Palmer.[39] By late 1919, both Brandeis and Holmes had fully changed their minds and were resolved to take a stronger position in the First Amendment cases still on the docket. Changing his mind was fairly unusual for Holmes, but not for Brandeis, who believed in the power of facts, education, and experience.[40]

The new term's docket held a second group of cases raising the same free speech issues as the four from March. The first of these was *Abrams v. United States*, decided in October 1919. The Court upheld Abrams' conviction under the Act, but Holmes dissented, arguing that the contested nature of truth meant that, absent an emergency, a "free trade in ideas" was required that prevented popular majorities from censoring minority views—even "opinions that we loathe and believe to be fraught with death."[41] Brandeis joined the dissent, telling Holmes privately that "I join you heartily & gratefully. This is fine—very."[42]

In cases following *Abrams*, Brandeis and Holmes developed these ideas, adding greater substance to Holmes's elegant but vague language.[43] Brandeis drafted important dissents in several free speech cases over the next decade, making major contributions to the idea of a more speech-protective First Amendment. In the same term as *Abrams*, he dissented in *Schaefer v. United States* (1920)[44] and *Pierce v. United States* (1920).[45] He also wrote important dissents in *Gilbert v. Minnesota* (1920)[46] and the *Milwaukee Leader* case (1921)[47] before his own free speech masterpiece in the Anita Whitney case (1927).[48] Holmes contributed two significant opinions following his masterpiece in *Abrams*, dissenting in *Gitlow v. New York* (1925)[49] and *United States v. Schwimmer* (1929).[50]

Brandeis and Holmes dissented together, but their opinions offered different reasons for why speech should get special constitutional protection. Holmes's theory was pragmatic and pessimistic; it justified free speech on the grounds that it advanced the search for truth in spite of Holmes's own resigned skepticism about the human ability to ever know the truth.[51] For Holmes, because people were frequently wrong, and truth was elusive, it seemed both futile and dangerous for judges to prohibit ideas that could turn out to be true.

By contrast, Brandeis developed a more idealistic conception of free speech rooted in its importance to democratic self-government. It is from this perspective that we should understand his opinion in *Whitney*. His "self-governance theory" of the First Amendment rested on four principles, each of which is important to an understanding of his view of the relationship between free speech and privacy.

The first principle justified free speech because it enabled citizens to make intelligent, informed decisions about *self-government*. Free speech was important not just as an *individual* right but also as a safeguard of the *social* processes of democracy.[52] In a self-governing society, discussion of public matters by citizens was essential. And the source of the facts and opinions those citizens needed to perform their civic duties was free speech. As a result, a government could only deny access to such information if there was a serious and imminent emergency threatening serious harm to persons or the state. This idea is at the heart of the famous excerpt from Brandeis's *Whitney* opinion quoted earlier—the idea that citizens like Anita Whitney had a duty to speak their mind about political matters, that others had a duty to listen, and that the state had a duty to stay out of it except in real emergencies.

Brandeis's second principle was to insist on the *absolute protection of opinion*, because of the difficulty judges and others might have in distinguishing between opinions and facts. *Pierce v. United States* upheld an Espionage Act conviction for the circulation of a Socialist Party leaflet charging that capitalists had started the war.[53] Brandeis insisted in dissent that the importance of a free press to a democratic society required the government to prove falsity, but he went further by suggesting that many opinions—like those relating to the cause of the war—cannot be proven false.[54] A rule that allowed juries to punish expressions of opinion would subject many leading politicians to possible criminal sanction. Even worse, it "would practically deny members of small political parties freedom of criticism and of discussion in times when feelings run high and the questions involved are deemed fundamental."[55]

Underscoring this conclusion is Brandeis's renewed skepticism about the ability of courts to make fine distinctions in free speech cases. In order for free speech to perform its democratic function of informing the electorate of new ideas, careful distinctions between protected and unprotected speech were impossible, and courts must defer to speakers. Just as he had suggested in *International News Service* that the public-private line was beyond judicial competence, in his First Amendment cases, Brandeis maintained that courts lacked the capacity to act as censors in matters of speech more generally. In *Pierce*, he declared that this was a First Amendment requirement.[56] Brandeis had thus abandoned the faith in judicial line-drawing on which *The Right to Privacy* depended.

The third innovation Brandeis made to free speech theory was the idea of *counter-speech*—that speakers and not the government must determine what is a fit subject for public debate. He argued that speakers, not courts, should police public debate, and that when dangerous speech is aired, the remedy should almost never be censorship by courts. "The fitting remedy for evil counsels," he argued in *Whitney*, "is good ones." In another part of that opinion, he explained further:

> If there be time to expose through discussion the falsehood and fallacies, to avert the evil by the processes of education, the remedy to be applied is more speech, not enforced silence. Only an emergency can justify repression.[57]

Brandeis argued that if we are to govern ourselves, we must be brave. We must trust our democratic institutions to survive dangerous speech and dangerous ideas, because the cost of suppressing them is greater than the benefit, especially in the long run.

Brandeis's fourth free speech principle was also novel: Free speech is important not just because it results in better democratic *decisions* but also because it produces better democratic *citizens*. This is what Brandeis meant in *Whitney* when he argued that liberty should be valued "both as an end and as a means."[58] The idea that law should promote good civic character had been with Brandeis for decades. In a letter he wrote to his future wife in 1890, he quoted the English poet Matthew Arnold that "[l]ife is not a having and a getting; but a being and a becoming."[59] In 1922 he wrote that in a democratic society, "the development of the individual is, thus, both a necessary means and the end sought. For our objective is the making of men and women who shall be free, self-respecting members of a democracy—and who shall be worthy of respect. . . . Success in any democratic undertaking must proceed from the individual."[60] In sum, then, Brandeis believed that free speech was important because it allowed citizens to make better democratic decisions, because it protected political opinions, because it let speakers, rather than governments check dangerous ideas, and because all of these activities produced better individual citizens.

Brandeis's opinion in *Whitney* illustrates the four themes and represents his fullest statement of the relationship between civic character and democratic self-governance. His argument was twofold: it was about the kinds of civic virtues necessary to promote effective self-governance and also about how the activities of self-governance reproduced those virtues in a democratic citizenry. Such a citizen believed "that public discussion is a political duty,"[61] and that we should not, as Vincent Blasi puts it, "underestimate the value of discussion, education, good counsels." Bad ideas are thus truly dangerous only when their "opponents lack the personal qualities of wisdom, creativity, and confidence."[62] And Brandeis argued that these virtues come from "discussion and education, not by lazy and impatient reliance on the coercive authority of the state."[63] Most fundamentally, Brandeis argued that when faced with dangerous and harmful speech, a democratic society should have faith in the strength and enduring goodness of its institutions, and should not fear the consequences of such speech. Thus, he could assert in *Schaefer* that the state must scrupulously prove the direct dangerousness of any leaflets it wished to punish, and he could assert his faith in *Whitney* that in order to suppress speech "there must be the probability of serious injury to the State. Among free men, the deterrents ordinarily to be applied to prevent crime are education and punishment for violations of the law, not abridgement of the rights of free speech and assembly."[64]

Each of Brandeis's First Amendment principles has become a foundational element of modern First Amendment law. The Supreme Court first adopted the *Schaefer* argument that scrupulous proof is required for any harms alleged to have been caused by speech. On the page immediately following the *Whitney* concurrence in *United States Reports* is the Court's opinion in *Fiske v. Kansas* (1927). *Fiske* invalidated a conviction for incitement on sufficiency of the evidence grounds under the Due

Process Clause of the Fourteenth Amendment.[65] Although the opinion does not speak explicitly in terms of free speech, it is fully consistent with Brandeis's approach in *Schaefer*. Ten years later, in *Herndon v. Lowry* (1937)[66] and *DeJonge v. Oregon* (1937),[67] the Court carefully scrutinized anti-incitement statutes under the First Amendment the way Brandeis had done in *Schaefer*, dismissing them for insufficient evidence of harm.[68]

Brandeis's second innovation—his concern that trial courts could not effectively police fine lines between protected and unprotected speech—was embraced by the Court in *New York Times v. Sullivan* (1964). That case gave constitutional protection to many kinds of false and defamatory statements in order to give "breathing space" to true statements by the press.[69] *Pierce*'s absolute protection of opinion was recognized by a later defamation case, *Gertz v. Robert Welch* (1974), which declared that "there is no such thing as a false idea."[70]

Brandeis's third suggestion that counter-speech should be the normal remedy for dangerous speech has likewise become a central element of First Amendment law, also established in *New York Times v. Sullivan*.[71] Justice Brennan's opinion quoted Brandeis's *Whitney* discussion of counter-speech at length before declaring that free speech on matters of public concern "should be uninhibited, robust, and wide-open."[72] *Sullivan*'s language about the nature of public debate, relying directly on Brandeis's counter-speech theory, is perhaps the most important and widely accepted statement of what the modern First Amendment requires.[73]

Finally, Brandeis's emphasis in *Whitney* on the link between free speech and civic character is a theme that runs throughout modern First Amendment law.[74] For example, in *Cohen v. California* (1971), the Supreme Court refused to accept any regulation of profane political speech on the grounds that it would offend the sensibilities of viewers or listeners:[75]

> The constitutional right of free expression is powerful medicine in a society as diverse and populous as ours. It is designed and intended to remove governmental restraints from the arena of public discussion, putting the decision as to what views shall be voiced largely into the hands of each of us, in the hope that use of such freedom will ultimately produce a more capable citizenry and more perfect polity and in

the belief that no other approach would comport with the premise of individual dignity and choice upon which our political system rests.[76]

This argument, of course, is precisely the one Brandeis made in *Whitney*. And taken together, his ideas about freedom of speech from the early twentieth century lie at the core of what the modern First Amendment protects. Both doctrinally and as a matter of theory, modern free speech law is inextricably linked with Brandeis's ideas about why speech matters and how it should be protected. We live under Brandeis's First Amendment.

***

Brandeis's relationships with two very different patrician women— Mabel Warren and Anita Whitney—thus came to influence the law of both privacy and freedom of speech. It is fair to say that there were two very different Brandeises as well—a young scholar imagining a right to privacy and an experienced jurist coming to realize the importance of freedom of speech in a democracy. But as we've seen, Brandeis's thinking changed over the course of the early twentieth century, such that his views on publicity, facts, and free speech became inconsistent with his earlier theory of tort privacy. In the next chapter, I explain the nature of this conflict in more detail, as well as how we should resolve it.

3

The Limits of Disclosure

The Welsh Wizard

Ryan Giggs was an immensely talented footballer who played for Manchester United from 1991 to 2014. He was one of the greatest ever Welsh players, second only to Ian Rush, who played for Liverpool in the 1980s and 1990s. Giggs was praised for his skillful handling of the ball, his leadership on the pitch, his personal modesty, and his stable personal life. But it turned out that, like many professional athletes, he wasn't quite the role model his publicists might have wanted us to believe. In fact, he had been engaged in a series of extramarital affairs, including one with British reality television star Imogen Thomas, meeting her in London hotel rooms for sex when United played away games in the capital. The affair ended badly, as affairs tend to do, and when it appeared that Thomas might go public about the affair, Giggs obtained an injunction on May 16, 2011, that prevented the press from reporting his name in connection with the news story.[1]

Such injunctions are recent innovations in English privacy law that allow celebrities to keep private, unflattering facts about themselves out of the newspapers. Most of these facts seem to involve sex. They have been used, for instance, to suppress unauthorized photographs of the wedding of film stars Michael Douglas and Catherine Zeta-Jones and footage of a kinky orgy involving Formula One head Max Mosley and a group of prostitutes.[2] Although English courts have permitted common law injunctions in kiss-and-tell cases for some time, the more recent cases have been justified by Article 8 of the European Convention on Human Rights, which has been part of English law since 2001.[3] Article 8 provides that "[e]veryone has the right to respect for his private and family life, his home and his correspondence."[4]

The story about Giggs eventually became public (or else I would not be able to name him in the UK edition of this book!). The injunction applied only to England and Wales, and an enterprising Scottish newspaper ran a thinly disguised picture of Giggs's famous face on its front page. English football is the most popular sport on the planet, and all over the world, tens of thousands of Twitter feeds and websites also identified Giggs as the mysterious footballer known only as "CTB" in court papers.[5] The story was public, but British newspapers were still barred from talking about it. As Prime Minister David Cameron told British television network ITV while the injunction was still in effect, he, "like everybody else," knew the identity of "CTB," but it was "rather unsustainable, this situation, where newspapers can't print something that clearly everybody else is talking about."[6] Finally, Member of Parliament John Hemming used parliamentary privilege to name Giggs on the floor of the House of Commons, which newspapers could report on without breaking the injunction. His secret out, Giggs threw himself into preparations for Manchester United's next game, the Champion's League Final at Wembley Stadium against Spanish champions Barcelona. United lost a badly one-sided game 3-1.[7]

The Child Prodigy

Under American law, a celebrity like Giggs who wanted to keep his name out of the press could bring a lawsuit under the Warren and Brandeis "disclosure tort." Unfortunately, the disclosure tort is directly at odds with the free press granted by the First Amendment. Consider the famous case of William Sidis, an American child prodigy who could read the *New York Times* at eighteen months and Greek and Latin at age three, and wrote childhood papers on mathematics, logarithms, anatomy, astronomy, and linguistics. Sidis enrolled at Harvard College at age eleven and was the subject of widespread media attention, including a front-page *New York Times* article.[8] But Sidis burned out; after his graduation from Harvard in 1914, he tired of media attention and became a recluse before he turned twenty. When *New Yorker* magazine ran a "where are they now?" feature on him in 1937 disclosing facts about his modest and somewhat sad life of underachievement, he sued under the disclosure tort.

The court, however, dismissed his claim. Even though Sidis has suffered emotional injury from the unwanted media attention, the court ruled that he could not recover because of the importance of a free press. Noting that Sidis had once been a "public figure," the court explained that

> Regrettably or not, the misfortunes and frailties of neighbors and "public figures" are subjects of considerable interest and discussion to the rest of the population. And when such are the mores of the community, it would be unwise for a court to bar their expression in the newspapers, books, and magazines of the day.[9]

The court concluded that while celebrities might be able to recover if the press printed "intimate" or "unwarranted" revelations that would "outrage the community's notions of decency," the public interest in discussion of famous people by a free press meant that the disclosure tort was of limited usefulness at best.

Driving the court's reasoning in *Sidis* was the belief—now a central tenet of First Amendment law—that public discussion of matters in the media are essential to democratic self-government.[10] By seeking to impose damages on the press, the disclosure tort was thus in direct conflict with the First Amendment.

Disclosure versus Speech

Let's look at modern American law now. Most states today apply the elements of the disclosure tort from the Second Restatement of Torts, which provides that

> One who gives publicity to a matter concerning the private life of another is subject to liability to the other for invasion of his privacy, if the matter publicized is of a kind that (a) would be highly offensive to a reasonable person, and (b) is not of legitimate concern to the public.[11]

Reorganizing this language slightly, we can think of the disclosure tort as having three basic elements: (1) *publicity* given to (2) *private facts* that aren't of legitimate concern to the public, and are (3) *highly offensive*. Remarkably, *each* of these elements creates First Amendment problems.

Publicity

Consider first the publicity element, usually interpreted to require "public communication." Under the Restatement approach, publicity "means that the matter is made public, by communicating it to the public at large, or to so many persons that the matter must be regarded as substantially certain to become one of public knowledge."[12] In practice this means something like an oral address to a large audience, or a publication in a newspaper or other form of mass media.[13] A few cases have read "publicity" more narrowly, allowing particularly harmful facts made known in a workplace, for instance.[14] But such cases remain a clear minority. The law continues to be faithful to Mabel Warren's ancient intentions: distrust of the press.

The disclosure tort thus targets by design precisely the kinds of defendants likely to raise First Amendment concerns: defendants (like newspapers) who spread truthful news to a wide audience. At the same time, the focus on mass publicity diverts attention away from other uses of words that may be both more injurious and less threatening to the First Amendment. Legal scholar Robert Post has explained that "[w]e often care more about what those within our 'group' think of us than we do about our reputation among the strangers who comprise the general public. Yet the publicity requirement, as defined by the Restatement, would impose sanctions for the disclosure of a husband's marital infidelity to the general public, but not for its disclosure to his wife."[15]

"Public" and "Private"

Now consider the tort's reliance on the old Warren and Brandeis line between private facts and public facts. The tort requires courts to separate facts that are private ("not of legitimate concern to the public") from facts that the public is allowed to know. In practice, this can be an impossible task. Information can be in both categories at once (think of Giggs's or Bill Clinton's extramarital affairs), or it can lie in the extremely fuzzy area between the two concepts, which are themselves poorly defined. My point is not that the public-private line is indefensible or always unworkable, but that the disclosure tort requires courts to engage in a process that is, as law professor Lior Strahilevitz puts it, an "abstract, circular, and highly indeterminate question."[16]

The public-private distinction's line-drawing problem is dwarfed by a much larger free speech problem. The idea that courts should police which publications are of "legitimate concern to the public" and which are not raises a serious risk of censorship. Warren and Brandeis acknowledged this problem in 1890 but had faith in the ability of courts to police the line in a fair and principled manner.[17] This is the assumption on which English courts rely in granting super-injunctions. But in the United States, it has been flatly rejected by the modern course of First Amendment law.

Brandeis, too, came to reject it. As we saw in the previous chapter, he questioned the ability of courts to police the news in the *International News Service v. Associated Press*, because in a complex society, "the public interest tends to become omnipresent."[18] Courts could not censor newspaper publications, he suggested, because news reports were the public interest *by definition*. In a democracy, it is not the job of the courts to say what is fit for the public to read, but is instead the job of those readers themselves. As I have shown in a study of Brandeis's free speech opinions, Brandeis's thinking along these lines continued to evolve so that by the end of his career, he was willing to contemplate only a tiny set of cases in which the disclosure tort was appropriate.[19]

Later privacy cases bore out the fear that although the line between public and private makes sense in the abstract, it is impossible to draw with any confidence or predictability in practice. Brandeis's two innovations—the disclosure tort and free speech—evolved at the same time, but free speech became dominant. In a fascinating study of disclosure tort cases from the mid-twentieth century, legal historian Samantha Barbas has shown how judges deciding disclosure tort press cases were actually thinking through the basic elements of freedom of speech. Those judges came to embrace a broad sense of what was of "legitimate concern to the public" in a democracy at the expense of Mabel Warren's aristocratic disclosure tort. Both judges and broader American society came to understand "the emergence of the concept of 'the public's right to know' about the world through the news media, and … that the purpose of the news is not only to inform citizens about the complex workings of modern society but to generate public discourse." For this to happen, there needed to be "robust legal and constitutional protection for a free press, and news content must be 'as extensive as the range of (the public's) interests and concerns.'"[20]

The Supreme Court has taken a similarly broad view of matters of "legitimate public concern" in First Amendment cases for the past fifty years. In *Time v. Hill*, an ordinary family that had been the victim of a famous kidnapping sued the producers of a drama about them under the "false light" privacy tort. The Court held that because of the importance of public discussion in the media, they had to meet the stringent standard of defamation law and show that the production was intentionally or recklessly false.[21] This was necessary because free discussion in a democratic society needs wide latitude, including the ability to discuss celebrities or private citizens whose lives become bound up in noteworthy events.[22]

This is a central principle of the modern First Amendment—the idea that free speech is valuable because it helps to preserve an informed citizenry, and the state should not attempt to proscribe the fit subjects for public debate.[23] *Snyder v. Phelps*, the Court's most recent word on tort privacy and free speech, also applied this standard, giving strong protection to even offensive and unrefined speech on matters "of interest to society at large."[24] The speech protected in that case was a "God Hates Fags" sign displayed by the roadside at a military funeral. This result is traceable back to Louis Brandeis, who argued that the remedy for bad speech is more speech. It also represents the germination of his mature free speech jurisprudence—ideas that are directly at odds with many of the assumptions and arguments of *The Right to Privacy*.[25]

Emotional Harm

Finally, consider the nature of the injury that the disclosure tort protects—the emotional harm of unwanted public disclosures. Remedying the emotional harm caused by words clashes directly with the modern First Amendment in yet another way. An additional pillar of modern First Amendment law is the idea that words causing hurt feelings, without more, cannot be punished by the state or made the basis for civil liability. As early as 1940, the Court held in *Cantwell v. Connecticut* that the First Amendment protected speakers who played a record aggressively denouncing the pope as evil, even though the record deeply offended the audience.[26]

The idea that emotional harm cannot trump free speech is one of the most important principles of First Amendment law. In *New York Times v. Sullivan* (1964), the Supreme Court announced what scholars called the "central meaning" of the modern First Amendment—that the best justification for free speech is that it protects democratic self-government by public discussion.[27] The *Sullivan* Court wanted to ensure that public debate be "uninhibited, robust, and wide-open," even if it might produce "vehement, caustic, and sometimes unpleasantly sharp attacks" on public men and women and their role in society.[28] Consequently, free speech has been strongly privileged at the expense of even serious emotional harm. It is no defense to speech on public matters to say that it hurt your feelings. This is not the case because emotional harm is trivial, since emotional harm is real harm. Instead, hurt feelings lose because public debate is ultimately more important. Emotional harm caused by public discussion is a price we pay for a free society.

Sullivan was not a privacy case, but dealt with the closely related law of defamation. Later cases made clear that the *Sullivan* privilege for speech over emotional harm applies in the privacy area as well. *Time v. Hill*, discussed earlier, extended the *Sullivan* rule to false light invasion of privacy claims against the press. Because both defamation and disclosure cause injuries through public speech, the Court reasoned, both torts needed to be limited in the interests of vibrant debate on public matters. In other cases, the Court explained that giving juries the power to award damages for speech that offends creates the risk of speakers being punished merely because their speech is unpopular.[29]

Thus, when the Court has heard cases pitting the disclosure tort against the First Amendment, the disclosure tort has consistently lost. Many of these cases have involved media disclosure of the names of rape victims. In these cases, the press learned the name of the victim from court files or the police and published it. In each of these cases, the Court ruled in favor of the First Amendment, though it has been careful not to declare the disclosure tort unconstitutional in every possible case.[30] The Court made this point most explicit in the *Florida Star* case, when it held that "if a newspaper lawfully obtains truthful information about a matter of public significance then state officials may not constitutionally punish publication of the information, absent a need to further a state interest of the highest order."[31] In this and other cases, the Court seems concerned about protecting truthful speech in a democracy, a fear of making the press timid in spreading the news, and also the fact that less restrictive means than censorship usually exist to protect privacy.

This last point about "less restrictive means" is particularly important. For example, in the *Cox* case, the press learned the name of the rape victim from publicly available court records. By protecting the press's publication of the name, the Court was essentially saying that if the state wants to protect the privacy of a secret in its possession, it needs to do more than the essentially lazy step of authorizing censorship. It must do something less threatening to a free press, like not putting the victim's name in the public record, or by requiring reporters accessing the record to agree not to publish the name as a condition of access. And, of course, the First Amendment places no bar on victims suing the state for negligent disclosures of their private facts. Some American courts have recognized a constitutional right of information privacy against state disclosures of embarrassing or harmful information.[32]

The strongest statement that remedies for words causing emotional harm threaten free speech is *Hustler Magazine v. Falwell* (1988).[33] The case involved a parody of televangelist Jerry Falwell in *Hustler Magazine* that made fun of Falwell's public moralizing. (It implied that he had had sex with his mother in an outhouse once they had evicted a goat from the premises.) But in spite of the nastiness of the parody and its intention to cause emotional harm, the Court unanimously protected the speech. At least where public figures are the subject of the intentional infliction of emotional distress, the First Amendment protects even "outrageous" attempts to cause emotional harm through crude caricature. Part of the problem is a practical one—it is difficult to separate out worthless speech causing emotional harm from valuable expression. Considering the question, Chief Justice William Rehnquist noted that "if it were possible by laying down a principled standard to separate the one from the other, public discourse would probably suffer little or no harm. But we doubt that there is any such standard, and we are quite sure that the pejorative description 'outrageous' does not supply one."[34] When it comes to separating emotional harassment from protected speech, then, we run into the same line-drawing problem as in the public-private distinction. In matters of public debate, it is impossible to draw any principled line between public and private, or reasonable and outrageous, so we must ultimately choose one value or the other.

The practical problem of separating the protected from the unprotected is hard enough for courts acting in good faith, but the murky legal standard creates a second problem—the risk of censorship on the basis of viewpoint or dislike of the speaker. In the *Hustler Magazine* case, the Court recognized this problem as well, noting that allowing recovery for "outrageous" speech has an inherent subjectiveness about it which would allow a jury to impose liability on the basis of the jurors' tastes or views, or perhaps on the basis of their dislike of a particular expression. An "outrageousness" standard thus runs afoul of our longstanding refusal to allow damages to be awarded because the speech in question may have an adverse emotional impact on the audience.[35]

In the recent case of *Snyder v. Phelps*, dealing with the protests of military funerals by the Westboro Baptist Church, the Court again protected highly offensive speech on this ground. It concluded that outrageous speech must be protected because of the risk that juries would punish speakers for their viewpoint rather than the harm they cause. When tort injury conflicts with free speech, the Court concluded, free speech must prevail because "in public debate we must tolerate insulting, and even outrageous speech in order to provide adequate 'breathing space' to the freedoms protected by the First Amendment."[36]

These three problems inherent in the design of the disclosure tort—the media as a target, the public-private problem, and damages based on emotional harm—mean that the disclosure tort is in direct conflict with the First Amendment. This is particularly true in the very cases that it was created to address—actions against the media for the publication of private facts that caused emotional harm. Perhaps ironically, disclosure-based theories of relief might be more applicable when the press is not involved because these scenarios don't involve public figures and seem to raise less of a First Amendment threat. Wal-Mart has much less right to disclose Elli Lake's nude shower pictures, for example, than the press have to report on Ryan Giggs or other people in the public eye.

The history of the development of disclosure privacy and free speech over the twentieth century thus reveals that we must ultimately make a choice—either categorically or on a case-by-case basis—between disclosure privacy and freedom of speech.

Choosing Free Speech over the Disclosure Tort

If we must choose between disclosure privacy and speech in most cases, what choice or choices should we make? I believe that American law's preference for free speech over disclosure privacy is basically correct: When free speech clashes with disclosure privacy, we should choose free expression, subject to a few limited exceptions. Mabel Warren's nineteenth-century class anxiety should not be the basis for privacy law in the twenty-first century. Nor should Ryan Giggs's image or emotional anxieties suffice.

The clash between the disclosure tort and free speech has occupied courts and scholars in the United States for decades.[37] But at the risk of oversimplifying, there are essentially two positions. On one side are First Amendment critics of disclosure privacy. These legal scholars argue that the disclosure tort is largely or entirely unconstitutional and should be jettisoned in the interests of free speech. As early as 1967, Harry Kalven argued that "fascination with the great Brandeis trade mark, excitement over the law at a point of growth, and appreciation of privacy as a key value have combined to dull the normal critical sense of judges and commentators and have caused them not to see the pettiness of the tort they have sponsored."[38] Fifteen years later, Diane Zimmerman went further and suggested that the disclosure tort was not only unworkable in practice, but "created a cause of action that, however formulated, cannot coexist with constitutional protections for freedom of speech and press."[39]

On the other side of the debate, many privacy scholars claim that disclosure privacy serves important social interests, and that we should be able to strike a balance between privacy and speech, preserving control over injurious gossip while maintaining a robust commitment to speech of legitimate public interest. Robert Post maintains that the disclosure tort serves a social purpose in the "maintenance of rules of civility" that protect human dignity.[40] Daniel Solove argues that the disclosure tort can be balanced with the First Amendment and can apply to "speech of private concern." He argues that Brandeis "reconciled free speech and privacy with the newsworthiness test"[41] and that the law should do a better job striking a "delicate balance" between speech and privacy in individual cases.

While my personal sympathies lie closer to the privacy scholars, the First Amendment critics have the better of the argument most of the time with respect to the disclosure tort. Protecting against emotional harm is important. But in a democratic society, it is just too dangerous to give courts a wide-ranging power in press cases to separate out "legitimate" truth from "illegitimate" truth that people have no right to hear.

Ultimately, as in other areas of freedom of speech, readers and viewers should be the judge of what is appropriate fodder for public debate.

Thus, when the First Amendment critique applies in the traditional disclosure context, it ought to triumph. Post is correct that, in its Gilded Age origins and in its protection of emotional harm and propriety, disclosure privacy protects against egregious breaches of etiquette. But that's precisely the problem. Because of the way it is structured to remedy emotional injury, the Warren and Brandeis privacy tort runs into unresolvable problems when it is applied against truth the public wants to know, whether published by the press or other speakers.[42] The problem with Post's theory is that the core of the modern First Amendment protects a right to offend in furtherance of the robust exchange of ideas and information. First Amendment rights must trump disclosure privacy except in cases of truly extraordinary disclosures of private information. This is the case because free speech is simply a more important value. Free speech can be costly, but we protect civil liberties in spite of their costs, not because those costs aren't real.

So what about the sort of "delicate balance" that Solove calls for? As I have shown, the design of the common law disclosure tort makes it highly amenable to abuse. It can be a pretext for censorship, but it can also be used by well-meaning judges to chill public debate. Consider Ryan Giggs, one of the most famous men in Britain, and a focus of discussion on matters of athletic excellence, fitness, and (like it or not) morality. In 2013, Giggs played his thousandth football match and was widely feted for his longevity and professional dedication. You could certainly talk about athletic longevity or infidelity without mentioning Giggs, but it makes it harder to do so. The injunction in the Giggs case cut off that debate. It is undoubtedly true that we talk too much about the sex lives of celebrities, and we may well build up our celebrities only to knock them down again to public delight. But judges (even well-meaning ones) should not be the ones to make a decision about fit topics for discussion for the entire public. And they should not have the ability to keep only negative stories about celebrities out of public debate. For better or worse, our society uses its celebrities (whether Giggs, the Kardashians, Justin Bieber, Rihanna and Chris Brown, or others) as people we "know" in common to discuss topics that matter to us all. Celebrities are common reference points around which we organize our public discussions, whether in the media or around the proverbial office water cooler. And when Giggs is used as a vehicle to discuss personal excellence, negative facts about him are just as relevant as positive ones. A judge could be wrong about whether the public needed to know about Giggs. This is in fact what happened in 2011, when much of the world was talking about his infidelity, but the English newspapers were enjoined from doing the same. As Brandeis realized in the *Associated Press* case, a "delicate balance" by judges is a dangerous power. In a democracy, individuals should be able to determine for themselves what is fit for public debate.

I should make three important qualifications to my argument at this point. First, I am talking primarily about celebrities at this stage. Disclosures about ordinary people are different. The public interest in discussing individual unremarkable people is less, and mass disclosure is needed to trigger at least the classic form of the disclosure tort.

Second, such disclosures about ordinary people frequently take place in the Internet context (whether on blogs or social media), which also presents a different case than newspapers. But the problem with crafting solutions to these issues is that we have thought about privacy in Mabel Warren's terms for more than a century. If we want to solve the new problems that are confronting modern society, we need to be able to put the model of disclosure privacy to one side so that we can think more imaginatively about what values we want to protect and how we should protect them.

The third qualification is that extraordinary cases involving (for instance) disclosures of explicit sex videos, present a different situation. Consider the recent debate about "revenge porn," the disclosure of sexual images of ordinary people (usually by former lovers) without their consent. While the upload of a sex video to a website would satisfy "publicity," it is difficult to make any credible case that our systems of free expression and self-government would be threatened by allowing liability for the emotional harm or breach of trust in the revenge porn phenomenon. Unwanted publication of a sex video would seem to cause much greater injury and to be far less necessary to public debate.

Protection against the nonconsensual distribution of sex videos could also extend to celebrities or other public figures. Consider also the case of *Bollea v. Gawker*, which is pending in the Florida courts. In that case, retired professional wrestler Terry Bollea (better known by his stage name Hulk Hogan) was secretly recorded having sex with a friend's wife in her private bedroom. The recording made its way into the hands of the celebrity gossip website Gawker.com, which published an edited sexually explicit version of the "highlights" of the sexual encounter in which Hogan's erect penis could be seen clearly. In such a case, the First Amendment would not prevent Bollea from recovering for the nonconsensual publication of the sex tape on the Internet. While it might create First Amendment difficulties for a court to impose damages or enjoin a gossip website's disclosure of the fact of a celebrity affair, the worldwide distribution of the accompanying sex video would be another matter entirely under the First Amendment. In fact, the defendants in that case seemed to recognize this fact when they labeled the video "NSFW," or "Not Safe For Work."

To return to the example with which this chapter began, naming Ryan Giggs as an adulterer is one thing; publishing high-resolution video of his sex acts would be another. Even courts in America are willing to grant relief in celebrity cases of this sort and impose liability for psychological injuries over free press challenges.[43] Take, for example, the infamous sex tape case involving the famous couple, actress Pamela Anderson Lee and rock star Bret Michaels. In that case, Michaels and Lee consensually made a video that depicted them having sex. The sex tape was obtained by an Internet video distributor, which intended to publish the video for profit. When they learned about the company's intentions, Lee and Michaels successfully obtained an injunction preventing the distribution under theories of invasion of privacy and copyright. With respect to the invasion of privacy claim, the court found that the disclosure of a privately recorded celebrity sex tape was not newsworthy, notwithstanding the fact that Lee had previously appeared nude in "magazines, movies, and publicly distributed videotapes." The court explained that merely because Lee had appeared nude as a professional actor in "roles involving sex and sexual appeal ... does not ... make her real sex life open to the public." This was the case even though a previous sex tape featuring Lee and her former husband, rock musician Tommy Lee, had also had a "wide distribution." The court also noted that Bret Michaels had a privacy interest in not having his sex life exposed, notwithstanding the fact that he was also a celebrity and a sex symbol. "While Michaels's voluntary assumption of fame as a rock star throws open his private life to some extent," the court explained, "even people who voluntarily enter the public sphere retain a privacy interest in the most intimate details of their lives." Thus, while the fact that the two celebrities were romantically involved along with the details of that involvement might be a matter of public interest, the video of their sex life (as the most intimate of human activities) was outside the scope of press privilege.[44]

To return once more to Ryan Giggs, we don't need to see him naked to discuss his infidelity. While barring him from a discussion of public morality is one thing, protecting even a celebrity from malicious revenge porn is another. Admittedly, even when we are talking about such extraordinary cases, the line being drawn is a blurred one. Such cases are likely to remain outliers, and appropriately so. As Brandeis himself grudgingly recognized later in life, a tort-based conception of privacy protecting against purely emotional harm must remain exceptional in a legal system regime dedicated to speech, publicity, and disclosure.[45] Nonconsensual distribution of sex videos is one exception, but there are unlikely to be many others.

Dignity

At this point, European (or European-minded) readers could offer a different defense of Ryan Giggs's press injunction. Even if Giggs's emotional harm would not be enough to trump the public interest in discussion of his sex life, he has suffered a different, more important injury from the emotional one that has preoccupied American law. In Europe, Giggs has a constitutional right to the protection of his family life, guaranteed by Article 8 of the European Convention of Human Rights. Putting his emotional distress to the side, the argument goes, doesn't Giggs have a right to human dignity that the press infringed by dragging his name through the mud?

As an interpretation of English (and Continental) privacy law, this argument would be correct. Under the European Convention, the Article 8 right of privacy and the Article 11 right of free speech are coequal and must be balanced with each other in a way that is consistent with a democratic society.[46] But this argument is not convincing. A regime of disclosure privacy is threatening to a free press regardless of how we dress up the interest on the other side. As Brandeis recognized long ago, in any democratic society, individual citizens and not the government must ultimately be the judge of what is a fit subject for public debate. As he explained in *Whitney*, freedom of speech in a democratic society rests on belief in our democratic institutions and the culture of counter-speech: "the fitting remedy for evil counsels is good ones [, not] silence coerced by law—the argument of force in its worst form."[47]

The power to mark certain subjects off limits—the power to gag a free press from reporting the truth—is the very essence of censorship. Ultimately, when it comes to determining matters of truth and matters of what is fit for public consumption, a free society must let the people decide rather than appointing elite judges (no matter how well-meaning) as censors. This is the only balance consistent with our values, whether under the First Amendment or Articles 8 and 11 of the European Convention on Human Rights.

To be clear, this is a value choice, just like the value choice between free speech and emotional harm. But if we value democracy, we should choose free speech again in this context. The dignity of a democratic society with a free press is more important than the dignity of a professional athlete using lawyers to protect his image from the truth, even when the press itself may be acting in ways that are undignified. This is true on both sides of the Atlantic.

More fundamentally, if we are seriously interested in tackling the problems of privacy in the digital age, Mabel Warren's genteel tort is wholly the wrong place to start. After refusing to recognize an American-style "right to privacy" for more than a century, English courts have decided to do just that, and they have adopted the Mabel Warren model. But these cases show two additional, different reasons why the Mabel Warren model is a bad idea, even if we phrase it as protecting "dignity."

First, the English privacy cases show how, in the age of the global web and social media, privacy injunctions are ineffective. Legal process alone cannot keep the truth from spreading, at least where lots of enquiring minds want to know that truth. This is one of the many lessons of the Giggs case, in which well-meaning judges trying to protect his dignity produced an absurd result, gagging newspapers, while gossip and Twitter spread the news through other channels. When the prime minister can go on television and talk about how everyone knows the truth but no one can talk about it, something is deeply broken in a free society committed to the open exchange of ideas and information about matters the public cares about.

The second lesson of the English privacy cases is that the sex lives of celebrities are a terrible model on which to build a regime of privacy protection. We should no more build our privacy law on Ryan Giggs as we should build it on Mabel Warren. If we want to protect the privacy of ordinary people, we should use ordinary people as the base from which we build our privacy law. The model for privacy law should be people whose dinner parties are not covered by the *New York Times* and people who play football (or other sports) for fun, not because Manchester United is paying them millions of pounds a year. Ordinary people cannot hold press conferences to rebut press coverage about them, nor hire high-priced counsel to litigate on a whim. We should build privacy law primarily for them, rather than for socialites or professional athletes. Most of all, we should build a regime of privacy protection for the media and problems of the twenty-first century, not the nineteenth.

***

Mabel Warren's aristocratic tort has grabbed the attention of courts and the public on both sides of the Atlantic for too long. Its fame has focused our attention on a kind of privacy that is of little use and that is threatening to a free press. More important, it has distracted us from thinking about other ways to protect privacy, and other kinds of privacy that are more important. We need to imagine other ways to protect privacy. The next two chapters take up this challenge of thinking about privacy beyond disclosure. They each show a different way to protect privacy in ways that are consistent with free speech. Chapter 4 shows ways to protect privacy consistent with the First Amendment by focusing on the collection, rather than the disclosure, of information, while chapter 5 shows that the First Amendment critique is much weaker outside the press context and does not doom other kinds of privacy law that try to regulate the commercial flow of data.

4

Invasion

The Dorm Room Camera

Tyler Clementi was a Rutgers University student in his first semester of college in the fall semester of 2010. Shy and somewhat awkward, he had come out to his parents as gay shortly before leaving for college. Although he'd had trouble making friends in high school, Tyler met a man shortly after starting college, and the two began an intimate relationship. On September 19, Tyler invited the man back to his dorm room and asked Dharun Ravi, his roommate, for some privacy. Dharun left the room, but didn't respect Tyler's privacy. Instead, he went to the room of his hall-mate, Molly Wei, where the two covertly watched some of Tyler's sexual encounter using the webcam on Dharun's computer. Dharun boasted about the incident online, tweeting, "Roommate asked for the room till midnight. I went into molly's room and turned on my webcam. I saw him making out with a dude. Yay."[1] A few days later, when Tyler again asked to have the room to himself for another meeting, Dharun made preparations to watch once more, inviting his Twitter followers to view streaming video of the sequel using the videoconferencing software iChat.

On September 22, apparently as a result of the torment caused by these events, Tyler Clementi jumped to his death from the George Washington Bridge.[2] Although no one saw him jump, his wallet and phone were found at the edge of the bridge, and his last words were the haunting Facebook status update "Jumping off the gw bridge sorry." His body was found a week later by a man taking a lunchtime walk.[3] It is not known whether Tyler's sexual orientation was a contributing factor in Dharun's actions, but the incident gained nationwide attention. Tyler's tragedy touched a nerve and prompted a national debate about harassment of young people on the basis of their sexuality. It gave impetus to the "It Gets Better Project" in support of gay youth, which became highly successful with its message to young gay men and women who might be the victims of bullying that life can and does get better.[4] Dharun Ravi was prosecuted in state court on fifteen charges, including criminal invasion of privacy. On March 16, 2012, he was convicted by a jury of all charges.

Disclosure of Sex Videos

Tyler Clementi was undoubtedly the victim of a wrong, but what was the nature of that wrong? To put the question more precisely, if we want to use the law to prevent situations like this from happening more frequently, how should we conceive of the wrong in legal terms? After all, if we want to craft a useful solution, we need to better understand the nature of the problem.

Press accounts in the aftermath of the tragedy focused largely on the wrongful disclosure of the video on Twitter, and Ravi's actions do fit the classic form of Warren and Brandeis.[5] In the previous chapter, I showed how the basic structure of the disclosure tort is inconsistent with the First Amendment, which generally protects truthful mass disclosures. I suggested, however, that the dissemination of sex tapes (especially those of ordinary people) might be different. Now is a good time to explain more completely why this is the case.

The disclosure tort (like all torts) remedies an injury. The injury Warren and Brandeis imagined was one to a person's personality caused by unwanted (and embarrassing) publicity. But we've seen that giving everyone a broad version of this right is often inconsistent with free speech. I've argued that this particular free speech critique of tort privacy should triumph where it applies. Nevertheless, the free speech critique has limits of its own. The First Amendment does not immunize *all* true statements by all speakers (or even all journalists). Even though Warren and Brandeis's core case of disclosure of private embarrassing facts by the press is largely unconstitutional, it certainly doesn't follow that all privacy claims (even against the press) are unconstitutional, too. Under current law, the well-established (and I think correct) rule is that if a speaker "lawfully obtains truthful information about a matter of public significance then state officials may not constitutionally punish publication of the information, absent a need ... of the highest order."[6] I want to unpack this language. When we do this, we'll see that under current law there are four important exceptions to the general principle that publication is always constitutionally protected.

1. *Falsity.* If the information disclosed is not true, all bets are off, and the applicable law would be defamation, which remedies false statements of fact. American defamation law after *New York Times v. Sullivan* is notoriously speaker-friendly, but where the information is false and intentionally disclosed, the speaker can be held liable under the actual malice standard for public figure plaintiffs, or lower standards for other plaintiffs.[7]

2. *"Not of Legitimate Concern to the Public."* A second exception under current law is that disclosures of private information not of legitimate concern to the public (not "newsworthy") are entitled to a lower level of First Amendment protection. Daniel Solove relies on this exception when he argues that because the Supreme Court has hinted that speech on matters of private concern is less protected than other kinds of speech, the Court "has thus left open an area for the public-disclosure tort to thrive."[8] This interpretation of the law probably overstates the vitality under American law of both the disclosure tort and disclosure-based theories of privacy more generally. The Supreme Court has been very reluctant in practice to second-guess the editorial judgments of journalists.[9] Similarly, most courts define what is newsworthy by what is published by the press, under the theory that the press is the best judge of what sells papers.

Nevertheless, a few kinds of truly outrageous disclosures have been found to be outside the public interest. In such extraordinary cases, usually involving sexually themed disclosures, tort privacy can survive a direct clash with the First Amendment protections given to the press. As discussed earlier, a few such cases impose liability for psychological injuries over free speech challenges, most famously one granting an injunction to actress Pamela Anderson Lee against the distribution of a graphic sex tape.[10] But, as noted in chapter 3 such cases must remain outliers. Insofar as the public disclosure tort remedies breaches of etiquette, only the most psychologically harmful and outrageous breaches of social norms would seem to satisfy this exception.

Courts are also reluctant to second-guess the views of individual citizens about what the legitimate topics of public debate really are. Thus, in *Snyder v. Phelps*, the Supreme Court deferred to the Westboro Baptist Church's argument that the "God Hates Fags" posters it displayed near a military funeral were speech on a matter of public concern.[11] (To be fair, if the Church is correct that an angry God is punishing America for its sexual licentiousness, most members of the public would want to know this fact.) The power to declare facts or topics to be off-limits to public discussion is, in a very real sense the power to censor. Modern First Amendment theory is built around Brandeis's argument in *Whitney* that individual citizens determine the appropriate limits of public debate, and the normal remedy for harmful or otherwise "bad" speech is counter-speech rather than censorship. Courts have also routinely held that even the publication of the name of a rape victim is "newsworthy." Given censorship concerns in this area, it is hard to imagine a category beyond the dissemination of videos of sexual or other intimate bodily activities that would satisfy this exception.

3. *Unlawfully Obtained Information.* There is a third and even more important exception to the general rule that truthful information can never be restricted. Even if the information disclosed is true, and even if it is newsworthy, disclosure can be punished if the information was unlawfully obtained. In the case of *Bartnicki v. Vopper*, radio DJ Mike Vopper broadcast a recording of an intercepted telephone call that an unknown person had sent him. The Court held that even though Vopper knew the conversation had been illegally obtained in violation of the federal Wiretap Act, the First Amendment protected his broadcast. This is consistent with the story we've developed so far. But the Court also explained that if Vopper had participated in or solicited the wiretap, the First Amendment wouldn't protect him from civil or criminal punishment:

> Our holding, of course, does not apply to punishing parties for obtaining the relevant information unlawfully. It would be frivolous to assert—and no one does in these cases—that the First Amendment,

in the interest of securing news or otherwise, confers a license on either the reporter or his news sources to violate valid criminal laws. Although stealing documents or private wiretapping could provide newsworthy information, neither reporter nor source is immune from conviction for such conduct, whatever the impact on the flow of news.[12]

This explanation illustrates the uncontroversial idea in First Amendment law that the press or other speakers have no exemption from "generally applicable laws." Speakers have wide discretion in being able to disseminate ideas and information, but this fact does not give the press or anyone else the right to disregard the ordinary tort, contract, property, and regulatory laws that govern all of us in our daily affairs. From this perspective, there is a crucial distinction between breaking the law to obtain information (whether by wiretapping, trespassing, hacking, or other means) and the innocent dissemination of news generated by that law-breaking.

4. *Compelling Government Interests.* The fourth and perhaps largest exception to the principle of protection for true facts is the presence of a state "interest of the highest order."[13] This is merely another way of saying that state restrictions on the publication of true, newsworthy, lawfully obtained facts invoke what constitutional law calls "strict scrutiny." When strict scrutiny applies to a law, it is presumed to be unconstitutional unless it is justified by a compelling government interest, and it is narrowly tailored to advance only that interest without otherwise burdening free speech (or whatever other constitutional interest is burdened).[14] But it is possible to imagine compelling government interests that could suffice to justify a speech restriction. For instance, national security could trump the First Amendment if a newspaper is disclosing the lawfully obtained names of spies, or the "publication of the sailing dates of transports or the number and location of troops" or other time-sensitive military secrets.[15]

In the *Pentagon Papers* case, the Court held that publication of Defense Department documents relating to the Vietnam War could not be enjoined unless the government proved a serious threat to national security. (The Court also held that the Nixon administration had failed to prove its case.) The famous case reveals that it can be hard to get an injunction before publication because of prior restraint concerns, but it says nothing authoritative about whether the press can be punished after publication for injuring national security.[16] Under current law, for example, it is a federal crime for anyone to disclose defense secrets that could be used to the "injury of the United States or to the advantage of any foreign nation."[17] This statute is likely constitutional even as applied to the disclosure of true, newsworthy, lawfully obtained facts, but only as applied to materials for which the government can prove an actual and serious threat to national security.

The problem with the "interest of the highest order" exception is that the showing necessary to satisfy the exception is extremely high—the compelling government interest and least-restrictive means required to satisfy First Amendment strict scrutiny. It is no coincidence that the standard example given here is harm to national security caused by the disclosure of defense secrets or dangerous technical information like the construction of bombs or weapons of mass destruction. In such cases the potential harm is lots of dead soldiers or civilians.

By contrast, the harm from unwanted disclosure could only qualify as a compelling interest in the most extraordinary of cases. There have been many cases seeking the censorship of true but harmful information, but few interests other than national security have survived the scrutiny that this exception requires. In the *Landmark Communications* case, for instance, the Court held that the confidentiality of a state judicial ethics investigation was an insufficiently strong interest to punish the press for divulging lawfully obtained information about an ongoing procedure.[18] Central to the Court's reasoning was the availability of a less restrictive means—rather than punishing the press for publishing the truth, it suggested, the state should first try the more modest step of attempting to reduce the likelihood of leaks from state employees to the press. In *Nebraska Press v. Stuart*, the state interest arrayed against the freedom of the press was of a constitutional magnitude—the fair trial rights of an accused defendant in a high-profile murder case whom the trial court sought to protect by enjoining reportage on his alleged confession.[19] The constitutional criminal procedure rights of the defendant would seem to be at least as strong as tort privacy rights.[20] But in this case as well, the Court held for the newspaper, reasoning that before taking the blunt step of restricting the free flow of true information in the press, the state could take other measures less restrictive of First Amendment rights, such as a change of venue, postponement of the trial until the media frenzy had abated, jury instructions to disregard facts learned outside the trial, or even sequestration of the jury. And in a more recent example, the WikiLeaks dispute produced much speculation about whether Julian Assange could be punished for the disclosure of diplomatic cables under this exception, and experts were divided about whether even this disclosure could be punished without additional factors present such as hacking or solicitation of leaks.[21]

We can now return to the question at hand—whether the disclosure tort (or something like it) would permit the punishment of something like the facts of the Tyler Clementi case as initially reported—the recording and sharing of a private video of sexual activity. Recall the elements of the tort—(1) *publicity* given to (2) *private facts* that aren't of legitimate concern to the public, but that are (3) *highly offensive*. Assuming that Dharun Ravi's tweet gave sufficient "publicity" to qualify for the disclosure tort, liability for a disclosure of this kind would be fairly straightforward under both the tort and the First Amendment. The video of Tyler Clementi's sexual activity is a private fact that is not of legitimate public concern (who, on September 19, 2010, had heard of Tyler?), and the dissemination of the video would be highly offensive to a reasonable person. Most people don't want their sexual activities secretly captured and publicized on Twitter. Thus, there would seem to be a cause of action under the disclosure tort for the release of a secretly recorded sex video.

But think again. What if the *New York Times* had published a lawfully obtained recording of Tyler's sexual encounter at the height of the "It Gets Better" campaign? Could the press be held liable for violating the disclosure tort in that case? If *Bartnicki* is any guide, the answer would appear to be "no." Because the press did not participate in the secret recording, the information would have been lawfully obtained by the press. Moreover, it is much harder in the case of press publication to argue that the tape would not now be "of legitimate concern to the public." When a video like Clementi's sparks a public debate on cyberbullying and acceptance of different sexual orientations, what was an easier case of non-newsworthiness for a non-press defendant becomes much more complicated because the video would then be at the center of a public debate. And when the debate centers on the content of the video ("What actually did happen in that dorm room? Was it kissing or sex? Enquiring and self-governing minds want to know!"), it becomes impossible to say that those contents are not of legitimate public concern. From the perspective of the First Amendment, we have (1) true (2) newsworthy facts that are (3) now lawfully obtained. Thus, even though the First Amendment might not protect Ravi's disclosure of a video he secretly recorded, it would protect the media from disclosing a copy of the video that it obtained lawfully, even when the emotional harm from a mass press disclosure would be far worse. The fact that the disclosure tort might fail to protect even its strongest case shows the limits of disclosure as a theory of liability. Perhaps we need a different theory of the injury in a case like this.

Invasions of Privacy

Let's think more about why we might want to restrict the circulation of a hypothetical recording of Tyler and his boyfriend being intimate. What is the wrong here? Intuitively, it seems to have something to do with Dharun Ravi invading Tyler Clementi's privacy and in making that invasion worse through the circulation of the video. I said that there might be a compelling government interest in "restricting the circulation of secretly recorded sex tapes." We can talk about the disclosure of the video as an invasion of privacy, but it isn't clear that all disclosures of this video might be wrongful (such as by the *New York Times* to better understand a compelling public issue). Moreover, after Tyler's tragic death, the disclosure of the video cannot harm him emotionally. (It might harm his surviving family members emotionally, but this harm is much less direct.)

Nevertheless, the initial (and indefensibly wrongful) harm in the Tyler Clementi case was not the disclosure but the secret recording. Secretly recording someone engaging in sexual activities in his or her bedroom is an *invasion of privacy* in the most natural sense of the phrase. But this invasion of privacy is a different kind of harm from the disclosure of private facts. It is a harm that comes from a secret *observation* and recording by video rather than the *sharing* of that video. This harm is an intrusive surveillance rather than an offensive disclosure. And it is a harm that the law in Britain and the United States has recognized for a very long time. William Blackstone, for instance, discussed the old common law action against eavesdroppers "who listen under walls or windows, to hearken after discourse, and thereupon to frame slanderous and mischievous tales."[22]

American tort law also reflects the idea that invasions of privacy are different from disclosures of private facts. Recall from chapter 1 that the Warren and Brandeis theory of privacy spoke in terms of disclosure, but actually spawned at least four separate torts—disclosure, of course, but also the appropriation of likeness, publicity placing the plaintiff in a "false light," and the tort of intrusion into seclusion. The idea of intrusion into seclusion tracks naturally our intuitive sense of an "invasion of privacy." As restated by William Prosser, the tort of intrusion of seclusion provides that "[o]ne who intentionally intrudes, physically or otherwise, upon the solitude or seclusion of another or his private affairs or concerns, is subject to liability to the other for invasion of his privacy, if the intrusion would be highly offensive to a reasonable person."[23]

As with the disclosure tort, we can reorganize this language slightly into three elements. In order to intrude into someone's seclusion, a defendant must (1) intentionally (2) intrude into solitude or private affairs, and such an intentional intrusion must be (3) highly offensive to a reasonable person. These elements are much closer to the essence of the wrong that Dharun Ravi inflicted on Tyler Clementi—Ravi (1) intentionally (2) observed Tyler's private affairs of a kind that (3) most ordinary people would find unreasonably offensive and emotionally distressing. From this perspective, whether Ravi recorded his invasion of privacy or whether he shared the invasion with others is irrelevant to whether an injury occurred. Recording or disclosure could make the injury worse, but the injury occurs merely from one person secretly observing another's sexual activity. Every additional fact beyond this point is merely a further detail.[24]

The classic case of *Hamberger v. Eastman* (1964) illustrates this point perfectly. Eastman, a landlord, installed a listening device in the bedroom of his married tenants, the Hambergers. For more than a year, Eastman was able to listen to the Hambergers' private conversations and intimate bedroom activities.[25] Recognizing the right of privacy, the New Hampshire Supreme Court noted that "the tort of intrusion upon a plaintiff's solitude or seclusion is not limited to a physical invasion of his room or his quarters," but could occur by electronic or other kinds of surveillance. Moreover, the kind of intrusion in this case—secret listening in a marital bedroom—would be highly "offensive to any person of ordinary sensibilities."[26] Eastman argued that he should prevail because the Hambergers had failed to claim that he had published the fruits of his surveillance or shared them with anyone else. But the court made clear that these facts (even if true) were irrelevant to the invasion of privacy here—an invasion of privacy occurred when the listening device was placed and used. Further disclosure of any recordings might increase the amount of damages owed but would be irrelevant to whether an invasion of privacy had occurred.[27] Unlike the disclosure tort, then, invasions of privacy are based upon an *intrusion* rather than a *disclosure*, an act of *unlawful gathering* rather than an act of *speaking*.

Such a theory of harm based upon invasion is much less troubling from a First Amendment perspective. It's hard to imagine a defendant making a credible argument that he had a First Amendment right to use a secret camera to view his tenant (or roommate) having sex. Even if the invader were a journalist using a secret camera to record an event, it's still hard to make a serious First Amendment argument in such a case. After all, what part of the freedom of the press allows a person to break generally applicable civil and criminal rules against trespass, surveillance, and wiretapping to report even a newsworthy story? Even if we could imagine some cases (say, videos of political corruption) where we might be sympathetic to journalistic surveillance, a free speech claim is still much weaker than the right of the press to *disclose* true facts about that political corruption. But recall that our concern here is ordinary people as much as it is journalists. It's very hard to make a credible argument that I have (for instance) a First Amendment right to hide a surveillance camera in your bedroom to watch you having sex. The point is that even if we can imagine cases where there might be a First Amendment interest in invasion, such cases will be far more infrequent than cases where there is a First Amendment interest in disclosure.

Cases dealing with investigative journalists have reflected this intuition that invasions of privacy are much less threatening to the First Amendment than disclosures of true but embarrassing facts. For example, in *Dietemann v. Time* (1971), reporters from *Life Magazine* entered into an agreement with the Los Angeles District Attorney's Office, under which they would investigate A. A. Dietemann, an unlicensed provider of alternative medicine. Dietemann was "a disabled veteran with little education ... engaged in the practice of healing with clay, minerals, and herbs—as practiced, simple quackery."[28] Pretending to be patients, the reporters—Jackie Metcalf and William Ray—entered Dietemann's home with his consent and asked him to diagnose an alleged lump on Metcalf's breast. Dietemann used a wand and other gadgets to tell Metcalf that the lump had been caused by her eating some rancid butter eleven years, nine months, and seven days before. While Dietemann was distracted, Ray used a hidden camera to photograph him, and that photo was later used in a *Life Magazine* story entitled "Crackdown on Quackery."

Dietemann sued for intrusion upon seclusion, and the court agreed that his privacy had been illegally invaded by the reporters. Invasion of privacy was an easy case because the "clandestine photography of the plaintiff in his den" without his consent was the kind of emotionally distressing injury that courts had recognized in the past. Particularly important was the reporters' use of the hidden camera to take pictures of Dietemann. As the court put it memorably:

> One who invites another to his home or office takes a risk that the visitor may not be what he seems, and that the visitor may repeat all he hears and observes when he leaves. But he does not and should not be required to take the risk that what is heard and seen will be transmitted by photograph or recording, or in our modern world, in full living color and hi-fi to the public at large or to any segment of it that the visitor may select. A different rule could have a most pernicious effect upon the dignity of man and it would surely lead to guarded conversations and conduct where candor is most valued, e.g., in the case of doctors and lawyers.[29]

A more difficult question was whether the First Amendment gave the reporters the right to invade Dietemann's privacy in pursuit of a story. But here, too, the court agreed with Dietemann and rejected the reporters' First Amendment argument. Although it recognized that newsgathering was essential to the dissemination of the news, the court refused to find that reporters had the privilege of disregarding ordinary tort or criminal law rules in the pursuit of a story. As for their argument that cameras are indispensable newsgathering tools, the court dismissed it coolly: "Investigative reporting is an ancient art; its successful practice long antecedes the invention of miniature cameras and electronic devices."[30]

Not all cases dealing with newsgathering are as dismissive of the press interests in information collection, whether as part of tort law or whether mandated by the First Amendment.[31] But in general, it is much harder for reporters (or others) to defeat intrusion claims on First Amendment grounds. In the case of *Shulman v. Group W Productions*, for example, reporters filmed and broadcast the scene of a horrific accident and conversations between the victim and a nurse. The victims sued under both disclosure and intrusion theories. The disclosure claim failed because of the public interest in the operation of emergency services, consistent with similar deference we have seen in other disclosure cases. By contrast, the intrusion claim was successful because there is no First Amendment defense to the recording of a private conversation in an ambulance helicopter between an accident victim and her nurse.[32] Invasion-based theories of privacy law, in fact, lie behind many of our privacy laws, from laws prohibiting eavesdropping and wiretapping, to those that outlaw video voyeurism and harassment by paparazzi.[33] So long as these laws protect reasonably understood zones of seclusion, there is little concern that they violate even broad understandings of the First Amendment.

The intuitive idea of an "invasion of privacy" also supplies the answer to the question of what harm Tyler Clementi suffered, and how to deal with problems of this sort going forward. Secretly recording or observing a sex act is an invasion of privacy in the most obvious sense of the phrase. And in terms of the elements of the intrusion tort, we have (1) an intrusion (the secret recording) into (2) seclusion or private affairs (having sex in one's bedroom) that is (3) highly offensive (most people would be outraged to find secret listeners or hidden cameras in their bedrooms). It is instructive that the state criminal law under which Ravi was convicted worked under precisely this theory. In New Jersey, it is a crime to observe or record another person's sexual activity without their consent under circumstances where they would reasonably expect not to be observed.[34]

Such a case is also an easy one under the First Amendment, as there is no credible First Amendment defense to secret recording in such circumstances. There is an important difference between intrusion and disclosure with First Amendment consequences—unlike disclosure, which requires the act of disclosure of words or images, no act of expression is necessary to satisfy the intrusion tort. Publication is only relevant to intrusion when damages are computed. Thus, unless we are prepared to recognize a First

Amendment right to break laws in pursuit of gathering news[35] or to take secret video,[36] the intrusion tort has been satisfied without implicating the First Amendment at all.

Let's sum up. Invasions of privacy are similar to the Warren and Brandeis disclosure theory—they both deal with private information, and they both deal with offensive breaches of social norms. But invasion and disclosure are different breaches of good manners. Disclosure protects against emotionally harmful gossip, while intrusion often protects against emotionally harmful *collection* of the gossip, by a secret recorder, secret listener, or other intruder.[37] Because the elements of the tort do not create civil liability for speech, thereby affecting public debate directly, the intrusion tort does not raise immediate First Amendment concerns.[38] More fundamentally, if we are interested in protecting against what we colloquially call "invasions of privacy," the intrusion model is a better fit with our intuitive understandings of that phrase. Secret cameras or other surveillance devices "intrude" on our privacy more directly than publications about us that hurt our feelings. Thus, as we structure legal protections to protect private information from disclosure, the law should perhaps focus more on preventing unwanted collections or accumulations of information rather than preventing the dissemination of already-collected information.

Invasion's Limits

Thinking more about invasions of privacy and less about disclosures of embarrassing facts is one fruitful way to reimagine privacy law going forward, especially if we want a privacy law that is sensitive to free speech. But I want to be clear about the future of privacy law—balancing privacy law with free speech and other interests (such as law enforcement, technological advances, and anti-terrorism) will be hard. In balancing privacy and the freedom of speech, there are no silver bullets, unless perhaps we decide to give up one value in favor of the other. Invasion of privacy theory is no exception. In fact, what reconciles it with the First Amendment are its in-built limitations. Before we leave invasion of privacy, it is worth highlighting two of these limitations. I'll call them the *downstream use problem* and the *seclusion limitation*.

Let's consider the downstream use problem first. Think about the wiretapping in *Bartnicki* or the secret recording and dissemination of a sex tape. In each of these cases, there are two wrongful acts—there is the secret recording of audio and video, and then a subsequent distribution of that recording. Invasion of privacy theory protects against the illegal recording, for the reasons we've seen. And if the person who makes or encourages the illegal recording also publishes or shares it, he or she can be held liable for the disclosure as well. The First Amendment doesn't bar punishment for this kind of disclosure because the recording was "unlawfully obtained." But what if the publisher of the recording isn't the same person who made it and didn't otherwise solicit or encourage the recording? This is the *downstream use* problem, and it's precisely the problem that the Wiretap Act faced in *Bartnicki*.

A downstream user of a recording hasn't invaded anyone's privacy as we normally use the phrase. In a case like this, the logical remedy would be the disclosure tort, and, as we've seen, this remedy is severely constrained by the First Amendment. A disclosure of even an illegal recording is protected by the First Amendment so long as it is otherwise newsworthy. In practice, this means that while illegal recording of information can be punished as an invasion of privacy, the theory of invasion of privacy only applies to those who invade privacy (and those who collaborate with or encourage them). It does not reach downstream uses of newsworthy information by true third parties like the radio DJ in the *Bartnicki* case, and it's an important limitation to keep in mind. Even under a legal regime where lots of things are "newsworthy," however, sex tapes should rarely qualify. This is especially the case where those tapes were unlawfully recorded, or of ordinary people.

The second important limitation on invasions of privacy is the seclusion limitation. Remember the essence of an invasion of privacy—an intrusion into a zone of solitude or seclusion. It is an invasion of privacy to wiretap someone's phone or to secretly record sound or video in their bedroom. Recognizing this, many US jurisdictions have passed laws outlawing so-called "video voyeurism," the recording in private of someone's nude or mostly nude body without their consent.[39]

But invasion of privacy only applies when we are talking about a private place or relationship. It might be rude to capture someone's photograph on a public street or in a restaurant, but it's probably not an illegal invasion of privacy. The seclusion limitation is the reminder that you can only invade privacy if you are invading something private that would be offensive to an ordinary person. Nude beaches might be different from bedrooms. Similarly, a law banning (for instance) the taking of someone's photograph without their consent would be much broader than a right based on merely invasion of privacy.

Consider how this principle applies in practice. In recent years, citizens armed with smartphones and other portable video cameras have taken to recording police as they perform their duties. Some police have argued that they have something like a right of privacy not to be monitored or recorded by the public when they are working. In the case of *ACLU v. Alvarez*, a federal court rejected this argument. The court made clear that while there was no absolute First Amendment right to make audio recordings, a law preventing citizens from recording police in public placed too great a burden on the ability of citizens to monitor and discuss police activities. An essential part of this conclusion was the idea that making recordings was inextricably entwined with the expressive value of those recordings. Thus, the government could no more outlaw photography in public places than it could prevent journalists from taking notes at public meetings. Equally important in the *Alvarez* case was the idea that the police have no right of privacy in the performance of their public duties. The court made clear that intrusions into the seclusion of ordinary citizens in their private affairs were consistent with the First Amendment. But it is another thing entirely (and a laughable thing at that) for police or public servants to assert a right of privacy against the very people they are entrusted with serving. The seclusion limitation was inapplicable, and so the First Amendment applied to the law with substantial force.[40] Brandeis would remind us here that public discussion is a political duty and that sunlight is necessary to keep government in check. In a self-governing society, after all, they work for us, not the other way around.

The seclusion limitation shows how it is not an intrusion into seclusion to be photographed in public. As we increasingly use portable and wearable computers to capture data about ourselves and others, questions of the appropriate limits on data collection in public will continue to arise. And since we often label problems of information collection as "privacy" problems, we will likely use notions of privacy to understand these problems. Problems of stalking by camera-equipped drones, or wishes not to be photographed or recorded in public, will continue to be real problems. But at least as I have used the term in this chapter, "invasion of privacy" is the wrong framework with which to understand this set of problems unless these activities happen within a zone we consider (or want to consider) private.

This means that invasion of privacy is only a limited tool to think about new problems posed by the pervasiveness of recording technologies in public, whether on drones, smartphones, Google Glass, or other wearable technologies that enable ubiquitous or pervasive data collection. These technologies raise many novel legal questions, but invasion of privacy will not be a useful tool to deal with them unless they are used to invade a recognized zone of seclusion, like the hidden camera in Dietemann's den or the webcam in Tyler Clementi's bedroom.

The limitations on invasion of privacy as a legal tool are important. At the level of legal doctrine, they focus on the ways a right to privacy in the Warren and Brandeis tradition can protect against emotional harm in manners that are consistent with even a robust commitment to free speech. But at a more general level, they show the complexity of the problems of privacy in a digital society, and they illustrate how all problems of privacy cannot be solved by a single tool, or even by Prosser's suite of four torts. This doesn't mean that we can't solve many of the problems of privacy (or free speech) through law. But it does mean that we must be careful about how we think about privacy and free speech, and we have to cautiously craft our legal tools to suit the job at hand.

5

Data

UP TO THIS point, I've shown how the classic notion of privacy—Warren and Brandeis's disclosure tort against the press—is largely inconsistent with the First Amendment as we understand it today. The main problem with the tort is that it targets the press for publishing the embarrassing truth under a blurry standard. But privacy can mean many things beyond the right to prevent the press from making embarrassing disclosures about us. We use the term "privacy" to refer to the many laws regulating personal data, including consumer credit and video rental information, and information given to doctors and lawyers. Are these data privacy rules unconstitutional, too?

Throughout the world, democratic societies regulate personal data using laws that embody the "Fair Information Practices." The "FIPs," as they are called by privacy professionals, are one of the most important concepts in privacy law. They are a set of principles that regulate the relationships between business and government entities that collect, use, and disclose personal information about "data subjects"—the ordinary people whose data is being collected and used. The FIPs, perhaps ironically, were developed in the 1970s by the US government, which wanted to establish some minimal best practices for the processing of personal data. The government report that announced them described the FIPs as "five basic principles" that automated data systems must ensure:

1. There must be no personal-data record-keeping systems whose very existence is secret.

2. There must be a way for an individual to find out what information about him is in a record and how it is used.

3. There must be a way for an individual to prevent information about him obtained for one purpose from being used or made available for other purposes without his consent.

4. There must be a way for an individual to correct or amend a record of identifiable information about him.

5. Any organization creating, maintaining, using, or disseminating records of identifiable personal data must assure the reliability of the data for their intended use and must take reasonable precautions to prevent misuse of the data.[1]

The FIPs were embodied into law in the United States in the Privacy Act and the Fair Credit Reporting Act, and then spread throughout the world.[2] They have different meanings in different places and contexts, but at bottom they guarantee that data is processed according to fair rules that give data subjects *notice* about how their data is collected and used, and some *choice* about certain uses of their data. They are the foundation of the OECD Privacy Guidelines and the basis for the 1995 EU Data Protection Directive, a framework governing data collection and use in the European Union that requires EU Member States to adopt their own country-specific data protection laws.[3] Legal scholar Joel Reidenberg has summarized the evolved FIPs as guaranteeing four basic protections against data misuse:

(1) standards for *data quality*, which ensure that data is acquired legitimately and is used in a manner consistent with the purpose for which it was acquired;

(2) standards for *transparency* or openness of processing, such as giving individuals meaningful notice regarding how their information is being used;

(3) special protections for *sensitive data* (for example, race, sexual preference, political views, or telephone numbers dialed), such as requiring opt-in consent before such data may be used or disclosed; and

(4) some standards of *enforcement* to ensure compliance.[4]

The FIPs have been remarkably durable, but other principles have been proposed from time to time. In January 2012 EU regulators proposed revisions to the almost twenty-year-old Data Protection Directive. The most controversial of these was for a new fair information principle, "*Le Droit à l'Oubli*," commonly translated into English as "The Right to Be Forgotten."[5] The Right to Be Forgotten is the idea that at some point, personal data should be deleted and not persist in databases forever. It was popularized by privacy scholar Viktor Mayer-Schönberger in his 2009 book *Delete*.[6] Implementation of this right into the FIPs could take several forms. On the one hand, it could be a somewhat innocuous general requirement that data not last forever, like the requirements in the Fair Credit Reporting Act or the Video Privacy Protection Act that records from background checks or of movie-watching be destroyed as soon as is practicable.[7] But on the other hand, the Right to Be Forgotten could be interpreted as a right to have websites remove personal data, or images, or news stories that a person thought violated his or her right to privacy. Under this view, the Right to Be Forgotten would turn the web into our own personal Wikipedia, giving us the right to edit data about ourselves as we like. The version of the right proposed by the EU in 2012 seems to be of this latter, stronger sort.[8]

Taking a step back, it's important to consider the constitutional status of these rules—not just the Right to Be Forgotten but also the FIPs as a whole. These are the questions I want to examine in this chapter, and they are some of the most important questions we face in our increasingly digital society. Do the FIPs restrict protected free speech? If so, are they unconstitutional in whole or in part? More generally, if Warren and Brandeis's conception of privacy is largely inconsistent with the First Amendment, what about rules that regulate the disclosure of personal data in the marketplace? Must we extend the First Amendment critique of privacy against the press to all nondisclosures rules? Is privacy always a threat to free speech?

I will argue in this chapter that the answers to these questions will generally be "no." Most data privacy regulations do not involve the First Amendment at all because they do not restrict the flow of data, much less the freedom of speech. Rules placing nondisclosure obligations on data processors will rarely place burdens on First Amendment values, especially if they are couched as confidentiality rules. A few such rules (such as a broad view of the Right to Be Forgotten) might certainly threaten free speech, especially as they come to look more like the disclosure tort. But in general, applying the FIPs to databases and data processing of ordinary commercial data is not censorship, and treating such rules as being outside the central concern of the First Amendment is consistent with the better reading of First Amendment law.

This conclusion is not just a better reading of the legal doctrine; the question of whether data privacy rules censor free speech raises the matter of whether we can regulate data flows at all. In a society in which data flows are becoming increasingly important, this is really akin to asking whether we can have commercial regulation at all. Good policy as well as our constitutional traditions of democratic self-government counsel against a broad and dangerous reading of the First Amendment that "data" is somehow "speech."

Let's begin with the FIPs. The FIPs are a code of best practices for the handling of personal information by businesses and government. But statutes embodying the FIPs do far more than merely regulate information flows or prevent disclosures. Legal scholar Paul Schwartz has shown that under Reidenberg's four-part taxonomy of fair information practices, principle one (ensuring data quality), principle two (ensuring transparency of processing), and principle four (ensuring enforcement) simply have nothing to do with speech under anyone's definition. Only principle three (providing protection against the use or disclosure of sensitive data) involves any restriction on the dissemination or communication of information.[9] Thus, even if you accept the idea that nondisclosure rules create First Amendment problems, major forms of information privacy protection envisioned by codes of fair information practices and protected by current laws have nothing whatsoever to do with the First Amendment under anyone's reading.[10]

As for rules regulating disclosure of commercial data transfers, the vast majority of these rules are consistent with the First Amendment. The obligation that a university should keep its students' records confidential, for example, is very different from the old Warren and Brandeis tort. It is one thing to gag the press in its entirety from reporting on Mabel Warren's dinner parties and quite another to require a university to keep its student records presumptively secret. This confidentiality rule does not target the press, it does not police an unwieldy line between public and private, and it does not remedy primarily emotional harm. Instead, the Family Educational Rights and Privacy Act (FERPA), the federal statute that imposes this requirement, regulates the "education records" of a university, carefully defines the records that are within its scope, and regulates the relationship between university and student, rather than imposing rules on the disclosure of grades (for example) under all circumstances.[11] Other statutes embodying the FIPs operate similarly and, rather than targeting news reports of celebrities, at their best, they protect the confidentiality of the information we need to live our lives, like our library, medical, and financial records.[12] Generally applicable regulation of commercial data simply doesn't raise the First Amendment concerns that the disclosure tort does.[13] And confidentiality rules that regulate the obligations of parties to a relationship rather than whether a fact can be published by anyone pose even fewer First Amendment problems.[14]

Not everyone agrees with me on this point, including some technologists, academics, and corporate lobbyists. For example, in an influential article, legal scholar Eugene Volokh argues that most privacy rules are inconsistent with free speech. Considering the various "codes of fair information practices" imposed by law upon commercial processors of personal data, Volokh asserts that "the right to information privacy—my right to control your communication of personally identifiable information about me—is a right to have the government stop you from speaking about me." He argues that although private agreements to restrict speech are enforceable under contract law, any broader, government-imposed code of fair information practices that restricts the ability of speakers to communicate truthful data about other people is inconsistent with the most basic principles of the First Amendment.[15] Although not all free speech or privacy scholars agree with Volokh, his argument (or ones like it) has been influential.[16] Others have questioned the constitutionality of something like the Right to Be Forgotten, calling it (in the words of one excited journalist) "the biggest threat to free speech on the Internet in the coming decade."[17]

The Supreme Court has not been quite so enthusiastic about the death of privacy. As previous chapters have explained, the Court has heard several cases pitting the disclosure tort or similar legal theories against First Amendment claims by the press.[18] But although free speech has usually defeated privacy in these cases, the Court's tradition has been to move carefully, refusing to rule categorically that claims by the press to publish true material always trump privacy claims. As the Court explained somewhat wordily in the *Bartnicki* case,

> [o]ur cases have carefully eschewed reaching this ultimate question, mindful that the future may bring scenarios which prudence counsels our not resolving anticipatorily.... We continue to believe that the sensitivity and significance of the interests presented in clashes between [the] First Amendment and privacy rights counsel relying on limited principles that sweep no more broadly than the appropriate context of the instant case.[19]

And in some of those additional contexts, the Court has rejected claims that other kinds of privacy violate the First Amendment. Trespass, eavesdropping, wiretapping, stalking, and industrial espionage do not receive special First Amendment scrutiny.[20] Nor do professional duties of confidentiality like the attorney-client privilege, or contractual agreements to not disclose information. Lawyers cannot credibly argue that they have a First Amendment right to divulge their client's confidences,[21] nor can reporters claim that the First Amendment gives them the right to break agreements with confidential sources that they will not disclose their identities.[22] Similarly, restrictions on the sale of targeted marketing lists under the Fair Credit Reporting Act have survived First Amendment attack, with the Supreme Court declining to get involved.[23]

This traditional approach makes a lot of sense. Privacy and free speech are both important human values, and it is important to tread carefully and not make overbroad claims about "the death of privacy" or the absolute protection afforded to speech. Both privacy and free speech claims can come in many guises and serve many different interests, and blunt pronouncements in this area have the power to cause significant harm. This is a complex issue, and it deserves a nuanced solution. But as I have shown in previous chapters, the First Amendment critique of privacy law is strong where the privacy claims resemble the traditional Warren and Brandeis argument for tort privacy. It is much weaker in other contexts. And it is hard to see how duties of confidentiality—whether imposed on banks, attorneys, or even data brokers—threaten First Amendment values. Under this traditional approach, the law is in balance—privacy claims that menace a free press are presumptively unconstitutional, but codes of fair information practices (the foundation of data privacy law) and professional duties of confidentiality are left intact.

Yet in 2011, the Supreme Court decided a case, *Sorrell v. IMS Health Inc.*, which some fear upset that balance in favor of broad First Amendment protection and against all privacy rules. *Sorrell* is the Court's most recent word on whether the First Amendment critique of privacy does (or should) apply to privacy law in the data context, so it is worth looking at in some detail.

The Data Broker

IMS Health calls itself a "health analytics company," which means it provides personal data, analysis, and other information services in the healthcare industry.[24] In common parlance, it is a "data broker," a company that sells information and answers to questions based on data. IMS is part of the so-called "Big Data" revolution. Its business is to collect information, assemble it into large databases, and mine it for insight by applying sophisticated analytic techniques. It specializes in analyzing trends in healthcare transactions so that the health companies that are its customers have more information about the market, the competition, and the human beings seeking health care (that is, essentially everyone).[25]

One of the services that IMS and other data brokers provide is data to support something called "physician detailing." You may have noticed representatives from pharmaceutical companies visiting your doctor. These "drug reps" drop off free samples of drugs along with branded pens and paper. More important, they are there to persuade your doctor to prescribe their company's drugs to you rather than another company's drugs (or no drugs at all). This direct marketing is known in the trade as "detailing," because drug reps give details about their products to the doctors. Detailing doesn't just rely on the personal charm and persuasive power of the drug reps. It depends also on another kind of detail—lots of data about what kinds of products to market to individual doctors.

This is where IMS and other data brokers come into the story. IMS buys prescription records from pharmacies in bulk and uses these records to assemble profiles of the prescribing patterns of individual doctors. Drug reps can then "detail" those doctors, knowing the habits of the doctor better than the doctor herself does. Detailing is a massive industry—one that is both data- and manpower-intensive. The multibillion-dollar costs of detailing (like advertising and other marketing costs) are ultimately passed on to the patients who buy the drug prescribed by the doctor from their pharmacy.[26] The pharmacies then sell the new records to data brokers, and the cycle continues.

Concerned about rising drug prices, Vermont and other New England states passed laws designed to restrict the costly practice of data-based detailing. They sought to drive down drug prices and to ensure that doctors made prescribing decisions on the basis of their own independent judgment rather than data-based persuasion by marketers. Vermont's Prescription Confidentiality Act prohibited pharmacies and health insurance companies from selling doctors' prescription data for marketing purposes and prohibited drug reps from using the data for marketing purposes, including detailing.[27]

Concerned about the effect of these laws on their profits, IMS and other data brokers challenged them in federal court. The First Circuit Court of Appeals upheld New Hampshire's law in the 2009 *Ayotte* case,[28] but in the 2011 *Sorrell* case, a deeply divided U.S. Supreme Court struck down the Vermont law under the First Amendment.[29]

Writing for a majority of six Justices, Justice Kennedy concluded that the Vermont law violated the First Amendment because it restricted the speech of marketers only, but not that of other speakers. As he put it succinctly, "[t]he state has burdened a form of protected expression that it found too persuasive. At the same time, the State has left unburdened those speakers whose messages are in accord with its own views. This the State cannot do."[30]

In reaching this conclusion, the Court ruled that the "sale, disclosure, and use of prescriber-identifying information" was protected by the First Amendment. Moreover, because the Prescription Confidentiality Act prohibited people from using the information for marketing, the Court found that the Act "disfavor[ed] marketing, that is, speech with a particular purpose. More than that, the statute disfavors particular speakers, namely pharmaceutical manufacturers."[31] The Court's logic was straightforward: because the sale of the data was protected by the First Amendment, and its use for marketing was prohibited, it created content- and viewpoint-based restrictions on expression. Under settled First Amendment law, content- and viewpoint-based discrimination is presumptively unconstitutional. And because Vermont could not give a sufficiently compelling reason to save the statute, it was invalid.

Two parts of this conclusion are significant. First, the principal defect with the Prescription Confidentiality Act was its *discrimination* against certain kinds of protected speech and certain kinds of protected speakers. This is a basic principle of First Amendment law—discrimination among types of speech ("content-based" restrictions) is usually invalid. Most especially, discrimination against particular speakers or messages ("viewpoint-based" restrictions) is virtually always invalid. For example, in the famous case of *R.A.V. v. City of St. Paul* (1992), the Court struck down a hate crime statute that had been used to prosecute a man who had burned a cross on the front lawn of an African-American family.[32] Cross-burning of this sort can be punished under a variety of theories, including threats, fighting words, and the intentional infliction of emotional distress. Cross-burning usually falls under what First Amendment parlance calls "unprotected speech." But the St. Paul law targeted only racist speech, and not the speech of toleration. (It punished racist cross-burning, but not other kinds of cross-burning, like the ones in Madonna's "Like a Prayer" video.) Because the law discriminated on the basis of viewpoint by treating racist viewpoints more harshly, it was unconstitutional.[33] Thus, viewpoint discrimination against speech that was *otherwise "unprotected" by the First Amendment* violated the First Amendment.

In *Sorrell*, the Court reached the same conclusion, relying explicitly on *R.A.V.*: The Prescription Confidentiality Act banned uses of the data in marketing communications, but not educational ones.[34] As the Court put it,

> it appears that Vermont could supply academic organizations with prescriber-identifying information to use in countering the messages of brand-name pharmaceutical manufacturers and in promoting the prescription of generic drugs. But § 4631(d) leaves detailers no means of purchasing, acquiring, or using prescriber-identifying information. The law on its face burdens disfavored speech by disfavored speakers.[35]

Because the law banned the use of data for speech by the marketers but allowed it for speech by their political opponents, it discriminated on the basis of viewpoint and was thus unconstitutional. Such a conclusion is a straightforward application of basic free speech law—the government can't tell human speakers what arguments they can and can't make and what data they can and can't rely on. And it can't discriminate between speakers, letting some but not others rely on a particular piece of information.

The second significant element of the opinion in *Sorrell* was a suggestion that the sale of a database was somehow "speech" protected by the First Amendment. Vermont had made the argument that the Prescription Confidentiality Act did not regulate speech, but merely conduct: the sale of information as a commodity. (The First Circuit in the New Hampshire *Ayotte* case had upheld New Hampshire's anti-detailing law on this exact basis.) As the U.S. Supreme Court put it:

> This Court has held that the creation and dissemination of information are speech within the meaning of the First Amendment.... Facts, after all, are the beginning point for much of the speech that is most essential to advance human knowledge and to conduct human affairs. There is thus a strong argument that prescriber-identifying information is speech for First Amendment purposes.[36]

But though the Court hinted that the sale of a database might be "speech," it stopped short of that sweeping conclusion, because the regulation's discrimination against marketers was a content- and viewpoint-based restriction.[37] In this respect, the Court continued its tradition of moving carefully and slowly in cases involving the conflict between privacy rules and freedom of speech.

What *Sorrell* Means

What is the significance of *Sorrell* for data privacy law? The short answer is that it's not clear, because the opinion itself isn't clear. From a First Amendment perspective, the Vermont statute was clumsily drafted, but the Court's opinion is hardly a model of clarity either. Moreover, Justices Breyer, Ginsburg, and Kagan would have upheld the Prescription Confidentiality Act notwithstanding its poor drafting, on the ground that the law was merely lawful regulation of a commercial enterprise and threatened the First Amendment barely, if at all.[38]

Nevertheless, some observers have suggested that *Sorrell* might mean the end of privacy law, because it assumed that data flows are "speech." The inevitable result of this conclusion, these scholars argue, is that all laws regulating the flows of data are now constitutionally suspect. Ashutosh Bhagwat worries that "the Court's hints in this regard have dramatic, and extremely troubling, implications for a broad range of existing and proposed rules that seek to control disclosure of personal information in order to protect privacy."[39] More generally, Jane Bambauer argues enthusiastically that "for all practical purposes, and in every context relevant to the privacy debates, data is speech. Privacy regulations are rarely (if ever) incidental burdens to knowledge. Instead, [they are] deliberately designed to disrupt knowledge-creation."[40] In their reading of *Sorrell* these scholars echo the earlier claim of Eugene Volokh that data privacy law under the FIPs is no more than "a right to stop people from talking about you."[41]

If this interpretation were to become the law, the implications would be striking. Information privacy law as we know it would be dead. If data is "speech," every restriction on the disclosure (not to mention the collection or use) of information would face heightened First Amendment scrutiny and be presumptively unconstitutional. This would jeopardize not just medical privacy rules but also most likely financial privacy rules, reader privacy rules, and any hope of imposing the FIPs to Internet data such as the logs ISPs and marketers keep of what websites we visit. Arguably, even such venerable nondisclosure rules like the attorney-client duty of confidentiality would also have to satisfy the demands of First Amendment scrutiny, for these rules also place nondisclosure obligations on lawyers not to speak confidences.

This reading of *Sorrell* has some support in dictum in Justice Kennedy's opinion, which suggests that regulation of information flows is indistinguishable from regulating "speech." But even Justice Kennedy was careful to make clear that the holding in *Sorrell* did not render privacy law unconstitutional in general. In particular, he suggested that if Vermont had addressed doctor confidentiality "through a more coherent policy" like the federal Health Insurance Portability and Accountability Act of 1996,[42] rather than (in his view) the haphazard methods it had used, the law would have been constitutional.[43]

There is thus another reading of both *Sorrell* and First Amendment law generally that is less menacing to data privacy law and to the FIPs. Under this reading, the problem with the Vermont law was not that it regulated data flows, but that it imposed viewpoint restrictions on "unprotected" speech. In other words, *Sorrell* is not the beginning of the end for data privacy law. Instead, like *R.A.V.*, the case is a reminder that the government cannot impose viewpoint restraints on particular speakers like marketers. Under this view, *Sorrell* invalidated one particularly clumsy attempt to regulate marketing, but it does not follow from this that data privacy law is largely unconstitutional. In fact, as Justice Kennedy suggested, the statute would have been less problematic if it had imposed *greater* duties of confidentiality on the data, rather than just restricting marketing uses. This was the case because "[p]rivacy is a concept too integral to the person and a right too essential to freedom to allow its manipulation to support just those ideas the government prefers."[44]

I think that this narrower reading of *Sorrell* is the better one, but ultimately *Sorrell* is just one case with a poorly explained holding. Yet it raises the broader question of how much force the First Amendment should play in the regulation of data privacy. Is the trade in personal data commercial regulation of the sort that does not and should not concern free expression doctrine? Or, as some commentators believe, is data "speech"? In the next two sections of this chapter, I want to show why "is data speech?" is a poor way to ask a very important question. I will also argue that however we frame the question, subjecting general nondisclosure rules on commercial data flows to the full force of the First Amendment would be a very bad idea. In fact, doing so would uproot one of the most basic foundations on which modern constitutional law has been built.

The Silliness of "Data = Speech"

The "data is speech" argument has a certain superficial appeal. After all, if the First Amendment is about protecting people's ability to share ideas and information, and data is information, then the First Amendment should protect people's ability to share data. The argument is clear, and it is consistent—everything is speech, and everything is protected.

But this argument's consistency is a foolish consistency. Just because something is "speech" doesn't mean it is beyond regulation. Nor does the fact that something is labeled "speech" qualify it for special protection by the First Amendment. Humans do lots of things every day with words— we talk on the phone, we write books and emails and blogs, we sing in the shower. But people also use words to hire assassins, engage in insider trading, sexually harass subordinates in the workplace, and verbally abuse their children. All of these are "speech," but many of them are well outside the main concerns of the First Amendment. We need to protect some, but we need to regulate others. This is a problem.

Fortunately, this kind of problem is one that law is used to dealing with. Other areas of constitutional law face the same issue. Take, for example, the Equal Protection Clause of the Fourteenth Amendment, which bars government from denying any person "the equal protection of the laws." A superficial reading of these words would be that the government cannot treat people differently, because to do so would deny them "the equal protection of the laws." Like the "data is speech" argument, this interpretation would have consistency, but it would be a foolish consistency. Governments treat their citizens differently all the time—they discriminate on the basis of age when allocating driver's licenses and health benefits like Medicare; they discriminate on the basis of wealth when setting tax rates, college financial aid, and welfare benefits; they discriminate on the basis of education and ability when allocating law and medical licenses; and they discriminate on the basis of criminal activity when deciding who can be free and who goes to prison. All of these actions discriminate, but none of them bring down the full weight of the Equal Protection Clause. As long as they are rational, these laws are constitutional. And that's a good thing, because a government that cannot treat people differently much of the time cannot regulate for the common good.

Equal protection law long ago created the idea of a "suspect classification": the government is allowed to discriminate among its citizens in lots of ways, but certain kinds of discrimination—classifications on the basis of race, gender, and national origin, for instance—are "suspect." When the government uses race to discriminate, we become suspicious, and judges scrutinize the laws much more carefully. This is why Jim Crow laws are unconstitutional and why even "benign" forms of discrimination like affirmative action must be carefully justified. For these laws to be constitutional they must be narrowly tailored to a compelling government interest.[45]

But because a small subset of suspect classifications is treated differently, the rest of the law can function. For example, the state can deny driver's licenses, tattoos, and beer to fifteen-year-olds. For these laws, so long as the law is rationally related to a legitimate government purpose, it is constitutional. There are certainly hard cases at the margins, but equal protection law has chosen common sense over a foolish consistency that would require courts to scrutinize every portion of every law that treats people differently.

To put the point succinctly: Discrimination is everywhere, but only those few kinds of discrimination that are especially dangerous get a hard look under the Equal Protection Clause. All discrimination implicates the Equal Protection Clause, but most kinds get only a cursory glance from courts. And the system works.

Something similar goes on in First Amendment law, though it does not get recognized as frequently.[46] Speech is everywhere, but only certain kinds of speech restrictions that are especially dangerous get looked at under the full force of the First Amendment. There are, of course, the famous categories of "unprotected speech"—incitement, obscenity, fighting words, threats, falsely shouting fire in theatres, and so forth. But these are just the tip of the iceberg. Under the surface, beneath our normal attention, there are product labeling requirements, murder for hire contracts, securities disclosures and nondisclosures, insider trading rules, agreements to restrain trade, sexually harassing speech that creates a hostile environment in the workplace, and regulations of truthful but misleading commercial offers.[47] Legal scholar Frederick Schauer has called this idea "First Amendment salience"—we are so used to regulations of words and information outside the normal attention of First Amendment law that we often don't notice them.[48] They aren't salient, so we don't notice them even though they are hiding in plain sight.

Faced with a similar choice between foolish consistency and common sense, First Amendment judges and scholars have overwhelmingly chosen the latter. The First Amendment has never been interpreted as an absolute protection for all uses of words, much less for automated and mechanized data flows or the sale of information as a commodity.[49] American lawyers are perhaps the group most protective of free speech in the history of the world.[50] But even in the United States, virtually all strong, speech-protective interpretations of the First Amendment carve out large chunks of the ways we use words or information from heightened First Amendment protection. They do this so that the First Amendment can do its job—protecting political and artistic expression—without swallowing the rest of the law. And the system works.

From this perspective, we can see why asking whether data is "speech" is the wrong question. Commercial data flows are certainly within the outermost bounds of the First Amendment, but so, too, are sexual harassment, criminal and antitrust contracting, threats, and securities disclosures. But putting data flows in this category merely means that the government can regulate them if it acts rationally to further a legitimate government purpose. Something more is needed to show that regulation of commercial data flows is suspect like regulation of traditional categories of expression, like political speech or protest, commentary on matters of public concern, artistic expression, or (less important) advertising to consumers that proposes a commercial transaction.[51]

One might ask a very good question at this point, which is why all "speech," broadly defined, isn't protected by the First Amendment. Let me offer two answers to this question, one simple and one more complicated. The simple answer is that because First Amendment lawyers don't want to leave important expressive activities or practices out of the First Amendment's protection, we tend to define speech rather broadly. For example, the Supreme Court has held a vast amount of things to be "speech" (or at least within the protection of the First Amendment), including cross burning, swearing, nude dancing, virtual child pornography, threats, lies, and often horrifying discrimination and hate speech.[52] Often, this is done for good reason: to protect potentially valuable dissenting political speech from the tyranny of the majority. But notice that when we expand the outermost bounds of what is "speech," there is a risk that everything becomes expressive or potentially expressive. The more this happens, the less room we have for ordinary legal rules, even ones that have no purpose or even effect of political or artistic censorship. All "speech," broadly defined, isn't protected by the First Amendment because if we define "speech" broadly enough, the First Amendment would swallow the law, making ordinary regulation impossible.

This brings us to the more complicated answer, which has to do with a basic tension in constitutional law. Constitutional rights are protected by judges by setting aside laws passed by the democratic process. Legal scholar Alexander Bickel famously called this the "counter-majoritarian difficulty": it is undemocratic for unelected judges to strike down laws passed by our elected representatives.[53] Judicial intervention is justified when it invalidates restrictions on free speech, voting, or political equality, because without such safeguards, we have reason to distrust all laws. If we can't speak out about unfair laws, it's hard to call those laws democratic. But the counter-majoritarian difficulty also suggests that exceptions to the basic idea that democratic laws are the law of the land must be limited. If judges made all of the law, we would no longer be living in a representative democracy, but in an oligarchy at best. Modern American constitutional law rests on the necessary compromise between democratic laws and undemocratic protection of civil liberties. For the system to work, it relies on the undemocratic exceptions being limited, and on them protecting democratic rights (like free speech). Central to this compromise is an important lesson from almost a century ago, to which we now turn.

Rejecting Digital *Lochner*

There's a famous parable in constitutional law that has been taught to virtually every first-year law student for decades. The parable goes something like this. In the late nineteenth and early twentieth centuries, the Industrial Revolution transformed American society. On the one hand, it produced great fortunes and technological innovation that made what had been impossible commonplace. These new innovations included factories, steam engines, railroads, cars, airplanes, and cheap textiles, and shaped the modern world into a form that we (or at least our parents) could recognize. But on the other hand, the Industrial Revolution produced enormous social costs, including huge wealth inequality, poverty, child labor, unsafe industrial working conditions, and pollution. Faced with these problems, Congress and the state legislatures tried to fix the issues of the perilous industrial workplace while preserving its benefits. Progressive legislators passed laws preventing child labor, regulating unsafe working conditions, and imposing minimum wage and maximum hours laws, overtime requirements, product labeling laws, and antitrust laws.[54] But the Supreme Court struck many of these laws down as infringements on personal liberty. Afraid that laws regulating economic transactions could lead to wealth redistribution or socialism, the Court held that much of this economic regulation violated the Fourteenth Amendment's Due Process Clause, infringing on the rights of workers and employers to what it called the "liberty of contract."[55]

This era in Supreme Court history is named after the infamous 1905 case of *Lochner v. New York*.[56] In *Lochner*, the Supreme Court struck down a New York law regulating the safety of bakers. *Lochner* was not the first Supreme Court case to protect economic rights against government regulation, nor was it the last, but it is the case that has given its name to the era of strong constitutional protection of economic rights, lasting from the late nineteenth century until the late 1930s.[57] The *Lochner* Court's economic libertarianism rested on the idea that private property was the bulwark of political liberty, and that a government that has the power to redistribute wealth is a grave threat to liberty.[58] These ideas have a strong tradition in Anglo-American political thought, but there was a problem. A broad government power to regulate economic matters also allows regulations such as minimum wages, maximum hours, workplace safety, and the right to collective bargaining. During the Industrial Revolution, the conservative economic, libertarian view of the Constitution became inconsistent with the needs of a modern, industrial economy. This inconsistency became most apparent during the Great Depression, when *Lochner*-style doctrines were used to invalidate portions of the New Deal.[59] Thus, in the industrial era, a libertarian view of industrial economic liberty made needed regulation impossible.

I fear that acceptance of the "data is speech" argument will repeat these errors of the Industrial Age for the Information Age. Today, great chunks of human society are being transformed into digital form, and we all leave digital footprints every day as we live our lives. It is essential that we preserve strong civil liberties in our digital future—much of this book is about how to do that in the context of thinking, reading, and speaking. But if the lessons of the twentieth century are that government regulation is sometimes necessary in an industrial economy, we should not forget those lessons in our information economy. In a 2005 article published before the *Sorrell* litigation, I made an argument along these lines.[60] Justice Breyer made a similar point in his *Sorrell* dissent, arguing that "[a]t best the Court opens a Pandora's Box of First Amendment challenges to many ordinary regulatory practices that may only incidentally affect a commercial message. At worst, it reawakens *Lochner's* pre-New Deal threat of substituting judicial for democratic decisionmaking where ordinary economic regulation is at issue."[61] The many new uses to which we can put data create new possibilities, but also new problems. We need to make choices as a society about what kinds of data privacy rules we should have, and about when data should flow freely. In fact, we might ultimately decide that the best policy is to have very little data privacy.

But however we as a society choose to regulate data flows, we *must* be able to choose. We must not be sidetracked by misleading First Amendment arguments, because the costs of not regulating the trade in commercial data are significant. As we enter the Information Age, where the trade in information is a multibillion-dollar industry, government should be able to regulate the huge flows of personal information as well as the uses to which this information can be put. Moreover, if our lives become digital, but if data is speech, regulation of many kinds of social problems will become impossible. There will certainly be cases at the borders, because of course data will sometimes be tied to important expression. But this is an insufficient reason to give up on regulation of our society as it digitizes. At the dawn of the Industrial Age, business interests persuaded the Supreme Court in the *Lochner* case that the freedom of contract should immunize them from regulation. We must reject the similar calls of modern advocates for digital *Lochner*.

Conclusion: The Right to Be Forgotten and Information Policy

Let me conclude with a few thoughts about the Right to Be Forgotten. I have argued that most commercial data flows regulated by information privacy law embodying the FIPs should be constitutional, but what about the "Right to Be Forgotten"? The answer to this question is more complicated because the Right to Be Forgotten is a poorly defined idea that can mean several different things. But the ambiguity of the Right to Be Forgotten is a helpful point on which to end this part of the book because it illustrates my general argument: Ordinary commercial regulations of the data trade are constitutional, but tort rights to censor the media aren't.

At the most basic level, the general encouragement that personal data *should* be deleted at some point poses no constitutional problems. As I will explain in chapter 11, our digital society cannot be regulated by legal rules alone, and the development of professional norms among data holders to protect values like the FIPs or some variant of the Right to

Be Forgotten will be an important part of any solution. This is particularly the case for so-called "sensitive data"—information that would be especially harmful if disclosed, such as health, political, or financial data. Governments could promote the importance of this social norm without mandating it, which would be clearly constitutional.

We could also imagine the Right to Be Forgotten being imposed on certain data holders as a consequence of their relationship with users who supply them with their data. For example, imagine a regulation of social networking sites that would require sites like Facebook to allow users to edit information they have supplied to the company, such as status updates or contact information. (Of course, most sites, including Facebook, already provide this feature, though the law does not require it.) This would be a more substantial requirement than merely promoting social norms, but it should also be constitutional as an ordinary regulation of a commercial relationship. Such rules could also be justified as placing an implied use condition on the receipt of information, the way the law imposes nondisclosure (and other) use conditions on information lawyers receive from their clients. The Fair Credit Reporting Act already gives consumers the ability to correct false information in their credit reports and places limits on the ability of credit reporting agencies to disclose old information about consumers, like criminal records and lawsuits older than seven years.[62] At least where there is an equivalently important relationship between consumers and data brokers, such regulations should be constitutional in most cases.

On the other hand, the Right to Be Forgotten runs into First Amendment problems when it starts to resemble the old disclosure tort. In fact, it is because the version of the right proposed for the revisions to the EU Directive has taken essentially this form that the proposal has generated so much free speech concern. The proposed regulation would allow anyone to require any online service provider to delete any information they had about them.[63] This is a much more sweeping version of the right, which would, for instance, allow the deletion of potentially newsworthy information about a person provided by others.[64] It is one thing to give Internet users the ability to restrict or retract information they provide in the context of a commercial relationship, and quite another to allow individuals the right to edit any and all information about them on the Internet. Such a broad power would turn the Internet into our own personal Wikipedias, and would represent a resuscitation of Mabel Warren's broad right to censor not merely commercial data but also potentially highly newsworthy expression.

But the fact that this strong form of the Right to Be Forgotten is a threat to free speech does not mean that milder forms of a right to delete are also problematic. Some of these weaker forms of *Le Droit à l'Oubli* might be a bad idea in theory or in actual implementation; they might increase costs, or deter innovations, or be counterproductive. But they are probably constitutional. Not everything that is a bad idea is unconstitutional, and in a democratic society in a time of technological change, we must be free to make policy mistakes. General principles or rights to make data mortal do not threaten free public debate or democratic self-government. One could imagine a Right to Be Forgotten that is bad policy, but in a democratic society, the basic contours of information policy must ultimately be up to the people, and not to unelected judges. Making policy mistakes is sometimes a price we pay for self-government.

PART II

The Promise of Intellectual Privacy

6

A Theory of Intellectual Privacy

UP TO THIS point, we've looked at the traditional way lawyers and scholars have thought about the relationship between privacy and speech. Under this view, tort privacy and free speech are values in conflict, and we have to choose between them in a kind of zero-sum game. I've tried to show that while the traditional way has been dominant in people's minds, it has been a failure as a practical matter and represents something of a dead end for our law.

In this part of the book, I want to show that there is a different way of thinking about privacy and speech. Instead of being conflicting values, privacy and speech can instead be mutually supportive. In fact, I want to argue that a certain kind of privacy is essential if we care about freedom of expression. This kind of privacy is different from tort privacy. Let's call it "intellectual privacy."

So what is intellectual privacy? Essentially, it's is a zone of protection that guards our ability to make up our minds freely. More formally, intellectual privacy is the protection from surveillance or unwanted interference by others when we are engaged in the processes of generating ideas and forming beliefs—when we're thinking, reading, and speaking with confidants before our ideas are ready for public consumption. Intellectual privacy is an old idea and shares its roots with some of our most ancient traditions of civil liberties. Curiously, like tort privacy, the germ of a theory of intellectual privacy can be traced in the writings of Louis Brandeis. In a series of constitutional law opinions in the 1920s, Brandeis argued for the protection of freedom of thought, intellect, and private speech as essential preconditions of freedom.

But although it is an old idea, intellectual privacy has remained under-appreciated and underdeveloped. This is not because intellectual privacy is trivial, but because until very recently, it has been difficult as a practical matter to interfere with the generation of ideas. The state, market, and our social contacts could not monitor our thoughts, our reading habits, and our private conversations, at least not in an efficient, comprehensive, and unobtrusive way. Law was not needed to tackle such a problem. But the context surrounding intellectual activities has changed dramatically, and the pace of this change is increasing. Continual always-on intellectual surveillance is increasingly possible, ironically as a result of the vast intellectual opportunities offered by the Internet.

Part II of this book is about this idea of intellectual privacy—what it is, where it comes from, and how it is increasingly under siege in our digital world. This chapter lays out the basic theory of intellectual privacy in our law and identifies three of its elements—the freedom of thought, the right to read, and the right to communicate in confidence. The three chapters that follow give greater content and context to each of the elements and develop the theory in greater detail.

Why Intellectual Privacy Matters

Where do new ideas come from? Think for a moment about how new ideas were generated in a pre-Internet era. Some new ideas are just thought up by clever people sitting alone in their offices or walking in the woods. This is the tradition of romantic individualism epitomized by Henry David Thoreau, who retreated to Walden Pond to think and to learn. As Thoreau put it, "I went to the woods because I wished to live deliberately, to front only the essential facts of life, and see if I could not learn what it had to teach, and not, when I came to die, discover that I had not lived."[1] When we are alone, we have time to think, to contemplate, to make sense of the world and our beliefs about it.

Contemplation is essential to a free and diverse society. It allows us to decide what we think about existing ideas, and to imagine new ones. The Canadian philosopher Timothy Macklem explains that "isolation is the source of human difference, for it is the exercise of creativity in isolation that makes it possible for people to reach different conclusions and thereby develop different ways of life, the ways of life that liberal societies draw upon for the diversity that makes freedom valuable there."[2]

In practice, of course, few ideas are just thought up by arboreal prodigies (or office-bound academics) working in isolation. Most human inventions are the product of building on the ideas of other people. This is as true of ideas like racial equality or freedom of speech as it is of innovations like the Internet or the iPad. The stuff of our culture—our ideas, our beliefs, our inventions—is invariably the product of a series of small improvements on the ideas of others. Essential to this process is the existence of a large body of work from other people against and upon which we can construct our own ideas. Legal scholar Jessica Litman expresses this point eloquently:

> Composers recombine sounds they have heard before; playwrights base their characters on bits and pieces drawn from real human beings and other playwrights' characters; novelists draw their plots from lives and other plots within their experience; software writers use the logic they find in other software; lawyers transform old arguments to fit new facts; cinematographers, actors, choreographers, architects, and sculptors all engage in the process of adapting, transforming, and recombining what is already "out there" in some other form. This is not parasitism: it is the essence of authorship.[3]

New ideas—political, scientific, artistic, or otherwise—thus depend on access to the ideas of others and the ability to engage with them. And to do this, we need to be able to read freely and then think privately about what we've read in our own time. In the past, access to ideas has come principally from print media—newsstands, bookstores, and libraries, but also from public speeches and performances, television, and radio. However, access to ideas is now increasingly digital—using computers, tablets, and smartphones to access search engines, websites, social networks, and to send texts, emails, and instant messages.

Even access to knowledge isn't by itself enough. We need places and spaces (real and virtual) in which to read, to think, to explore. The process of idea generation is one of trial and error. Very often, what seems like a good idea at the time turns out to be a terrible one after testing or further reflection. But to test or examine ideas, we again turn to other people—our friends and confidants, our family and colleagues. We rely on these people for their frank and confidential assessments of whether we're on to something, or whether we're crazy.

It's not just new ideas that get tested this way. When we're trying to make up our minds about whether we like government policy, a war, a movie, or even our appearance, we often test novelty with our intimates. We share with our small groups before we are ready to share with the world. We trust them to keep our half-formed notions and beliefs confidential and not to share them with others. At the same time, we also expect that when we are talking to our confidants, third parties are not listening in or recording what we say. These activities and expectations allow us to discuss, test, and reevaluate our ideas before they are ready for public exposure. Intellectual privacy, then, is the protection of all of these individual and social processes, so we may, as Brandeis put it in *Whitney*, have the "freedom to think as [we] will and to speak as [we] think."[4]

If we're interested in the creation of new ideas, we should want people to experiment with controversial ideas. But this notion has not been deeply developed in First Amendment law or theory. First Amendment cases and scholarship are full of explanations about *why* we allow the expression of large amounts of often offensive and harmful speech—for instance, because lots of speech enhances the search for truth, the processes of democratic self-government, or individual autonomy.[5] By contrast, discussions of free speech have only rarely addressed the question of *how* we ensure that new and interesting ideas get generated.

This is a curious omission, because if we care about free speech, we should care about speakers having something interesting to say. Many of today's most cherished ideas were once highly controversial. Consider the notion that governments should be elected by the people, or the separation of church and state, or the idea of the equality of all people under law regardless of race, sex, or religion. At various times, believing or promoting each of these ideas was to be done at your peril. Think of the thousands of people killed in early modern Europe for believing differently in matters of faith, or the violent persecution of American civil rights activists who believed in racial equality. Ideas matter because they can be destabilizing, which explains why those in power have resorted to extreme measures—burnings at the stake, lynchings, Selma Bridge—to keep those destabilizing ideas in check.

Modern First Amendment law has broadly rejected the notion that brute force can be used to keep dangerous ideas out of public debate. And this idea has significant social support. We now believe that in a free society, individuals can be trusted to sort out good ideas from evil ones, and that the state cannot keep an idea from the people on the ground that they cannot be trusted to handle it. A free society that does not allow its people to think for themselves does not seem particularly free. As the Anglo-American philosopher Alexander Meiklejohn put it, "to be afraid of ideas—any idea—is to be unfit for self-government."[6]

Recall the leading justifications for freedom of speech from chapter 2—truth, self-government, and autonomy. The generation of new ideas is central to each of them. Consider the search for truth rationale first. In his famous dissent in *Abrams v. United States*, Justice Holmes eloquently expressed the idea that people in a free society cannot be persecuted based on the beliefs that they hold or the words that they say:

> [W]hen men have realized that time has upset many fighting faiths, they may come to believe even more than they believe the very foundations of their own conduct that the ultimate good desired is better reached by free trade in ideas—that the best test of truth is the power of the thought to get itself accepted in the competition of the market. . . . [W]e should be eternally vigilant against attempts to check the expression of opinions that we loathe and believe to be fraught with death, unless they so imminently threaten immediate interference with the lawful and pressing purposes of the law that an immediate check is required to save the country. [7]

Holmes believed that free societies must resist the urge to oppress those who believe differently from the majority. Those in power might feel certain that they are right and that the dissidents are crazy and dangerous, holding opinions "that we loathe and believe to be fraught with death."[8] But any sense of moral certainty must be tempered by the indisputable fact that most firmly held beliefs from the past ("fighting faiths") have been rejected and abandoned over the years. Faced with this evidence, we must acknowledge the doubt that our ideas, too, might be found false or incomplete in the future. We must let the dissidents believe their beliefs and have their say.[9]

The self-governance and autonomy rationales for free expression are also consistent with a commitment to the generation of new ideas and the protection of the processes of belief formation. Self-governance theory suggests that democratic citizens need a wide variety of perspectives and information to make the informed decisions that are essential to good government. Because it depends upon the informed decisions of the citizenry, the processes of belief formation and decision making are *the* critical element of self-governance, as Brandeis reminded us in *Whitney*.

More directly, if we can't make up our minds freely and without constraint or surveillance, self-government is impossible. This is why democracies protect the privacy of voting through the secret ballot and the voting booth—we make the decisions of self-governance in a private, unmonitored, untracked place. Similarly, the government is forbidden from freely listening in on private conversations about politics, or monitoring the meetings of political groups. Autonomy theory is even easier to square with autonomous belief formation—why else would we want people to think for themselves or develop their individuality if not to generate new ideas and new forms of identity and expression?

Intellectual freedom thus requires more than just protection from censorship or punishment for unpopular speech. If we are interested in the kind of new ideas that cause us to revise or displace existing "fighting faiths," we need to go beyond protecting merely the *expression* of dissident ideas and think about their *production*. The existing theories of why we care about free expression may not have spoken directly in terms of the production of new ideas and the processes of how they come to be accepted. But this is because oppressive regimes in the past have taken the easier step of censoring speech directly rather than the more difficult (and expensive) means of monitoring or constraining individual thoughts and preferences. But under any theory, the creation and acceptance of new ideas are critical to the reasons we protect freedom of expression.

Imagine a society in which there were few if any barriers to the airing of racist, hurtful, or shocking speech. In such a society, citizens could speak on virtually any matter secure from the risk that the content of their expression would subject them to imprisonment, criminal fines, or civil liability. Unpopular or radical speech might face social sanction, but incur no legal liability. But imagine further that in this society the government had access to all sorts of information about the reading habits and private communications of individuals. One might imagine the state engaging in this kind of surveillance to protect intellectual property from infringement, deter the consumption of obscenity and child pornography, and prevent acts of crime and terror. We would have a society in which there was little punishment by the state for spoken words, but heavy intellectual surveillance.

By the standards of current law, we would probably say that this was a highly speech-protective society. A society with little legal punishment for harmful speech is speech-protective almost by definition. But in such a society, something important is missing, which is intellectual privacy. Intellectual privacy matters because it gives new and possibly heretical ideas room to develop and grow before they are ready for publication. Intellectual privacy gives us the ability to make up our minds about controversial ideas by ourselves or with a few trusted confidants, free from being watched or discovered by others. By contrast, surveillance of intellectual activity deters people from engaging with new ideas and inclines our intellectual explorations to the boring, the bland, and the mainstream. If we know that someone is watching and listening, we will be careful with not just what we say but also what we read and even what we think.

Intellectual surveillance gives the watcher great power over the watched. Even when what we read or think or say privately might not subject us to imprisonment or liability, the threat of its disclosure could nevertheless cause us to guard our words or thoughts. A watcher can use the threat of disclosure to discredit political opponents. Imagine if there were a public critic of government policy on race relations who was subject to pervasive electronic surveillance. By watching what she read and what she said, the government would not only have an advantage in any debate with this dissident, but it could also use the threat of disclosure of her reading habits to keep her in check. One can imagine such a critic of government policy, if she were aware of surveillance, not only being careful of what she said privately to her confidants but also being careful in what she read and what websites she visited. Without some meaningful guarantee of intellectual privacy, political freedom as we understand it could become impossible.

This "hypothetical" society is arguably very similar to the one we live in today. By almost any traditional standard, modern American law is highly protective of free speech restrictions by the state. Recall the *Snyder v. Phelps* case, which protected a horrific funeral protest that caused serious emotional harm to the family of a deceased soldier.[10] More generally, modern American society is exceptionally speech protective, even by the standards of modern Western democracies. In Europe and Canada, the government can regulate and even censor speech that is racist or hurtful. By contrast, in the United States, such speech is protected, frequently to the horror of Canadian or European observers, who believe that a free and civilized society must protect its citizens from hate speech and other forms of dignitary or emotional harm.[11]

Reasonable societies can certainly disagree about the extent to which government can restrict certain kinds of harmful speech to promote the public good; such a conversation has taken place in the United States and is ongoing in the context of cyber hate speech.[12] But I would maintain that some commitment to intellectual privacy is a necessary requirement for the kinds of democratic freedom that all Western societies aspire to.

The aforementioned surveillance example might sound far-fetched, but it is not. For example, concerned that Martin Luther King Jr. was a threat to public order, the FBI listened in to his private telephone conversations in order to seek information with which to blackmail him. As the official government investigation into the King wiretaps concluded in 1976:

> The FBI collected information about Dr. King's plans and activities through an extensive surveillance program, employing nearly every intelligence-gathering technique at the Bureau's disposal. Wiretaps, which were initially approved by Attorney General Robert F. Kennedy, were maintained on Dr. King's home telephone from October 1963 until mid-1965; the SCLC headquarter's telephones were covered by wiretaps for an even longer period. Phones in the homes and offices of some of Dr. King's close advisers were also wiretapped. The FBI has acknowledged 16 occasions on which microphones were hidden in Dr. King's hotel and motel rooms in an "attempt" to obtain information about the "private activities of King and his advisers" for use to "completely discredit" them.[13]

Imagine a dissident like King living in today's information age. Government officials (or political opponents) who wanted him silenced might be able to obtain not just access to his telephone conversations but also his reading habits and emails. Our critic could be blackmailed outright, or he could be discredited by disclosure of the information as an example to others. Perhaps he has not been having an affair but has some other secret. Maybe he is gay, or has a medical condition, or visits embarrassing websites, or has cheated on his expenses or his taxes. All of us have secrets we would prefer not be made public. Surveillance allows those secrets greater opportunities to come out, and it gives the watchers power that can be used nefariously.[14]

Of course, we have laws protecting against some kinds of surveillance and information collection by individuals and the state, such as the federal Electronic Communications Privacy Act.[15] But when revelations about secret government spying come out, we sometimes lack a vocabulary to explain why it is wrong. My goal here is to illustrate exactly *why* we have these kinds of laws and the important constitutional values they serve. We normally justify the protection of thinking, reading, and private communication under a vague rubric of "privacy," but as we have seen, privacy can mean many things. Looking at these questions from the perspective of *intellectual* privacy illuminates not only the importance of these sorts of legal rules but also how they contribute directly to the kinds of political freedom we often take for granted. It can also point the way toward thinking about how and why we should expand these kinds of protections to take account of gaps in their coverage and changes in technology.

All Western societies share a foundational commitment to the freedom of speech on public matters—a belief that new ideas should be aired and given their say.[16] But if we are interested in freedom of speech and the ability to express new and possibly heretical ideas, we should care about the social processes by which these ideas are originated, nurtured, and developed. After all, a society that cares about the free exchange of ideas should be committed to producing new ideas and not just in shouting the same old ones as loudly as possible.

How Intellectual Privacy Works

Intellectual privacy rests on the intuition that new ideas often develop best away from the intense scrutiny of public exposure; that people should be able to make up their minds at times and places of their own choosing;

and that a meaningful guarantee of privacy—protection from surveillance or interference—is necessary to promote this kind of intellectual freedom. It rests on the belief that free minds are the foundation of a free society, and that surveillance of the activities of belief formation and idea generation can affect those activities profoundly and for the worse.

Writers have long noted the intuition that when we are watched, our behavior inclines to the mainstream, the inoffensive, and the "normal." This is the insight behind Jeremy Bentham's famous image of the Panopticon, a circular prison designed around a central surveillance tower that could see into all of the cells in such a way as to create a sense of permanent surveillance on the part of the prisoners.[17] The wardens could watch any prisoner at any time, but each individual prisoner had no idea when or even if he was being watched. The purpose of this arrangement was to create an environment of permanent surveillance in the minds of the prisoners so they would behave in the manner that the wardens desired.

Bentham's invention was famously explored by French philosopher Michel Foucault, who dramatically described the Panopticon as follows:

> We know the principle: at the periphery, an annular building; at the center, a tower. . . . All that is needed, then, is to place a supervisor in a central tower and to confine in each cell a madman, someone sick, someone condemned, a worker, or a schoolboy. By the effect of backlighting, one can observe from the tower, standing out precisely against the light, the small captive silhouettes in the cells of the periphery. They are like so many cages, so many small theatres, in which each actor is alone, perfectly individualized and constantly visible.[18]

The Panopticon's purpose was to change behavior; those in the cells were aware that they could be watched at any one time. This was a calculated design feature intended to create the sense of pervasive surveillance at any time. As Bentham himself put it, "[t]he fundamental advantage of the Panopticon is so evident that one is in danger of obscuring it in the desire to prove it. To be incessantly under the eyes of the inspector is to lose in effect the power to do evil and almost the thought of wanting to do it."[19]

The most striking illustration of the Panopticon in Western culture is George Orwell's description of the mechanics of surveillance in his novel *Nineteen Eighty-Four*.[20] Orwell famously depicted a society of total state surveillance, designed to produce not just obedience on the part of the people but uniformity of thought. In Orwell's society, it was not just a crime to express dissent against the state, but a crime to think such an idea—a "Thoughtcrime." Orwell's fictional state—personified by the sinister image of "Big Brother"—achieved its control over the mouths and minds of its people through old-fashioned methods such as human informers and a secret police, but also through the technology of the "telescreen." This omnipresent tool operated like a videoconferencing device—broadcasting propaganda outward, but also monitoring all that happened within view of its cameras. Orwell describes the operation of the telescreens as experienced by his protagonist, Winston Smith, as follows:

> The telescreen received and transmitted simultaneously. Any sound that Winston made, above the level of a very low whisper, would be picked up by it, moreover, so long as he remained within the field of vision which the metal plaque commanded, he could be seen as well as heard. There was of course no way of knowing whether you were being watched at any given moment. How often, or on what system, the Thought Police plugged in on any individual wire was guesswork. It was even conceivable that they watched everybody all the time. But at any rate they could plug in your wire whenever they wanted to. You had to live—did live, from habit that became instinct—in the assumption that every sound you made was overheard, and, except in darkness, every movement scrutinized.[21]

By eliminating any vestige of intellectual privacy in this and other ways, Big Brother sought—successfully in Orwell's work of fiction—to shrink the freedoms of thought and speech through surveillance, and to eliminate any possibility of intellectual or political freedom for the people under its sway.

The commitment to intellectual freedom outlined here is a moral one—that we should protect intellectual freedom and intellectual privacy because they are necessary elements of a good and free society. But my claim about surveillance chilling intellectual experimentation contains a factual assertion as well—that intellectual surveillance deprives people of the privacy they need to make up their minds autonomously. When our intellectual activities are secretly watched, this is an injury to our civil liberties, but my argument that the processes of intellectual experimentation and belief formation are deterred and affected for the worse by surveillance depends upon (1) subjects being watched; (2) the subjects knowing or fearing that they are being watched; and (3) the surveillance causing a disruption in their intellectual activities.

At one level, it would seem obvious that surveillance chills and deters free thought, reading, and communications. This is the long-standing insight of Bentham, Foucault, and Orwell. But there is other interesting evidence that people under surveillance change their behavior toward the ordinary and the inoffensive. Over the last twenty years, a burgeoning academic literature of "surveillance studies" in sociology and other fields has attempted to document the effect of surveillance on a wide variety of human activities.[22] Although the starting point for this body of work has been the classic image of the Panopticon, this literature has explored and illustrated the normalizing effects of surveillance in a wide variety of settings. These scholars have studied the effects on behavior from (for example) state monitoring of welfare recipients and the use of undercover policing and closed-circuit television systems to deter sex in public places, public urination, and crime in general.[23] Other scholars have documented the effects and the implications of electronic and other forms of "new surveillance" in our increasingly information-based society.[24] One experiment revealed that workers put more money in a break room honesty box as requested by a sign when the background of the sign had eyeballs on it.[25] When we feel we are being watched, we act differently.

Of course, the normalizing effects of surveillance can sometimes be a good thing—one of the reasons we have police in uniform is to encourage people to obey the law and stop them from speeding or engaging in robbery. Surveillance can deter unpopular bad behavior as well as unpopular good behavior. As sociologist David Lyon explains, "surveillance is not unambiguously good or bad."[26] A recent study of the use of CCTV in holding cells, for example, found that the presence of a camera restrained the violent behavior of both police and arrestees.[27] As we saw in chapter 2, even Brandeis himself remarked shortly after publishing *The Right to Privacy* that surveillance could be beneficial at keeping wrongdoers in check; that sunlight is the best of disinfectants.

Crimes and frauds are one thing. But questions of civil liberties, of speech and thought, are quite another. When the tools of criminal deterrence affect civil liberties, we need to treat them with care. Like other Western societies, we have made a commitment to civil liberties that requires us to keep the state out of such matters. We allow the state to watch us when we might be speeding, but not when we might be voting against the party in power. Surveillance and observation are powerful tools. But their power requires us as a society to keep them within carefully circumscribed limits, and especially away from our most cherished civil liberties.

First Amendment law reflects this insight. We let the state regulate the content of nutritional labels on cereal, but not the editorials in newspapers or the placards of protestors. One of the basic elements of First Amendment law is the idea that when people are subject to punishment for speaking, there is a "chilling effect" on the exercise of their constitutional right to free expression. In First Amendment freedom of speech cases, courts rarely require proof of a chilling effect. For example, in *Hustler Magazine v. Falwell*, Chief Justice Rehnquist, writing for the Court, accepted without proof the idea that a civil liability rule for journalists would have a chilling effect, even when the journalists were not telling the truth.[28] The late Chief Justice was not usually a defender of a robust First Amendment. Nevertheless, even he treated it as a given that "a rule that would impose strict liability on a publisher for false factual assertions would have an undoubted 'chilling' effect on speech relating to public figures that does have constitutional value."[29] If I am correct that free thinking and free reading are critical to the exercise of First Amendment rights, then it would logically follow that government surveillance causing a chill to intellectual experimentation would violate the First Amendment. The law on this point is currently unclear, though a few courts have suggested something along these lines.[30] But if we think that surveillance by companies or other private actors would affect our reading and thinking as well, then we should be concerned about a threat to our culture of free speech, even if the First Amendment does not apply as a formal matter.

Keeping out those who would monitor our reading and private communications is essential if we want to generate new ideas, a fact our law has long recognized in subtle and sometimes underappreciated ways. Timothy Macklem has argued that "[t]he isolating shield of privacy enables people to develop and exchange ideas, or to foster and share activities, that the presence or even awareness of other people might stifle. For better and for worse, then, privacy is sponsor and guardian to the creative and subversive."[31] When there is protection from surveillance, new ideas can be entertained, even when they might be deeply subversive or threatening to conventional beliefs. If we value a pluralistic society or the mental processes that produce new ideas, then some measure of intellectual privacy, some respite from cognitive surveillance, is essential. Any meaningful freedom of speech requires an underlying culture of vibrant intellectual innovation. Intellectual privacy nurtures that innovation, protecting the engine of expression—the imagination of the human mind. To the extent our existing theories of law—First Amendment, Fourth Amendment, or otherwise—are under-protective of intellectual privacy, we must rehabilitate them to take these vital processes into account.

The Elements of Intellectual Privacy

Let's recap my argument. Intellectual privacy has at least three related dimensions—(1) the freedom of thought and belief, (2) the right to read and engage in intellectual exploration, and (3) the confidentiality of communications. Each of these elements is needed for intellectual privacy to work, and all of them are related and build on the others. Thus, while *freedom of thought and belief* is the core of a free society, developing our thoughts and opinions requires access to the ideas of others. So that we can read and follow the dictates of our conscience and imagination, *the right to read freely* protects our ability to read without being deterred by the observation, disapproval, or interference of others. Finally, before our ideas are ready for public consumption, it is often helpful to test them privately in discussions with our trusted intimates, which requires the *confidentiality of communication*. Intellectual privacy may require other things to be fully protected—access to education or associational liberties, or a place to read privately, for example—but the three elements I identify in this book are the most important, and the easiest for the state or private parties to undermine. Each of the next three chapters addresses an element of intellectual privacy, shows how they are mutually supportive, and gives examples of why they matter and how they are increasingly coming under threat in our digital world.

7

Thinking

The Search Subpoena

The Justice Department's subpoena was straightforward enough. It directed Google to disclose to the U.S. government every search query that had been entered into its search engine for a two-month period, and to disclose every Internet address that could be accessed from the search engine. Google refused to comply. And so on Wednesday January 18, 2006, the Department of Justice filed a court motion in California, seeking an order that would force Google to comply with a similar request—a random sample of a million URLs from its search engine database, along with the text of every "search string entered onto Google's search engine over a one-week period."[1] The Justice Department was interested in how many Internet users were looking for pornography, and it thought that analyzing the search queries of ordinary Internet users was the best way to figure this out. Google, which had a 45-percent market share at the time,[2] was not the only search engine to receive the subpoena. The Justice Department also requested search records from AOL, Yahoo!, and Microsoft. Only Google declined the initial request and opposed it, which is the only reason we are aware that the secret request was ever made in the first place.[3]

The government's request for massive amounts of search history from ordinary users requires some explanation. It has to do with the federal government's interest in online pornography, which has a long history, at least in Internet time. In 1995 *Time Magazine* ran its famous "Cyberporn" cover, depicting a shocked young boy staring into a computer monitor, his eyes wide, his mouth agape, and his skin illuminated by the eerie glow of the screen. The cover was part of a national panic about online pornography, to which Congress responded by passing the federal Communications Decency Act (CDA) the following year. This infamous law prevented all websites from publishing "patently offensive" content without first verifying the age and identity of its readers, and the sending of indecent communications to anyone under eighteen.[4] It tried to transform the Internet into a public space that was always fit for children by default.

The CDA prompted massive protests (and litigation) charging the government with censorship.[5] The Supreme Court agreed in the landmark case of *Reno v. ACLU* (1997), which struck down the CDA's decency provisions. In his opinion for the Court, Justice John Paul Stevens explained that regulating the content of Internet expression is no different from regulating the content of newspapers.[6] The case is arguably the most significant free speech decision over the past half century since it expanded the full protection of the First Amendment to Internet expression, rather than treating the Internet like television or radio, whose content may be regulated more extensively. In language that might sound dated, Justice Stevens announced a principle that has endured: "Through the use of chat rooms, any person with a phone line can become a town crier with a voice that resonates farther than it could from any soapbox. Through the use of web pages, mail exploders, and newsgroups, the same individual can become a pamphleteer."[7] The Internet, in other words, was now an essential forum for free speech.

In the aftermath of *Reno*, Congress gave up on policing Internet indecency, but continued to focus on child protection. In 1998 it passed the Children's Online Protection Act, also known as COPA. COPA punished those who engaged in web communications made "for commercial purposes" that were accessible and "harmful to minors" with a $50,000 fine and prison terms of up to six months.[8] After extensive litigation, the Supreme Court in *Ashcroft v. ACLU* (2004) upheld a preliminary injunction preventing the government from enforcing the law.[9] The Court reasoned that the government hadn't proved that an outright ban of "harmful to minors" material was necessary. It suggested that Congress could have instead required the use of blocking or filtering software, which would have had less of an impact on free speech than a ban, and it remanded the case for further proceedings.[10] Back in the lower court, the government wanted to create a study showing that filtering would be ineffective, which is why it wanted the search queries from Google and the other search engine companies in 2006.[11]

Judge James Ware ruled on the subpoena on March 17, 2006, and denied most of the government's demands.[12] He granted the release of only 5 percent of the requested randomly selected anonymous search results and none of the actual search queries.[13] Much of the reason for approving only a tiny sample of the de-identified search requests had to do with privacy. Google had not made a direct privacy argument, on the grounds that de-identified search queries were not "personal information," but it argued that disclosure of the records would expose its trade secrets and harm its goodwill from users who believed that their searches were confidential. Judge Ware accepted this oddly phrased privacy claim, and added one of his own that Google had missed. The judge explained that Google users have a privacy interest in the confidentiality of their searches because a user's identity could be reconstructed from their queries and because disclosure of such queries could lead to embarrassment (searches for, e.g., pornography or abortions) or criminal liability (searches for, e.g., "bomb placement white house"). He also placed the list of disclosed website addresses under a protective order to safeguard Google's trade secrets.[14]

Two facets of Judge Ware's short opinion in the "Search Subpoena Case" are noteworthy. First, the judge was quite correct that even search requests that have had their user's identities removed are not anonymous, as it is surprisingly easy to re-identify this kind of data. The queries we enter into search engines like Google often unwittingly reveal our identities. Most commonly, we search our own names, out of vanity, curiosity, or to discover if there are false or embarrassing facts or images of us online. But other parts of our searches can reveal our identities as well. A few months after the Search Subpoena Case, AOL made public twenty million search queries from 650,000 users of its search engine users. AOL was hoping this disclosure would help researchers and had replaced its users' names with numerical IDs to protect their privacy. But two *New York Times* reporters showed just how easy it could be to re-identify them. They tracked down AOL user number 4417749 and identified her as Thelma Arnold, a sixty-two-year old widow in Lilburn, Georgia. Thelma had made hundreds of searches including "numb fingers," "60 single men," and "dog that urinates on everything."[15] The *New York Times* reporters used old-fashioned investigative techniques, but modern sophisticated computer science tools make re-identification of such information even easier. One such technique allowed computer scientists to re-identify users in the Netflix movie-watching database, which that company made public to researchers in 2006.[16]

The second interesting facet of the Search Subpoena Case is its theory of privacy. Google won because the disclosure threatened its trade secrets (a commercial privacy, of sorts) and its business goodwill (which relied on its users believing that their searches were private). Judge Ware suggested that a more direct kind of user privacy was at stake, but was not specific beyond some generalized fear of embarrassment (echoing the old theory of tort privacy) or criminal prosecution (evoking the "reasonable expectation of privacy" theme from criminal law). Most people no doubt have an intuitive sense that their Internet searches are "private," but neither our intuitions nor the Search Subpoena Case tell us why. This is a common problem in discussions of privacy. We often use the word "privacy" without being clear about what we mean or why it matters. We can do better.

Internet searches implicate our intellectual privacy. We use tools like Google Search to make sense of the world, and intellectual privacy is needed when we are making sense of the world. Our curiosity is essential, and it should be unfettered. As I'll show in this chapter, search queries implicate a special kind of intellectual privacy, which is the freedom of thought.

Freedom of thought and belief is the core of our intellectual privacy. This freedom is the defining characteristic of a free society and our most cherished civil liberty. This right encompasses the range of thoughts and beliefs that a person might hold or develop, dealing with matters that are trivial and important, secular and profane. And it protects the individual's thoughts from scrutiny or coercion by anyone, whether a government official or a private actor such as an employer, a friend, or a spouse. At the level of law, if there is any constitutional right that is absolute, it is this one, which is the precondition for other political and religious rights guaranteed by the Western tradition. Yet curiously, although freedom of thought is widely regarded as our most important civil liberty, it has not been protected in our

move "Why how" section to be part C
   of Problems? or right after that
   section. ~

_____

p. 96 def. of intellectual privacy
p. 98 how new ideas happen matters
p. 107
p. 107 chilling effect

MADELEINE L'ENGLE's 1962 fantasy *A Wrinkle in Time* has enjoyed some out-of-this-world success. Astronaut Janice Voss credits the book with inspiring her career choice, which saw her spend over forty-nine days in space. In 2013, the International Astronomical Union (IAU) honored the late author by naming a crater on Mercury's south pole "L'Engle."

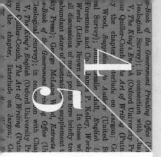

law as much as other rights, in part because it has been very difficult for the state or others to monitor thoughts and beliefs even if they wanted to.

Freedom of Thought and Intellectual Privacy

In 1913 the eminent Anglo-Irish historian J. B. Bury published *A History of Freedom of Thought*, in which he surveyed the importance of freedom of thought in the Western tradition, from the ancient Greeks to the twentieth century. According to Bury, the conclusion that individuals should have an absolute right to their beliefs free of state or other forms of coercion "is the most important ever reached by men."[17] Bury was not the only scholar to have observed that freedom of thought (or belief, or conscience) is at the core of Western civil liberties. Recognitions of this sort are commonplace and have been made by many of our greatest minds. René Descartes's maxim, "I think, therefore I am," identifies the power of individual thought at the core of our existence.[18] John Milton praised in *Areopagitica* "the liberty to know, to utter, and to argue freely according to conscience, above all [other] liberties."[19]

In the nineteenth century, John Stuart Mill developed a broad notion of freedom of thought as an essential element of his theory of human liberty, which comprised "the inward domain of consciousness; demanding liberty of conscience, in the most comprehensive sense; liberty of thought and feeling; absolute freedom of opinion and sentiment on all subjects, practical or speculative, scientific, moral, or theological."[20] In Mill's view, free thought was inextricably linked to and mutually dependent upon free speech, with the two concepts being a part of a broader idea of political liberty. Moreover, Mill recognized that private parties as well as the state could chill free expression and thought.[21]

Law in Britain and America has embraced the central importance of free thought as the civil liberty on which all others depend. But it was not always so. People who cannot think for themselves, after all, are incapable of self-government. In the Middle Ages, the crime of "constructive treason" outlawed "imagining the death of the king" as a crime that was punishable by death.[22] Thomas Jefferson later reflected that this crime "had drawn the Blood of the best and honestest Men in the Kingdom."[23] The impulse for political uniformity was related to the impulse for religious uniformity, whose story is one of martyrdom and burnings of the stake. As Supreme Court Justice William O. Douglas put it in 1963:

> While kings were fearful of treason, theologians were bent on stamping out heresy.... The Reformation is associated with Martin Luther. But prior to him it broke out many times only to be crushed. When in time the Protestants gained control, they tried to crush the Catholics; and when the Catholics gained the upper hand, they ferreted out the Protestants. Many devices were used. Heretical books were destroyed and heretics were burned at the stake or banished. The rack, the thumbscrew, the wheel on which men were stretched, these were part of the paraphernalia.[24]

Thankfully, the excesses of such a dangerous government power were recognized over the centuries, and thought crimes were abolished. Thus, William Blackstone's influential *Commentaries* stressed the importance of the common law protection for the freedom of thought and inquiry, even under a system that allowed subsequent punishment for seditious and other kinds of dangerous speech. Blackstone explained that:

> Neither is any restraint hereby laid upon freedom of thought or inquiry: liberty of private sentiment is still left; the disseminating, or making public, of bad sentiments, destructive of the ends of society, is the crime which society corrects. A man (says a fine writer on this subject) may be allowed to keep poisons in his closet, but not publicly to vend them as cordials.[25]

Even during a time when English law allowed civil and criminal punishment for many kinds of speech that would be protected today, including blasphemy, obscenity, seditious libel, and vocal criticism of the government, jurists recognized the importance of free thought and gave it special, separate protection in both the legal and cultural traditions.

The poisons metaphor Blackstone used, for example, was adapted from Jonathan Swift's *Gulliver's Travels*, from a line that the King of Brobdingnag delivers to Gulliver.[26] Blackstone's treatment of freedom of thought was itself adopted by Joseph Story in his own *Commentaries*, the leading American treatise on constitutional law in the early Republic.[27] Thomas Jefferson and James Madison also embraced freedom of thought. Jefferson's famous Virginia Statute for Religious Freedom enshrined religious liberty around the declaration that "Almighty God hath created the mind free,"[28] and James Madison forcefully called for freedom of thought and conscience in his *Memorial and Remonstrance Against Religious Assessments.*[29]

Freedom of thought thus came to be protected directly as a prohibition on state coercion of truth or belief. It was one of a handful of rights protected by the original Constitution even before the ratification of the Bill of Rights. Article VI provides that "state and federal legislators, as well as officers of the United States, shall be bound by oath or affirmation, to support this Constitution; but no religious test shall ever be required as a qualification to any office or public trust under the United States."[30] This provision, known as the "religious test clause," ensured that religious orthodoxy could not be imposed as a requirement for governance, a further protection of the freedom of thought (or, in this case, its closely related cousin, the freedom of conscience). The Constitution also gives special protection against the crime of treason, by defining it to exclude thought crimes and providing special evidentiary protections:

> Treason against the United States, shall consist only in levying war against them, or in adhering to their enemies, giving them aid and comfort. No person shall be convicted of treason unless on the testimony of two witnesses to the same overt act, or on confession in open court.[31]

By eliminating religious tests and by defining the crime of treason as one of guilty actions rather than merely guilty minds, the Constitution was thus steadfastly part of the tradition giving exceptional protection to the freedom of thought.

Nevertheless, even when governments could not directly coerce the uniformity of beliefs, a person's thoughts remained relevant to both law and social control. A person's thoughts could reveal political or religious disloyalty, or they could be relevant to a defendant's mental state in committing a crime or other legal wrong. And while thoughts could not be revealed directly, they could be discovered by indirect means. For example, thoughts could be inferred either from a person's testimony or confessions, or by access to their papers and diaries. But both the English common law and the American Bill of Rights came to protect against these intrusions into the freedom of the mind as well.

The most direct way to obtain knowledge about a person's thoughts would be to haul him before a magistrate as a witness and ask him under penalty of law. The English ecclesiastical courts used the "oath ex officio" for precisely this purpose.[32] But as historian Leonard Levy has explained, this practice came under assault in Britain as invading the freedom of thought and belief. As the eminent jurist Lord Coke later declared, "no free man should be compelled to answer for his secret thoughts and opinions."[33] The practice of the oath was ultimately abolished in England in the cases of John Lilburne and John Entick, men who were political dissidents rather than religious heretics.[34]

In the new United States, the Fifth Amendment guarantee that "No person ... shall be compelled in any criminal case to be a witness against himself" can also be seen as a resounding rejection of this sort of practice in favor of the freedom of thought.[35] Law of course evolves, and current Fifth Amendment doctrine focuses on the consequences of a confession rather than on mental privacy,[36] but the origins of the Fifth Amendment are part of a broad commitment to freedom of thought that runs through our law. The late criminal law scholar William Stuntz has shown that this tradition was not merely a procedural protection for all, but a substantive limitation on the power of the state to force its enemies to reveal their unpopular or heretical thoughts.[37] As he put the point colorfully, "[i]t is no coincidence that the privilege's origins read like a catalogue of religious and political persecution."[38]

Another way to obtain a person's thoughts would be by reading their diaries or other papers. Consider the Fourth Amendment, which protects a person from unreasonable searches and seizures by the police:

> The right of the people to be secure in their persons, houses, papers, and effects, against unreasonable searches and seizures, shall not be violated, and no Warrants shall issue, but upon probable cause, supported by Oath or affirmation, and particularly describing the place to be searched, and the persons or things to be seized.[39]

Today we think about the Fourth Amendment as providing protection for the home and the person chiefly against unreasonable searches for contraband like guns or drugs.[40] But the Fourth Amendment's origins come not from drug cases but as a bulwark against intellectual surveillance by the state.[41] In the eighteenth century, the English Crown had sought to quash political and religious dissent through the use of "general warrants," legal documents that gave agents of the Crown the authority to search the homes of suspected dissidents for incriminating papers.[42]

Perhaps the most infamous dissident of the time was John Wilkes. Wilkes was a progressive critic of Crown policy and a political rogue whose public tribulations, wit, and famed personal ugliness made him a celebrity throughout the English-speaking world. Wilkes was the editor of a progressive newspaper, the *North Briton*, a member of Parliament, and an outspoken critic of government policy. He was deeply critical of the 1763 Treaty of Paris ending the Seven Years War with France, a conflict known in North America as the French and Indian War. Wilkes's damning articles angered King George, who ordered the arrest of Wilkes and his co-publishers of the *North Briton*, authorizing general warrants to search their papers for evidence of treason and sedition. The government ransacked numerous private homes and printers' shops, scrutinizing personal papers for any signs of incriminating evidence. In all, forty-nine people were arrested, and Wilkes himself was charged with seditious libel, prompting a long and inconclusive legal battle of suits and countersuits.[43]

By taking a stand against the king and intrusive searches, Wilkes became a *cause célèbre* among Britons at home and in the colonies. This was particularly true for many American colonists, whose own objections to British tax policy following the Treaty of Paris culminated in the American Revolution. The rebellious colonists drew from the Wilkes case the importance of political dissent as well as the need to protect dissenting citizens from unreasonable (and politically motivated) searches and seizures.[44]

The Fourth Amendment was intended to address this problem by inscribing legal protection for "persons, houses, papers, and effects" into the Bill of Rights. A government that could not search the homes and read the papers of its citizens would be less able to engage in intellectual tyranny and enforce intellectual orthodoxy.[45] In a pre-electronic world, the Fourth Amendment kept out the state, while trespass and other property laws kept private parties out of our homes, paper, and effects.

The Fourth and Fifth Amendments thus protect the freedom of thought at their core. As Stuntz explains, the early English cases establishing these principles were "classic First Amendment cases in a system with no First Amendment."[46] Even in a legal regime without protection for dissidents who expressed unpopular political or religious opinions, the English system protected those dissidents in their private beliefs, as well as the papers and other documents that might reveal those beliefs.

In American law, an even stronger protection for freedom of thought can be found in the First Amendment. Although the First Amendment text speaks of free speech, press, and assembly, the freedom of thought is unquestionably at the core of these guarantees, and courts and scholars have consistently recognized this fact. In fact, the freedom of thought and belief is the closest thing to an absolute right guaranteed by the Constitution. The Supreme Court first recognized it in the 1878 Mormon polygamy case of *Reynolds v. United States*,[47] which ruled that although law could regulate religiously inspired actions such as polygamy, it was powerless to control "mere religious belief and opinions."[48] As we saw in chapter 2 freedom of thought in secular matters was identified by Justices Holmes and Brandeis as part of their dissenting tradition in free speech cases in the 1910s and 1920s. Holmes declared crisply in *United States v. Schwimmer* that "if there is any principle of the Constitution that more imperatively calls for attachment than any other it is the principle of free thought—not free thought for those who agree with us but freedom for the thought that we hate."[49] And in his dissent in the Fourth Amendment wiretapping case of *Olmstead v. United States*, Brandeis argued that the framers of the Constitution "sought to protect Americans in their beliefs, their thoughts, their emotions and their sensations."[50] As we shall see in chapter 9, Brandeis's dissent in *Olmstead* adapted his theory of tort privacy into federal constitutional law around the principle of freedom of thought.

Freedom of thought became permanently enshrined in constitutional law during a series of mid-twentieth century cases that charted the contours of the modern First Amendment. In *Palko v. Connecticut*, Justice Cardozo characterized freedom of thought as "the matrix, the indispensable condition, of nearly every other form of freedom."[51] And in a series of cases involving Jehovah's Witnesses, the Court developed a theory of the First Amendment under which the rights of free thought, speech, press, and exercise of religion were placed in a "preferred position."[52] Freedom of thought was central to this new theory of the First Amendment,[53] exemplified by Justice Jackson's opinion in *West Virginia State Board of Education v. Barnette*,[54] which invalidated a state regulation requiring that public school children salute the flag each morning. Jackson declared that:

> If there is any fixed star in our constitutional constellation, it is that no official, high or petty, can prescribe what shall be orthodox in politics, nationalism, religion, or other matters of opinion or force citizens to confess by word or act their faith therein....
>
> [The flag-salute statute] transcends constitutional limitations on [legislative] power and invades the sphere of intellect and spirit which it is the purpose of the First Amendment to our Constitution to reserve from all official control.[55]

Modern cases continue to reflect this legacy. The Court has repeatedly declared that the constitutional guarantee of freedom of thought is at the foundation of what it means to have a free society.[56] In particular, freedom of thought has been invoked as a principal justification for preventing punishment based upon possessing or reading dangerous media. Thus, the government cannot punish a person for merely possessing unpopular or dangerous books or images based upon their content.[57] As Alexander Meiklejohn put it succinctly, the First Amendment protects, first and foremost, "the thinking process of the community."[58]

Freedom of thought thus remains, as it has for centuries, the foundation of the Anglo-American tradition of civil liberties. It is also the core of intellectual privacy.

"The New Home of Mind"

"Governments of the Industrial World, you weary giants of flesh and steel, I come from Cyberspace, the new home of Mind." So began "A Declaration of Independence of Cyberspace," a 1996 manifesto responding to the Communications Decency Act and other attempts by government to regulate the online world and stamp out indecency. The Declaration's author was John Perry Barlow, a founder of the influential Electronic Frontier Foundation and a former lyricist for the Grateful Dead.[59] Barlow argued that "[c]yberspace consists of transactions, relationships, and thought itself, arrayed like a standing wave in the web of our communications. Ours is a world that is both everywhere and nowhere, but it is not where bodies live."[60] This definition of the Internet as a realm of pure thought was quickly followed by an affirmation of the importance of the freedom of thought. Barlow insisted that in Cyberspace "anyone, anywhere may express his or her beliefs, no matter how singular, without fear of being coerced into silence or conformity."[61] The Declaration concluded on the same theme: "We will spread ourselves across the Planet so that no one can arrest our thoughts. We will create a civilization of the Mind in Cyberspace. May it be more humane and fair than the world your governments have made before."[62]

In his Declaration, Barlow joined a tradition of many (including many of the most important thinkers and creators of the digital world) who have expressed the idea that networked computing can be a place of "thought itself." As early as 1960, the great computing visionary J. C. R. Licklider imagined that "in not too many years, human brains and computing machines will be coupled together very tightly, and that the resulting partnership will think as no human brain has ever thought."[63] Tim Berners-Lee, the architect of the World Wide Web, envisioned his creation as one that would bring "the workings of society closer to the workings of our minds."[64]

Barlow's utopian demand that governments leave the electronic realm alone was only partially successful. The Communications Decency Act was, as we have seen, struck down by the Supreme Court, but today many laws regulate the Internet, such as the U.S. Digital Millenium Copyright Act[65] and the EU Data Retention Directive.[66] The Internet has become more (and less) than Barlow's utopian vision—a place of business as well as of thinking.[67] But Barlow's description of the Internet as a world of the mind remains resonant today.

It is undeniable that today millions of people use computers as aids to their thinking. In the digital age, computers are an essential and intertwined supplement to our thoughts and our memories. Discussing Licklider's prophesy from half a century ago, legal scholar Tim Wu notes that virtually every computer "program we use is a type of thinking aid—whether the task is to remember things (an address book), to orga-
ize prose (a word processor), or to keep track of friends (social network

software)."[68] These technologies have become not just aids to thought but also part of the thinking process itself. In the past, we invented paper and books, and then sound and video recordings to preserve knowledge and make it easier for us as individuals and societies to remember information. Digital technologies have made remembering even easier, by providing cheap storage, inexpensive retrieval, and global reach.[69] Consider the Kindle, a cheap electronic reader that can hold 1,100 books, or even cheaper external hard drives that can hold hundreds of hours of high-definition video in a box the size of a paperback novel.[70]

Even the words we use to describe our digital products and experiences reflect our understanding that computers and cyberspace are devices and places of the mind. IBM has famously called its laptops "ThinkPads," and many of us use "smartphones." Other technologies have been named in ways that affirm their status as tools of the mind—notebooks, ultrabooks, tablets, and browsers. Apple Computer produces iPads and MacBooks and has long sold its products under the slogan, "Think Different." Google historian John Battelle has famously termed Google's search records to be a "database of intentions."[71] Google's own slogan for its web browser Chrome is "browse the web as fast as you think," revealing how web browsing itself is not just a form of reading, but a kind of thinking itself. My point here is not just that common usage or marketing slogans connect Internet use to thinking, but a more important one: Our use of these words reflects a reality. We are increasingly using digital technologies not just as aids to our memories but also as an essential part of the ways we think.

Search engines in particular bear a special connection to the processes of thought. How many of us have asked a factual question among friends, only for smartphones to appear as our friends race to see who can look up the answer the fastest? In private, we use search engines to learn about the world. If you have a moment, pull up your own search history on your phone, tablet, or computer, and recall your past queries. It usually makes for interesting reading—a history of your thoughts and wonderings.

But the ease with which we can pull up such a transcript reveals another fundamental feature of digital technologies—they are designed to create records of their use. Think again about the profile a search engine like Google has for you. A transcript of search queries and links followed is a close approximation to a transcript of the operation of your mind. In the logs of search engine companies are vast repositories of intellectual wonderings, questions asked, and mental whims followed. Similar logs exist for Internet service providers and other new technology companies. And the data contained in such logs is eagerly sought by government and private entities interested in monitoring intellectual activity, whether for behavioral advertising, crime and terrorism prevention, and possibly other, more sinister purposes.

Searching Is Thinking

With these two points in mind—the importance of freedom of thought and the idea of the Internet as a place where thought occurs—we can now return to the Google Search Subpoena with which this chapter opened. Judge Ware's opinion revealed an intuitive understanding that the disclosure of search records was threatening to privacy, but was not clear about what kind of privacy was involved or why it matters.

Intellectual privacy, in particular the freedom of thought, supplies the answer to this problem. We use search engines to learn about and make sense of the world, to answer our questions, and as aids to our thinking. Searching, then, in a very real sense is a kind of thinking. And we have a long tradition of protecting the privacy and confidentiality of our thoughts from the scrutiny of others. It is precisely because of the importance of search records to human thought that the Justice Department wanted to access the records. But if our search records were more public, we wouldn't merely be exposed to embarrassment like Thelma Arnold of Lilburn, Georgia. We would be less likely to search for unpopular or deviant or dangerous topics. Yet in a free society, we need to be able to think freely about any ideas, no matter how dangerous or unpopular. If we care about freedom of thought—and our political institutions are built on the assumption that we do—we should care about the privacy of electronic records that reveal our thoughts. Search records illustrate the point well, but this idea is not just limited to that one important technology. My argument about freedom of thought in the digital age is this: Any technology that we use in our thinking implicates our intellectual privacy, and if we want to preserve our ability to think fearlessly, free of monitoring, interference, or repercussion, we should embody these technologies with a meaningful measure of intellectual privacy.

8

Reading

The Naughty Book

Fifty Shades of Grey was an unlikely cultural phenomenon. E. L. James's S&M romance started its life, oddly enough, as a work of fan fiction based on Stephenie Meyer's vampire-themed *Twilight* series. After circulating early versions on fan sites, James revised her manuscript, ditched the vampires, and submitted it to publishers. The major houses passed on her work, but a small independent Australian publisher eventually agreed to publish it. The book was poorly received by critics. Salman Rushdie declared, for example, that "I've never read anything so badly written that got published. It made *Twilight* look like *War and Peace*."[1]

Yet despite the odds, the alternative love story of Anastasia Steele and Christian Grey touched a nerve with readers. Though print editions were hard to find in Britain and the United States, the book sold millions of copies as an e-book. Its largely female readership repeatedly praised the privacy that the e-book version allowed. And as more people started to read the book, it became more socially acceptable to be seen with a thick paperback book of what was essentially S&M pornography. Random House sold millions of print copies, with the book being prominently displayed at the front of bookstores. But the book's print success would perhaps never have happened without the easy privacy afforded by its digital editions. As James's agent noted, "in the 21st century, women have the ability to read this kind of material without anybody knowing what they're reading, because they can read them on their iPads and Kindles."[2]

Most people are familiar with the story of E. L. James's Naughty Book, but in this chapter, I'm going to use its story to show three things about reading and intellectual privacy. First, I will argue that *private reading matters*; that it is an important civil liberty, because we need access to the ideas of others on our own terms in order to make sense of the world. My second claim is something I shall call the *e-reader paradox*, which is that electronic readers create the illusion of intellectual privacy in the physical world, while they threaten intellectual privacy in the digital one. Finally, I will argue that digital text is bringing about a revolution in reading as profound as the printing press. This *digital reading revolution* brings into question many of the assumptions about privacy and reading that we have protected for a long time. And it requires us to make a choice now about whether future reading will be protected by intellectual privacy.

Why Private Reading Matters

Reading is important. I argued in chapter 6 that if we are interested in understanding the world around us, or in the creation of new ideas, we need access to the ideas of others. We can do this by talking and listening, but reading has real advantages over the spoken word. We can only listen at the speed of the speaker, but we can read (and reread) at our own pace. Reading also lets us access the words and ideas of other people who aren't available. These people may be separated across space, like writers in another part of our country, or another part of the world. Or they may be separated across time, like Ernest Hemingway, Jane Austen, Thomas Jefferson, William Shakespeare, or the authors of the Bible. Ideas or facts that are believed to be important get written down so that they can be read in different places and different times. And if we want these ideas to last, we've tended to put them in books. The late historian Barbara Tuchman expressed the point nicely: "Books are the carriers of civilization. Without books, history is silent, literature dumb, science crippled, thought and speculation at a standstill. They are engines of change, windows on the world, lighthouses erected in the sea of time."[3]

Unlike thinking or speaking, reading is not a natural skill for humans. We are born wired to speak and to think, but we are not born with a natural aptitude for reading. Reading requires study, and it is hard work to train our brains to absorb text—a skill that requires years of practice to become proficient in, and further years to master. Neuroscientists have discovered that learning to read rewires the way that our brains are put together. We are thus in a very real sense shaped by what we read.[4] Reading is therefore socially and environmentally constructed in even more ways than thought and language are. What this means is that the norms and rules that govern reading are up for grabs—they can be affected by our social norms, our laws, and our technologies.

This brings me to the first argument I'll make in this chapter—private reading is an important civil liberty, because we need access to the ideas of others *on our own terms* in order to make sense of the world. And those terms should include a meaningful amount of privacy, especially when readers are reading dangerous or unpopular ideas. After all, because reading is particularly socially constructed, it is particularly fragile as a social practice.

The social and technological practices of reading have changed substantially over the millennia. Early forms of writing on clay and papyrus gave way to the codex—our familiar object of pieces of paper bound together to form a book. But the culture of reading early books was not private; readers would read them out loud regardless of whether they were with a group or alone.[5] Saint Augustine famously recounted his surprise in the year 380 when he observed Ambrose, the Bishop of Milan, reading silently to himself: "When he read, his eyes scanned the page and his heart explored the meaning, but his voice was silent and his tongue was still."[6] Early books were notoriously expensive and often confined to topics of government and religion. Only with the explosion of book publishing after the introduction of the printing press could books become cheap enough for mass consumption. And that mass consumption dramatically changed the nature of books, creating markets for radical political commentary, daily newspapers, and the novel. Such books could be read in solitude and privacy, whether in a library, a study, the train, or a park bench.

The development of private reading was one of the most significant technological advances in human history. It democratized knowledge and allowed readers to privately engage with ideas on their own terms. It transformed society, politics, and religious belief. Private reading also enabled thinking of a new, critical, and active kind. Nicholas Carr explains eloquently what happens during this kind of active but private reading:

> The bond between book reader and book writer has always been a tightly symbiotic one, a means of intellectual and artistic cross-fertilization. The words of a writer act as a catalyst in the mind of

the reader, inspiring new insights, associations, and perceptions, sometimes even epiphanies. And the very existence of the attentive, critical reader provides the spur for the writer's work. It gives the author the confidence to explore new forms of expression, to blaze difficult and demanding paths of thought, to venture into uncharted and sometimes hazardous territory.[7]

Essential to this relationship is the location in which it happens—in the minds of author and reader, secure from the monitoring or interference of others. The act of reading a book is a kind of thinking and a quintessentially private activity, whether it occurs in an office, a study, or under the covers of a bed by flashlight. To read is to think, to question, and to make sense of the world for ourselves. It is both social and private at the same time.

Unsurprisingly, given its importance, there are laws that protect reader privacy. In the United States, the most important of these is the First Amendment, which protects the right to read as well as the right to speak and think. The right to read freely developed in a number of areas, but perhaps the most important battlefield for the right has been in the context of obscene publications. Obscene books (and other publications) are those that depict hard-core pornographic acts—the idea Justice Potter Stewart was searching for when he famously described obscenity as lacking definition, writing: "I shall not today attempt further to define the kinds of material I understand to be embraced within that shorthand description, and perhaps I could never succeed in intelligibly doing so. But I know it when I see it, and the motion picture involved in this case is not that."[8]

For the last four decades, sexually themed books and films have been protected by the First Amendment unless they fall under the definition of "obscenity" in *Miller v. California* (1973), which requires that a work (1) appeal to the "prurient interest" in (2) a "patently offensive" way and (3) that the work taken as a whole "lacks serious literary, artistic, political, or scientific value."[9] The *Miller* test has been highly protective of sexually themed literature, in part because the first two elements require an apparent absurdity. As Kathleen Sullivan put it well, to be obscene, the work must "turn you on" and "gross you out" at the same time![10]

The most important case about the right to read is *Stanley v. Georgia* (1969).[11] Robert Eli Stanley was a Georgia resident the IRS believed to be engaged in illegal gambling. Concerned that he wasn't paying tax on his illegal earnings, the IRS obtained a search warrant for Stanley's home. The police searched the house, but found no evidence of illegal gambling or bookmaking activity, or of any tax avoidance. However, while searching an upstairs bedroom, they did find three cans of 8mm film, which piqued their curiosity. The police discovered a film projector in Stanley's closet, which they set up and used to watch the films while still in his home. The films featured "nude men and women engaged in acts of sexual intercourse and sodomy" and "successive orgies of seduction, sodomy and sexual intercourse." Believing the films to be obscene, the police charged Stanley with the possession of obscenity.[12]

Stanley was convicted and appealed his conviction to the US Supreme Court, arguing that he had a constitutional right to possess any books or films he liked in the privacy of his home.[13] The Supreme Court agreed.[14] In ringing language, Justice Thurgood Marshall ruled that the First Amendment protects a person's right to read or watch whatever he or she might want without government interference. The First Amendment, he ruled, protects the right to receive information, which is "fundamental to a free society." This was particularly important in a case like *Stanley*, which involved the prosecution for "mere possession of printed or filmed matter in the privacy of a person's own home."[15] Both the First Amendment and constitutional privacy interests supported Stanley's "right to satisfy his intellectual and emotional needs in the privacy of his own home [and his] right to be free from state inquiry into the contents of his library." Justice Marshall concluded with a broad declaration of the right to read: "If the First Amendment means anything, it means that a State has no business telling a man, sitting alone in his own house, what books he may read or what films he may watch. Our whole constitutional heritage rebels at the thought of giving government the power to control men's minds."[16]

Controlling what a person can read is controlling the moral content of their thoughts. Although there are some exceptions to the right to possess what books you want in your own home, this principle from *Stanley* has endured for half a century. There is no right to possess stolen books, for example. Nor does *Stanley* extend to the possession of child pornography that depicts actual child abuse.[17] But the reason these are exceptions to *Stanley* is because these cases are justified on grounds other than thought control. The child pornography cases allow punishment for possession only because the interest in protecting children from sexual abuse means that there is no right to possess actual records of child abuse. But if no children were involved in the production of the pornography (for example, through animation or the use of young-looking adults), then the government cannot punish its possession in the home either.[18] Even though the idea of child sexuality is repugnant to many, the First Amendment protects the right to read and view materials that explore deviant ideas, no matter how unpopular those ideas may be.

Let's recap my argument so far. The right to read is an important civil liberty, and the unfettered right to read whatever we want is the hallmark of a free society. The case of the Naughty Book with which this chapter opened illustrates this principle quite nicely. It turned out that an awful lot of women wanted to read a salacious book by a female author—a book that contemporary social norms might consider deviant. But even though many people might disapprove of *Fifty Shades of Grey* on moral or literary grounds, the government lacks the power to censor such a book unless it is obscene and lacking social value. Otherwise, we are free to read what we want. From this perspective, the tale of the Naughty Book is a victory for the right to read.

What's particularly interesting about the *Fifty Shades of Grey* phenomenon is that it showed how the availability of e-books has made it easier to acquire and read unpopular or potentially embarrassing books in public. A reader who wants to purchase an embarrassing book on an e-reader can do so without going into a bookstore, facing a human clerk, and leaving with the book in a bag. All she needs to do is to use the shopping application built into her reader, and the book is hers to read in moments. As our reading habits increasingly embrace not just the codex but the Kindle as well, technology can be a powerful aid to the right to read privately.

The e-Reader Paradox

The privacy implications of e-readers are complex, and digging into this complexity reveals what I'll refer to as the *e-reader paradox*. E-readers certainly advance privacy in the physical context of readers and books. When you read your Kindle, Nook, or iPad on the subway, no one knows what (or even if) you are reading. In this respect, E. L. James's agent was exactly right about the privacy advantages of e-readers.

But in another more important way, she was completely wrong. Consider our hypothetical early reader of *Fifty Shades of Grey*, carrying her Kindle on the London Tube. The other passengers might have no idea what she is reading, but Amazon does. The way that its Kindle is engineered allows Amazon to know not just what she is reading, but whether she has finished the book, what page she is on, how long she has spent on each page, and which passages she might have highlighted.[19] Some of this information-collection is necessary to allow certain Kindle features to function, like the syncing of which page she is on among the physical Kindle and virtual Kindle apps on her iPad, PC, or smartphone. But functional necessity doesn't change the fact that the Kindle is creating highly detailed records of her reading habits, linking them to her real name and Amazon account, and preserving them for posterity. This is the e-reader paradox: e-readers create an illusion of physical reader privacy while they threaten the very existence of any kind of digital reader privacy.

The e-reader paradox isn't just limited to electronic books. Many of our digital technologies open up new opportunities to read and interact with ideas while simultaneously creating records of reading habits and intellectual explorations. Digital bookstores, websites, social media sites, and other electronic media companies collect vastly more data than old-fashioned libraries and bookstores. In addition to its Kindle data, for example, Amazon uses cookies and other monitoring technologies to track not just what books, films, and other products its customers purchase, but also what they browse on its website and for how long.[20] The vast amount of data about reading habits that these technologies collect is starting to be subjected to analytic technologies, promising the creation of ever-more detailed profiles of reader behavior as these technologies mature and readers increasingly migrate to digital books.[21]

While we have always read newspapers, increasingly, they are reading us as well. On newspaper and many other websites, targeted advertising is fueled by a variety of technologies and companies that track, assemble, and analyze the web-surfing and reading habits of Internet users to enable "behavioral" personalized advertisements.[22] These companies monitor your web travels and serve you ads that fit your profile, ads that can follow you around the web as you move from site to site. Consider also the ubiquitous Facebook "like" and "recommend" buttons that appear on millions of news, lifestyle, and sports pages across the web. When a Facebook user clicks the "like" button on one of these websites, embedded software code sends the information back to Facebook in order to publish the event on the user's profile page. But how did Facebook know in the first place which user clicked the button? The answer is that Facebook knows which of its users are on what pages throughout the web in order to serve up their personalized buttons in the first place.[23] As *The New York Times* concluded, "Facebook is collecting a vast amount of data about the web travels of some 800 million people worldwide with the buttons, unbeknownst to most of them. And other social networks are starting to do the same."[24] A key design feature of Facebook makes its tracking and profiling even more problematic. Unlike traditional behavioral advertising, which is linked to a cookie on a computer that may have several users, Facebook accounts are linked to a person's real name, a practice that the company aggressively defends.[25] In 2011 Facebook deactivated Salman Rushdie's account, not because of his critical views on *Fifty Shades of Grey*, but because he didn't register as "Ahmed Rushdie," the name on his passport.[26] For many of its users, then, Facebook knows what they are reading, and it knows them precisely by name.

Perhaps surprisingly, in the United States at least, reading records—book purchases, as well as data about online or digital reading habits—often receive only minimal legal protection. In many cases, such records can be collected, assembled, circulated, sold, or given to the government with almost no regulation.[27] Even physical book purchases are sometimes without legal protection. For example, during the investigations of President Clinton that led to his impeachment, the independent counsel sought to compel Kramerbooks in Washington, DC, to release Monica Lewinsky's book purchase records.[28] Kramerbooks refused on the grounds that it would hurt its business, and both the bookstore and Lewinsky argued that the release of those records would infringe their First Amendment rights. These arguments met with some success in court, but they did not stop the independent counsel from obtaining the records directly from Lewinsky. Ultimately, the independent counsel, Kenneth Starr, was able to get Lewinsky to concede that she had purchased erotic literature for Bill Clinton, including Nicholson Baker's phone sex novella *Vox*.[29] But the important lesson is that if it had wanted to, or if its commercial interests favored disclosure, Kramerbooks could have made any of its records public, free of any legal obligation. It could do so tomorrow, as well.[30]

While companies claim they will respect the confidentiality of such records, in reality these records are subject to a very low level of legal protection. For these records, the only constraints on disclosure are the corporate self-interest and the promises in company-drafted privacy policies. In an age where personal information is a profitable industry, corporate self-restraint can be a very weak constraint. As for privacy policies, few people read them, and their terms can be easily changed.

Moreover, other legal requirements such as copyright and child protection laws impose a logic of surveillance that can become highly intrusive. The Digital Millenium Copyright Act requires the unmasking of anonymous users in order to protect copyright holders from infringement.[31] And in order to protect children from adult content, users of youtube.com who wish to access content flagged as indecent must register with YouTube and create accounts that allow even greater surveillance and identification of their viewing habits. This creates the irony of greater intellectual privacy protections for users who read and view only the non-objectionable content, and creates a chill on the unfettered right to read anonymously.

Yet there are some legal protections for reader records. The most common way that the law protects them is by imposing a *confidentiality rule*. These rules place obligations on the people and organizations who receive personal information not to disclose it without our consent.[32] I'll talk more about confidentiality in the next chapter, but it's worth noting that the idea of confidentiality recognizes the fact that information is usually neither wholly public nor wholly private. We often share information (or gossip) with others under the expectation that our confidants will keep the information to themselves. We sometimes impose legal obligations to back up our social intuitions, too. Familiar examples of such confidentiality rules include professional duties of confidentiality imposed on doctors, lawyers, accountants, and ministers.[33]

Confidentiality rules recognize that sharing of information with trusted confidants is important, and that an assurance of confidentiality is necessary in order to enable full and frank sharing of information. Rules of this sort encourage us to tell our doctors potentially embarrassing medical details so that they can assemble a complete clinical picture to treat our ailments better. We also protect the honest discussions essential to healthy marital relationships by preventing spouses from being called to testify against each other in many legal matters.[34]

Some confidentiality rules apply to reader records. The most famous of these rules is the federal Video Privacy Protection Act (VPPA), colloquially known as the "Bork Bill." The VPPA prohibits online and physical video stores from sharing the video rental histories of their customers without their consent.[35] The law came about when Michael Dolan, a reporter from the alternative *Washington City Paper*, went to Potomac Video in Washington, DC, and obtained and published the rental records of Supreme Court nominee Robert Bork's family. Ironically enough, Dolan's intent was to expose Bork because of the nominee's public rejection of any right to privacy.[36] Dolan's article, *The Bork Tapes Saga*, was subtitled "Never mind his writings on *Roe vs. Wade*. The Inner Workings of Robert Bork's Mind Are Revealed by the Videos He Rents." Dolan argued that Bork's 146 film rentals revealed him to be a boring and middlebrow Anglophile, afraid of sex and violence, who mainly watched movies starring men, and who was better suited to being a "Supreme Couch Potato" than a Supreme Court Justice. The article ended with a threat to disclose the viewing habits of other politicians, describing the project as a possible "life's work."[37]

Despite the fact that the most sensational disclosure in the Bork files was John Hughes's *Sixteen Candles* (presumably rented not by Bork, but by his teenage daughter), a horrified Congress quickly passed the VPPA, perhaps fearing the disclosure of more interesting film preferences should politicians be targeted next. The VPPA's legislative history reveals a real concern for the privacy of reader records, broadly defined. The Senate Report accompanying the Act justified the protection of rental records on the grounds that they reveal the core of who we are as individuals; it argued that

> [our] right to privacy protects the choice of movies that we watch with our family in our own homes. And it protects the selection of books that we choose to read. These activities are at the core of any definition of personhood. They reveal our likes and dislikes, our interests and our whims. They say a great deal about our dreams and ambitions, our fears and our hopes. They reflect our individuality, and they describe us as people.[38]

The VPPA mandates that anyone in the business of the renting or selling of "prerecorded video cassette tapes or similar audio visual materials" may only disclose the sale or rental records of a customer "with the informed, written consent of the consumer given at the time the disclosure is sought."[39] The law also requires that law enforcement seeking access to video rental records provide a warrant supported by probable cause that the "records or other information sought are relevant to a legitimate law enforcement inquiry." Anyone aggrieved by the disclosure of their viewing records can sue to recover at least $2,500 for each violation.[40] Courts applying the VPPA have read it broadly, interpreting its guarantee of intellectual privacy to resist disclosure of records to state tax authorities,[41] to sue those who induce breaches of confidentiality,[42] and to cover not just physical media but also streaming online video by services such as hulu.com.[43]

State law sometimes provides even greater protections than the federal VPPA.[44] Maryland and Connecticut treat video records as confidential, prohibit their sale, and impose criminal penalties in cases of unlawful sale or disclosure.[45] Other states with video privacy laws include California, Delaware, Iowa, Louisiana, New York, and Rhode Island.[46] Notably, Michigan has a particularly broad law, which protects the confidentiality of records of the sale, rental, and borrowing of books, in addition to videos.[47]

There is little protection for book privacy under federal law, but some states protect books even more strongly than videos. In Colorado, the state constitution's free speech guarantee limits government access to bookstore records.[48] Perhaps the strongest book privacy law is California's Reader Privacy Act of 2012,[49] which places a confidentiality rule on books, broadly defined to include emerging technologies such as e-books.[50] It prohibits the disclosure of reader information except where stringent requirements are met, such as a court order for disclosure to government or to a private entity only where the user has given her "informed, affirmative consent to the specific disclosure for a particular purpose."[51]

Beyond video and book statutes, most states protect the confidentiality of library records from sale or other disclosure.[52] A typical example, the Missouri library confidentiality statute provides that "no library or employee or agent of a library shall be required to release or disclose a library record or portion of a library record to any person or persons," except where the person gives written request to the disclosure or subject to a court order.[53] Moreover, the scope of what constitutes "library material" is very broad, covering books, films, music, art works, or any "other library property which a patron may use, borrow or request."[54]

Yet legal protection for the data produced by electronic reading is limited. The e-reader paradox reveals that e-readers have created an information privacy problem and the law has yet to comprehensively deal with this problem. We thus have a situation where data about video and library rentals are highly protected, but book purchases and reading records from the Internet receive almost no protection. Technology has exposed a kind of privacy we took for granted because invading it was impossible. Reader privacy is up for grabs.

The Digital Reading Revolution

This leads me to the third and final argument I'd like to make about reading and intellectual privacy. The transformation in reading we are witnessing as we move from print to pixels is a revolution in how we read. It is as significant as the revolution caused by the introduction of the printing press. The tale of the Naughty Book reveals how radically we are seeing change in what we read and how we read it. And the digital data trail created by our digital reading revolution threatens to make reading—once that most private and solitary of activities—social or even public. Consider Facebook's ill-fated attempt to make the activity of reading social, in which what we read was shared "frictionlessly" with our "friends."[55] The social reading experiment fizzled once its initial sheen wore off, as readers remembered that they did not want to automatically share everything they read with everyone they knew. Reading remains a private activity, at least in the minds of many.

As with other digital revolutions, the digital reading revolution will challenge the assumptions about privacy and reading that we have protected for decades, and in some cases for centuries. New things will be possible, and we will need to decide whether we want them. The social fabric of reading is up for grabs in a way that it has never been before. We have to make a choice about the rules we will read by in the digital environment. And we should choose to preserve a meaningful guarantee of intellectual privacy for readers.

At the same time, it's important to understand that we have a choice. The digital reading revolution is not a natural phenomenon, like the processes of evolution or the laws of physics. The digital reading revolution is being constructed every day by humans making choices in how they read, in how they build reading technologies, and in what laws they enact. The extent to which intellectual privacy is protected (or not) in our reading future is a choice that we will have to make as a society. If we don't have the conversation about why reading and reader privacy matter, the choice will still be made, but it will be made only by technology companies interacting with the market. This is a sea change for the publishing industry and for the social practices of reading—a time of opportunity and a scary time all at once. We need not fear the new opportunities our technologies have created, but we shouldn't abandon the wisdom of the past either.

Let me conclude by saying a little about *why* we should protect the intellectual privacy of readers. (I will pick up the question of *how* we should protect it in part III.) My argument can be stated simply: disclosure of our reading habits—whether through social reading, government surveillance, or the trade in personal data that feeds online advertising—menaces our intellectual privacy. If we leave these activities unchecked, we risk creating a digital society in which the tyranny of the social threatens the private and unfettered exploration of unpopular ideas. Rather than passively accepting the default sharing of our mental activities, we should reject a world of automatic or haphazard disclosure. We should demand meaningful notice of when our reading and viewing habits might be shared and the meaningful ability to share consciously or not at all. And we should ensure that our reading and viewing habits are treated as confidential, to be shared only when we give real consent. Digital reading expands our ability to read, but while we are enjoying the convenience of pixels, we should continue to insist on the privacy of paper. The importance of private reading as a dimension of intellectual privacy demands no less.

9

Confiding

The Snake Oil Salesman

The Warshak family was in the penis enlargement business. Stephen Warshak owned and operated Berkeley Premium Nutraceuticals, Inc., which sold a variety of herbal supplements and other products. Berkeley was very much a family affair; Stephen's mother, Harriet, processed credit card payments for the company, and his sister and brother-in-law also had important roles within the business. Berkeley's flagship product was Enzyte, a supplement that allegedly increased the size of a man's penis. If you live in North America, you may remember Enzyte's television commercials, which featured a character called "Smilin' Bob," a man who went through his day with a beaming grin on his face, ostensibly because Enzyte had significantly improved his sex life.[1]

But Enzyte and Berkeley turned out to be a house of cards. Enzyte was marketed on the basis of several false claims about its medical effectiveness and customer satisfaction. And much of Berkeley's profitability came from a practice known as "auto-ship," in which a customer who bought Enzyte was automatically enrolled (and billed monthly) for a subscription to Enzyte until they told Berkeley to stop. The auto-ship program was the secret to Enzyte's profitability, but complaints about the practice mounted.[2] The business depended on the ability to accept credit card payments, but as customers increasingly began disputing their credit card charges, the Bank of Kentucky terminated its relationship with Berkeley. Stephen and Harriet Warshak filed new applications for credit, but allegedy falsified items on the credit applications, including whether Berkeley had ever had an account terminated.[3]

In 2006 Stephen and Harriet Warshak were indicted on federal fraud charges. The government had built a strong case against them, relying in large part on 27,000 of Stephen Warshak's emails that it had subpoenaed from his Internet service provider, NuVox. Under the Fourth Amendment, the government can get a warrant to obtain privately held evidence if it can prove probable cause that it is relevant to the investigation of a crime. But the government hadn't obtained a warrant to get the emails; it had acquired them under the less onerous subpoena standard. The case against the Warshaks thus turned on a simple legal question: Does the Fourth Amendment require the government to get a warrant supported by probable cause before it can seize a person's email from an ISP, or do emails fall outside the protection of the Fourth Amendment?

The Warshaks argued that an email was like the contents of a letter or a telephone call, which the government, under long-standing law, must get a warrant to obtain. By contrast, the government contended that the Fourth Amendment doesn't protect email. Emails, it argued, are shared with an ISP, and this act of sharing waives any reasonable expectation of privacy a person might have in their emails. This argument is not as outlandish as it might first appear; in several cases, the Supreme Court has held that the Fourth Amendment does not protect information shared with a third party when the government obtains the evidence from that third party. Thus, the government does not have to get a warrant before it hears a suspect's confession from a jailhouse snitch[4] or obtains financial records from a bank to see if a person has paid their taxes.[5] In the famous case of *Smith v. Maryland*, involving a stalker who made menacing phone calls, police installed a device without a warrant at the phone company to monitor the phone calls made by the suspected stalker. The Supreme Court held that because telephone users share the phone numbers they call with the phone company, they waive any expectation of privacy they might have in the phone numbers they dial. Accordingly, the installation of the device without a warrant did not violate the Fourth Amendment.[6] Criminal lawyers call this rule the "Third-Party Doctrine."

In the *Warshak* case, the government claimed that the Third-Party Doctrine applied. It argued that an email is shared with an ISP and is thus no different from jailhouse confessions, bank records, or telephone call histories. As a consequence, when customers send an email using their

ISP, they waive any expectation of privacy that they might have in the contents of that email.

The federal Court of Appeals in *Warshak* disagreed with the government. It ruled that the Fourth Amendment does protect email, and that the police must get a warrant before they can obtain your email from your ISP. It noted that "the very fact that information is being passed through a communications network is a paramount Fourth Amendment consideration." More important, it recognized that "the Fourth Amendment must keep pace with the inexorable march of technological progress, or its guarantees will wither and perish." Because emails have become the primary form of modern confidential communications, the court reasoned that the Fourth Amendment should protect an email just as it protects its antecedents, including letters and phone calls. Any other conclusion would "defy common sense" and destroy the Fourth Amendment's longstanding purpose of protecting private communications.[7] The Third-Party Doctrine thus does not apply to email.

That simple question raised by the *Warshak* case—are emails protected by the Fourth Amendment?—turned out to be surprisingly complex. It is also vastly more important than whether the Snake Oil Salesman went to prison or not. In an age when most of our communications and documents are made possible or stored with the help of technological intermediaries, this issue will settle the question of whether and to what extent we will have any privacy in our digital communications. The Supreme Court has yet to rule on this question, and we lack a fuller account why email matters and why or whether it should be treated as private or confidential.

That is my goal in this chapter, the final part of my argument about the nature and importance of intellectual privacy before we move on in part III to talk about solutions. I'll attempt to show why the case of the Snake Oil Salesman correctly decided that an email is more like a letter than a bank record and is worthy of legal protection. But I want to go further than that. I want to show why communications more generally deserve the promise and protection of confidentiality.

Confidentiality protects the relationships in which information is shared, allowing candid discussion away from the prying ears of others. It allows us to ask our questions and build tentative conclusions with confidence that our thoughts will not be made public until we are ready.

Confidentiality protects the disclosure of our shared secrets in a number of ways, although two are especially relevant here: (1) preventing *interception* of our communications by third parties and (2) sometimes also preventing *betrayal* of confidences by our confidants. A good example is a telephone call, where confidentiality rules prevent wiretapping by third parties and prevent the telephone company from sharing the contents of our communications. Under some circumstances, such as when we talk to our lawyers, our confidant is also prohibited from disclosing our communications.

I want to show that confiding, like thinking and reading, is an essential element of intellectual privacy, and I'll explain why we should continue to protect it in the digital age. In a nutshell, we should protect private communications for the same reason we should protect thinking and reading—they are the ways we make up our minds about the world. As chapter 6 explained, thinking and reading are essential to our intellectual explorations, but sometimes we want to share our half-baked ideas with others before they are ready for public consumption. We make sense of the world in our minds and through our reading habits, but sometimes we also need to confide in trusted intimates—our spouses, partners, friends, priests, and lawyers. Confidential communications are thus a fundamental civil liberty and deserve protection in the digital age, just as they have been protected in the past. Confidentiality doesn't just protect *information*; it also protects *relationships*. It protects the trust we place in each other. Our story of confidentiality and intellectual privacy begins, coincidentally, like our story of tort privacy did, with Louis Brandeis.

Brandeis and the Bootlegger

To call Roy Olmstead merely a bootlegger would be to insult his ambition. The core of Olmstead's business was alcohol, illegal in the United States since the ratification of the Eighteenth Amendment in 1919. Olmstead was a former Seattle police officer who, during Prohibition, had built a large criminal empire in the Pacific Northwest. At one point, he was believed to be the largest employer in the whole Puget Sound area, controlling not just the liquor trade but, through corruption, many of the operations of the government itself. After a lengthy investigation into his illegal liquor operation by the police, Olmstead was arrested and charged under the National Prohibition Act.[8] The government's case rested largely upon evidence produced from extensive (and warrantless) wiretapping of Olmstead's home and office.[9]

Olmstead was convicted of the charges against him. He appealed his conviction to the Supreme Court, which ruled in 1928 that because wiretaps required neither physical trespass nor seizure of "tangible material effects," the Fourth Amendment didn't apply to them. Warrants might be necessary when the police enter your home, but not when they listen to your phone conversations.[10]

The only member of the Court to dissent was Louis Brandeis, who argued forcefully that warrantless wiretaps were an intolerable invasion of privacy that violated the Fourth Amendment. [11] Two principles motivated Brandeis's dissent—the need for law to adapt to changing times and the importance of individual civil rights against the state.[12] Brandeis explained at the outset that the Constitution should evolve to reflect social realities. Both the language and purpose of the Fourth and Fifth Amendments and prior cases guaranteed against "invasion of the sanctities of a man's home and the privacies of life."[13] Unfortunately, Brandeis noted, these protections were threatened by changing circumstances, and changes in technology had enabled "[s]ubtler and more far-reaching means of invading privacy.... Discovery and invention have made it possible for the Government, by means far more effective than stretching upon the rack, to obtain disclosure in court of what is whispered in the closet."[14]

He also suggested prophetically that science would likely give future governments even more invasive and secret methods of surveillance than wiretaps. Echoing his commitment to free thought from his free speech cases, he warned that:

> Ways may someday be developed by which the Government, without removing papers from secret drawers, can reproduce them in court, and by which it will be enabled to expose to a jury the most intimate occurrences of the home. Advances in the psychic and related sciences may bring means of exploring unexpressed beliefs, thoughts and emotions.[15]

The chief problem with the Court's opinion in *Olmstead*, Brandeis believed, was that it clung to a narrow and outmoded view of the Fourth Amendment as protecting only tangible property.[16] The law needed to evolve in the face of changing technology to protect timeless values, including "the significance of man's spiritual nature, of his feelings and of his intellect." [17] He went on to argue that the drafters of the Constitution "knew that only a part of the pain, pleasure and satisfactions of life are to be found in material things. They sought to protect Americans in their beliefs, their thoughts, their emotions and their sensations."[18] At the level of legal doctrine, this meant that "every unjustifiable intrusion by the government upon the privacy of the individual, whatever the means employed, must be deemed a violation of the Fourth Amendment. And the use, as evidence in a criminal proceeding, of facts ascertained by such intrusion must be deemed a violation of the Fifth."[19]

Reading *Olmstead* in connection with Brandeis's First Amendment opinions suggests that he was not merely restating his old ideas about tort privacy, but sketching something new: a basic theory of intellectual privacy. Unlike the tort privacy of 1890, Brandeis's idea of intellectual privacy sought to protect the thoughts and communications of self-governing citizens from the state. It thus reinforces, rather than conflicts with, the First Amendment values that Brandeis found so compelling in his *Whitney* opinion.

Unlike tort privacy, which clashes with the First Amendment, intellectual privacy in thinking, reading, and confiding actually protects it. *Olmstead* protects privacy against surveillance and disclosure by the state, rather than disclosure by newspapers, and it justifies the protection of thoughts and emotions as a civil liberty rather than a private right in tort. As a civil liberty, the right is not merely to protect against hurt feelings, but rather to keep "unexpressed beliefs, thoughts and emotions" away from the gaze of an all-seeing state.[20] Privacy expressed in this way is not primarily about maintaining the status of elites, but preserving the autonomy and political capacity of all citizens—the people who read the newspapers, and not just the ones who appear in their society pages.

Brandeis's point in *Olmstead* about the important connections between privacy and free speech appear in his free speech opinions as well. *Gilbert v. Minnesota* (1920) involved a man who had spoken at a rally against the First World War and conscription, and been convicted under a state law prohibiting persuading others against enlistment in the armed forces.[21] Although the Court upheld the conviction, Brandeis dissented, explaining the mutually reinforcing relationship between privacy and free speech. He noted that American citizens govern themselves by participating in lawmaking, and that this "necessarily includes the right to speak or write about them, to endeavor *to make his own opinion* concerning laws existing or contemplated prevail, and, to this end, to teach the truth as he sees it.... In frank expression of conflicting opinion lies the greatest promise of wisdom in governmental action, and in suppression lies ordinarily the greatest peril."[22] As he argued in his later *Whitney* opinion, freedom of thought and counter-speech were essential to one another, so that each citizen could fulfill his political duty to "make his own opinion" freely and without constraint.

The problem with the law in *Gilbert* was the burden it placed upon free thought and private discussion. This burden on civil liberties fell not just in public but also upon the privacy of the home and the family. The law Gilbert had violated forbade speaking out against enlistment in any place where five or more people had gathered together. And it applied regardless of the intention or purposes of the speaker. Brandeis lamented that the law applied "alike to the preacher in the pulpit, the professor at the university, the speaker at a political meeting, the lecturer at a society or club gathering. Whatever the nature of the meeting and whether it be public or private, the prohibition is absolute."[23] Worse still, he argued, another provision of the statute made it punishable to

> teach in any place a single person that a citizen should not aid in carrying on a war, no matter what the relation of the parties may be. Thus the statute *invades the privacy and freedom of the home.* Father and mother may not follow the promptings of religious belief, of conscience or of conviction, and teach son or daughter the doctrine of pacifism. If they do, any police officer may summarily arrest them.[24]

The Minnesota law not only interfered with the civic duty of public discussion and deliberation, but even worse, it criminalized and deterred such discussions in the privacy of the home. Privacy and speech, under this view, were complementary and reinforcing concepts.

Reading *Olmstead* and *Gilbert* together reveals an important set of connections between privacy and free speech. In these opinions, Brandeis suggests that unfettered and unmonitored private activity is essential to democratic liberty. From this perspective, civil liberty requires not only an absence of government monitoring of individual activity but also the opportunity for talking, listening, and teaching before public speech takes place. His suggestion in these cases is that the First Amendment requires not only protection for *outputs* such as speeches and newspaper articles but also attentiveness to *inputs* and the process by which opinions are formed and beliefs are transmitted.

Brandeis worried about inputs a lot. In a 1906 speech, he argued that democracy mandated that "every man is of the ruling class." "Our education and condition of life," he continued, "must be such as become a ruler. Our great beneficent experiment in democracy will fail unless the people, our rulers, are developed in character and intelligence." To properly engage in the processes of self-governance, Brandeis argued, the eight-hour workday was critically important in providing members of the public with the time and energy for reading, thinking, and other civic responsibilities.[25]

Once he had "thought through" the First Amendment, Brandeis realized that these issues were ones of constitutional magnitude. Law professor Robert Cover noted "Brandeis' chief free speech refrain—not that truth will prevail in some market place of ideas but that free input is necessary to deliberative politics."[26] In the *Schaefer* case, Brandeis worried about the ability of "an intolerant majority, swayed by passion or fear, ... to stamp as disloyal opinions with which it disagrees. Convictions such as these, besides abridging freedom of speech, threaten freedom of thought and of belief."[27] In the *Burleson* case, he canvassed the history of federal postal policy to show that socialist literature should not be denied access to the mail.[28] At stake was the need of citizens to receive information, for the power to deny access to the mail based on content "would prove an effective censorship and would seriously abridge freedom of expression."[29] The *Whitney* opinion also recognizes the importance of expressive inputs and the development of democratic character through public or private discussion, deliberation, and education.[30]

Brandeis linked speech and education in other areas. He privately told his colleague Felix Frankfurter in 1923 that although he was usually opposed to the Court's majority in civil liberties cases, four rights were "fundamental"—most importantly the "right to speech" and the "right to education."[31] Thus Brandeis could join conservative Justice James Clark McReynolds's opinion in *Meyer v. Nebraska*, which struck down a state law banning the teaching of foreign languages in schools.[32] Brandeis may have been appalled by McReynolds's other applications of the Constitution, but he believed more strongly in the right of private citizens to teach and learn without interference from the state and that this right was inseparable from his broader interests in free speech and free thought.[33]

Brandeis suggested that self-government requires not just free speech, but freedom to communicate and explore even dangerous or subversive ideas in private. He believed that meaningful self-governance requires the protection of private thinking and reading, and of teaching and discussion between parent and child, teacher and student, among friends, or between strangers. He was also certain that the entire experiment of self-governance requires the "right to be let alone" by government when citizens think and examine ideas privately for themselves.

To make these claims, Brandeis drew on a variant of the privacy right he had called for in 1890. But this constitutional, intellectual right to be let alone was a sharply different one from tort privacy. Three differences spring immediately to mind. First, intellectual privacy initially involves threats to privacy by the state and not the press, a fact that removes much of the threat that privacy poses to First Amendment values. Second, Brandeis's conception of intellectual privacy supports First Amendment processes of belief formation and helps to produce a self-governing citizenry, one that is intelligent, courageous, and able to think for itself. By contrast, tort privacy is ordinarily opposed to publication of the truth, usually by the press. Third, Brandeis's mature version of privacy transforms the nature of the injury. To be sure, both tort and intellectual privacy address damage to the human psyche. But whereas the tort conception protects the interest in being free from unwanted press disclosures and the emotional harm that ensues, intellectual privacy protects individuals' emotional and intellectual *processes* so that they can think for themselves. Rather than being opposed to the interests in free expression, constitutional interests in privacy mandate space for new ideas to develop.

Brandeis's impassioned dissent in the *Olmstead* case ultimately prevailed in the law. In *Katz v. United States* (1967), the Supreme Court adopted his view that the Fourth Amendment requires the police to obtain a warrant before they wiretap a person's telephone calls.[34] The case is also significant because it made privacy, rather than trespass, the cornerstone of the Fourth Amendment, protecting "reasonable expectations of privacy" against electronic as well as physical intrusions, and requiring a warrant before the police could monitor the contents of a telephone conversation, even if the call was made from a pay phone.[35]

But although Brandeis prevailed on the narrower issue of wiretapping, Fourth Amendment law has embraced his concerns about intellectual privacy less obviously. This isn't to say that the law has rejected intellectual privacy, but rather that a full affirmation of intellectual privacy has been unnecessary. Trespass law (and Fourth Amendment protection for letters carried by government postmen) protected our papers and communications before the advent of the telephone. And the rule in *Katz* protected the intellectual privacy of our communications before the advent of email. Moreover, the privacy of communications has been protected by statute as well as constitutional law. In 1968, Congress passed the federal Wiretap Act, giving statutory protection to *Katz*'s constitutional rule.[36] And in 1986 it amended the Wiretap Act with the Electronic Communications Privacy Act, which extended the warrant requirement to "electronic communications" in transit.[37] The privacy guarantees of the Fourth Amendment are thus implemented in more specific detail by federal law.

The Supreme Court has recognized this point as well. In the famous *Keith* case (1972), the Supreme Court unanimously declared that the Fourth Amendment applies to cases of domestic surveillance of terrorists.[38] In doing so, it affirmed the central importance of the Wiretap Act as "a comprehensive attempt by Congress to promote more effective control of crime while protecting the privacy of individual thought and expression."[39] Many years after his death, Brandeis's conception of intellectual privacy against the state had thus prevailed.

But the fact that Louis Brandeis sketched out a theory of intellectual privacy, standing alone, doesn't tell us anything about whether we should adopt such a theory in our time. In the remainder of this chapter, I want to explain why the confidentiality of communications is important for our time.

Why Confidentiality Matters

Confidentiality matters to intellectual privacy for two very different reasons. The first reason is *descriptive*. Confidentiality illustrates a very important fact about information: Information is rarely completely public or private, but exists in a middle ground between being truly secret and being known to the world. The second reason is *prescriptive*. Confidentiality is important because it allows us to generate and develop our beliefs with trusted confidants. It is an important element of intellectual privacy as a guarantee for the civil liberties of freedom of thought and speech.

Let's start with the descriptive reason first: confidentiality reveals the fact that information is rarely truly secret. Most information exists in an intermediate state where it is known to or accessible by some people, but not all people. For example, we often communicate information to a few people that we don't want the whole world to know. Sometimes we call this information a "secret," but in everyday usage, a secret remains a secret when we relate it to a confidant. My telling you something and telling you it is a secret communicates a piece of information, but also relays my expectation that sharing it with you is not intended to share it with the world. A different kind of secret—a government secret—is shared among officials with a certain level of security clearance. When there is an outcry by the government about a security leak—whether Bradley Manning to WikiLeaks or Edward Snowden to the *Guardian*—it is a recognition that government secrets are known by many, but not intended to be known by all. Whether it is a personal or state secret, then, a secret is something some but not all people know. Until there is a breach of confidentiality, the secret remains in an intermediate level between purely private and wholly public.

Most communications also exist in an intermediate state between completely private and wholly public because they rely on *intermediaries* to deliver them. Consider an old-fashioned letter, which is written, placed in a thin paper envelope, and mailed to a confidant. The letter is collected by the postman and carried to its destination. We tend to think about letters as being quintessentially private. But even the most private of letters is carried by an intermediary—either a private messenger or a government-employed postal carrier. For letter communications to work as we intend them, we need to be able to trust that our intermediary will faithfully deliver the letter. And for the letter to be confidential, we need to be able to assume that the intermediary will respect our confidentiality. Paradoxically, when we have such an assurance, we may be more likely to disclose, to communicate. The promise of confidentiality allows this.

But the important point is that in the case of a letter, the presence of an intermediary doesn't change the fact that the contents of the letter are confidential.

Other forms of communications require intermediaries. Telegraphs were read and forwarded by telegraph operators. Telephone calls are made possible along the phone lines (and mobile phone towers) owned, operated, and maintained by telephone companies. Stephen Warshak had to trust his ISP to send his emails. Emails require not only an email account but also a provider of Internet service and use of the wires, switches, and other physical infrastructure of the Internet, each of which could be owned by a different company or even government entity. All of these communications thus require intermediaries, and all of the communications exist in the large middle ground between wholly private and wholly public.

Let's turn to the second, prescriptive reason: that the confidentiality of communications is important. Confidential communications matter because they enable us to share our tentative, half-formed, or possibly heretical ideas with a few trusted confidants before they are ready for public disclosure. But if other people are listening to our telephone calls or reading our paper or electronic mail, we are less likely to share those ideas. We lose the ability to test them out, and our confidants might lose the benefit of our insight.

Think for a moment about professional confidences. If we have unusual medical symptoms, we tell a doctor. If we fear legal liability, we might confide in a lawyer. We might share our financial information with an accountant, or our moral doubts or failings with a psychologist, priest, or other counselor. In each case, the promise of some level of confidentiality encourages us to share our information, and it paradoxically encourages us to share more freely, honestly, and completely. When we talk to a doctor about a medical ailment, the doctor needs to know the complete truth, no matter how embarrassing, in order to better treat us. And we want to get the best treatment possible. The presence of the medical duty of confidentiality allows us to share more fully, secure that the knowledge will go no further than our physician. And we get better medical treatment based upon better information. Confidentiality rules reveal not only that information exists in an intermediate state between public and private but also that promises of confidentiality can result in useful (but limited) disclosures of information to our benefit. Let's call this the *information-sharing function of confidentiality.* If we know our secret will be held in confidence, we're more likely to share it with our confidant.

The confidentiality of communications also relies on the information-sharing function of confidentiality. Put simply, we protect the confidentiality of communications to encourage free sharing of ideas and information. In a *Wired Magazine* article in 2006[40], security expert Bruce Schneier asked

> How many of us have paused during conversation in the past four-and-a-half years, suddenly aware that we might be eavesdropped on? Probably it was a phone conversation, although maybe it was an e-mail or instant-message exchange or a conversation in a public place. Maybe the topic was terrorism, or politics, or Islam. We stop suddenly, momentarily afraid that our words might be taken out of context, then we laugh at our paranoia and go on. But our demeanor has changed, and our words are subtly altered.

Schneier was writing even before Edward Snowden's revelations about government surveillance, but his question illustrates the relationship between confidential communications and intellectual privacy. This is an idea with a long legal heritage, although the government was confused about this point in the case of the Snake Oil Salesman. But the point should be clear: The value promoted by our long legal tradition of confidential communications is intellectual privacy.

Recall our example of the old-fashioned letter. We know that letter-writers entrust the contents of their letters to government postmen, but what kind of confidentiality should a letter-writer expect? As a practical matter, the postman could easily fail to deliver the letter, and he or she could easily tear the envelope—that thin layer of paper and glue to which we have entrusted the confidentiality of many communications over the centuries. But they don't, and the norm of confidentiality of communications supplies the answer why.

It turns out that the thin layer of paper and glue is backed up by both law and tradition. The legal tradition of confidentiality in the Anglo-American common law is ancient and is centuries older than the idea of privacy.[41] In the United States, the contents of letters have been protected by law in a variety of ways since colonial times, including criminal laws prohibiting opening other people's letters. The initial source of this tradition in the United States was not constitutional law, but policy choices by the post office in the late eighteenth century. Early Congresses and postmasters built postal privacy into the new American postal system, drawing both on English traditions of postal privacy and memories of the American revolutionary experience, in which confidential written correspondence was intimately associated with political liberty.[42]

The tradition of postal privacy ultimately came to be understood as part of the American constitutional tradition. In 1877 the Supreme Court ruled in *Ex parte Jackson* that the Fourth Amendment prohibited federal agents from inspecting letters without a warrant.[43] Such a decision was understood by the public as obviously correct. Nineteenth-century public opinion treated the confidentiality of communications as having the utmost importance, and the "sanctity of the mails" was often treated as having an almost religious quality, in part because of its connectedness to freedom of thought.[44] As one postal official put it: "The laws of the land are intended not only to preserve the person and material property of every citizen sacred from intrusion, but to secure the privacy of his thoughts, so far as he sees fit to withhold them from others."[45]

Confidential communications are essential to meaningful intellectual privacy. Our *confidants* are a source of new ideas and information, but without confidentiality they may be reluctant to share subversive or deviant thoughts with us lest others overhear. On the other hand, without the ability to speak with trusted confidants, we lack the capacity to develop our own ideas in collaboration with others before we are ready to share them publicly.[46] Consultation with intimates allows us to better determine if an idea is a good one, and to gauge some expectation of how it will be received if we finally decide to share or publish it. Without a meaningful expectation of confidentiality, then, we would have fewer ideas, and those that we did have might be unlikely to be shared.

Of course, to say that confidentiality of communications should be meaningful is not to say that it must be absolute—there is certainly a legitimate government interest in being able to investigate those suspected of plotting criminal acts that justifies some inroads into absolute confidentiality. But given the importance of confidentiality to intellectual privacy and the First Amendment values that support it, such inroads must be carefully managed. There are good reasons why government should be able to monitor particular communications where it has a reasonable (but specific) belief that they are being used to facilitate illegal activity. But a broad-ranging and unconstrained power to monitor secretly (or monitor everything) is an entirely different proposition—one that is deeply corrosive of the kind of trust and reliance necessary for the development of ideas.[47] Indeed, although largely forgotten today, such concerns were at the core of why the Supreme Court adopted Brandeis's interpretation of the Fourth Amendment in *Katz*, and why Congress passed the Wiretap Act the next year.[48] A presidential commission at the time put it aptly: "In a democratic society privacy of communication is essential if citizens are to think and act creatively and constructively. Fear or suspicion that one's speech is being monitored by a stranger, even without the reality of such activity, can have a seriously inhibiting effect upon the willingness to voice critical and constructive ideas."[49]

This, then, is the answer to why the case of the Snake Oil Salesman was correctly decided. To put it simply, if we care about intellectual freedom, we need intellectual privacy, and intellectual privacy would be impossible in a world without confidential communications. We have long protected the ability to confide using letters, telegrams, and telephones. The migration of communications to electronic platforms doesn't eliminate the need to extend our old, tested values to those platforms. When we send electronic mail, we should be able to rely on a meaningful guarantee that our email is confidential, for the same reasons we have long had those guarantees for paper mail. Intellectual privacy requires the ability to communicate in confidence.

PART III

Information Policy and Civil Liberties

10

Beyond Tort Privacy

IN THIS BOOK, I have made two relatively simple arguments. First, when free speech and tort privacy come into conflict, especially in the form of the old Warren and Brandeis disclosure tort, free speech should almost always win. I made three qualifications to this claim. I conceded that a few kinds of particularly bad disclosures of private facts could survive a free speech claim (for example, sex tapes about ordinary people). I suggested that there are ways other than the disclosure tort to remedy disclosures of information that cause emotional harm, such as invasion of privacy or confidentiality. And I asserted that even though the disclosure tort is threatening to civil liberties, we should be careful not to make too much of the threat beyond its original context, or any regulation of the digital age would be impossible. This was my argument in part I.

My second claim was that a different kind of privacy—intellectual privacy—is not only consistent with free speech but is also essential to it. I suggested that freedom from interference or surveillance when we are engaging with ideas and beliefs is essential to both free speech and a democratic culture. I explored this idea in three different contexts—thinking, reading, and confidential communications—and I showed how intellectual privacy is coming under threat by technological and social developments in the information age. This was my argument in part II.

My argument up to now has been about different ways of thinking about privacy and freedom of speech, the ways in which they conflict, and the ways in which they support each other. My goal has been to explore the complexities of privacy and speech in our increasingly digital age. I've suggested that we need to protect the time-honored values of the past, but adapt them so that they can survive in the future. In the remainder of the book (part III), I'll attempt to sketch out ways that this can be done.

Since I am a law professor, in this chapter I'll suggest ways in which the law can go beyond tort privacy to promote both privacy and freedom of speech. But the problems of civil liberties in the digital age are too important to be left just to lawyers. In the final chapter, I suggest ways that we should promote these values beyond law itself.

Beyond "Information as Speech"

Let's start with a fairly simple observation. Sometimes we use law to restrict information flows, like making or selling the video of Tyler Clementi, or records of reading The Naughty Book. We often make these restrictions in the name of "privacy." Sometimes, we use law to say that certain kinds of information cannot be regulated, like Anita Whitney's criticism of the government, or the Westboro Baptist Church's distasteful funeral protests. We make these restrictions in the name of "free speech."

All of these rules deal with the collection or flow of information—privacy rules restricting it while free speech rules enable it. They are all information rules. From this perspective, privacy and free speech are simply two sides of the same coin. As our society becomes increasingly digital, information rules are going to become increasingly important. Sometimes we'll want to restrict harmful or dangerous flows of information. Other times, we'll want to constitutionally protect them, to put them beyond the reach of legal rules. But most of the time, we'll want the option to regulate them to some extent, some of the time. But as I argued in chapter 5 with the story of the Data Broker, if we treat all information flows the way we treat Anita Whitney's protest against racism, we will have a society in which regulation of any kind of information flow is impossible. In a digital society, this will be a lawless society.

I'm not arguing that we should necessarily have more regulation of data. Rather, I'm arguing, first and foremost, that a democratic society should have the *option* to treat certain kinds of (especially commercial or dangerous) data flows differently from political dissent. We may ultimately decide that the benefits of freely flowing data outweigh the benefits of regulation in some or most cases. But we should have the ability to make that choice. Just because data may have expressive value in some cases does not mean that we should be afraid to experiment with legal tools in others. But I do believe that we should reject the idea that just because some restrictions on information flows threaten free speech, they all do. And as we build a digital future, we should not be afraid of using law to shape that future in pursuit of human values like privacy, equality, dignity, and of course free speech.

Beyond Disclosure: The Information Torts

If we are to use law to protect privacy, how should we do it? The most important single thing that legal protections for privacy can do is to move beyond the disclosure tort and its fixation on tort-style harm. We saw in chapter 1 that Warren and Brandeis's tort protected, at its core, elites from emotional harm against the press. As I explained in chapters 2 and 3 such an idea of privacy is inconsistent with a broad right of free speech in a democratic society. A free press should not be held hostage to (for example) Ryan Giggs's attempts to craft a family-friendly persona by hiding the truth. Mabel Warren's elitist dream of keeping the democratic press in its place is inconsistent with the broad right of a free press that the First Amendment protects.

But although the core case for disclosure privacy is inconsistent with modern understandings of free speech, Mabel Warren's dream continues to shape the way we understand privacy, driving privacy law into avoidable confrontations with free speech. We still think of privacy as a binary option of public or private, when our everyday experiences remind us that virtually all information that matters exists in intermediate states between these two extremes. We still think of privacy as protecting individual emotional harm in the first place, when our understandings of the harms of information flows should be broader in form and scope. And we still think of privacy as being a right against true disclosures, when privacy law (or information law) should embrace the full sweep of the Fair Information Principles.

The disclosure tort is only of minimal usefulness today. To get over the hurdle (correctly) imposed by the First Amendment, a disclosure of private facts needs to be one that is both outrageous and not a fit subject for public discussion. Given the deference that courts (correctly) grant to deciding what is a fit matter for public discussion, the only place where the disclosure tort might fit is the dissemination of pictures of people involving nudity, bodily functions, or sexual activity. Only in this limited set of cases should the privacy interest be able to survive against a free speech challenge, and the disclosure tort will be a useful tool in the important battle against such nonconsensual pornography. Otherwise, the disclosure tort should be unavailable to plaintiffs. We should let Mabel's dream go and think about protecting privacy in the twenty-first century rather than the nineteenth. We need to think beyond the disclosure tort.

One way to do this would be to think about the four privacy torts that William Prosser identified. Prosser brought the privacy torts into the mainstream of American law, but still defined them fairly narrowly as the four torts of disclosure, appropriation, intrusion, and false light. Prosser gave tort privacy respectability, something that could be (and still is) taught to first-year law students. But he robbed privacy of its vitality—its ability to change.[1] We should think more broadly about tort privacy, especially the intrusion tort or, as it is more intuitively understood, as invasions of privacy.

In chapter 4 I used the tragic case of Tyler Clementi to show that invasions of privacy are a much more fruitful way of regulating personal privacy than the old disclosure model. Restricting the collection of information or capture of images in places of seclusion fits better with our intuitive understandings of privacy and free speech than the old disclosure model. Invasion of privacy is a useful way of thinking about legal restrictions on secret surveillance or bugging, whether by other people, by the government, or by drones. But intrusion alone will not be enough to solve all of the problems of information collection and dissemination. As we also saw in chapter 4 some of the features of an invasion of privacy model that make it consistent with free speech also limit its effectiveness as a legal tool. Invasion, for example, only applies to someone who invades privacy in order to collect information unlawfully; it does not apply to those who might receive that same information lawfully from the invader or a third party. Similarly, invasion only applies where there is an invasion of a place (or perhaps a relationship) that we can say to be "private." A conclusion that something is "private" is a function of both social norms and technologies. As the tiny cameras on mobile phones, tablets, drones, and other devices become more common in our society, it is likely we will expect fewer places to be "private," or at least free of the risk of recording. Such places will not vanish entirely, but we must remember that understandings of privacy are socially and technologically constructed, and that they vary across societies and change over time.

Going beyond intrusion, there are other ways to remedy privacy harms that create fewer constitutional problems than the disclosure tort. We have become accustomed to thinking about privacy in terms of Prosser's four torts, but there are other torts sharing elements with some or all of the privacy torts that can also be used to regulate information. For example, there is the "right of publicity," an offshoot of the appropriation tort that gives celebrities the exclusive property right to use their image for endorsements, whereas appropriation lets private people prevent unwanted (and emotionally harmful) use of their images in advertising. More generally, the intentional infliction of emotional distress tort prevents attempts to cause outrageous emotional harm by any means, including the use of words, images, or information.[2] Similarly, there is a close analogy between intrusion and trespass, with the primary difference being that intrusion protects emotional harm from invasions into private areas or relationships, while trespass protects property rights from similar invasions. But trespass is, in reality, a kind of privacy tort as well—protecting the privacy of the home from invasion and another tort that creates fewer First Amendment problems than disclosure.

Breach of confidence is another privacy tool to regulate disclosures of embarrassing or harmful information that we have largely overlooked.[3] A breach of confidence requires a disclosure of information in violation of a duty of confidence.[4] Recall that in the press privacy cases, police departments that wanted to keep the names of rape victims out of the press could have required the press to agree to confidentiality agreements before they inspected the police files. Such rules would allow the regulation of disclosure in a way that is less troubling from a First Amendment perspective than the disclosure tort. This is the case because confidentiality remedies not the emotional injury of published words, but instead the breach of an assumed duty or trust.[5] Confidentiality has limits, too; most notably, it typically applies only to duties that are voluntarily assumed as part of relationships. But unlike the limits of disclosure, the limits of confidentiality enhance its consistency with our First Amendment commitments to robust public debate, for reasons we saw in chapter 9.[6]

In fact, though Prosser insisted that tort privacy was "not one tort, but a complex of four" that had little in common, he was mistaken.[7] Tort privacy should actually be understood as encompassing at least *twice as many torts*, including the intentional infliction of emotional distress, breach of confidence, the "right of publicity," defamation, and trespass. All of these "information torts" share some (but not all) of a relatively small number of elements, including private facts, private places, publication, harm to emotions, harm to a property interest, or reliance on a trust. At the risk of technicality, I have summarized these torts in table 10.1.

A return to the Tyler Clementi example will illustrate my point that we should think about the broader group of "information torts." We saw in chapters 3 and 4 how the disclosure tort would apply to the disclosure of a secretly recorded video of sexual activity, but that intrusion/invasion was a better legal theory to understand the true nature of the injury—the secret capture of the images themselves. If a person enters onto another person's property to place or use a camera, they have also committed a trespass. And if sexually explicit pictures or video are disclosed in order to embarrass or mortify another person, the intentional infliction of emotional distress tort would apply (at least so long as the disclosure wasn't newsworthy).

Table 10.1 The Information Torts: An Expanded Set of "Privacy Torts"[a]

	Private Facts	Private Place	Emotional Harm	Disclosure	Property Harm	Reliance/ Duty
Disclosure	X		X	X		
False Light	X		X	X		
Appropriation	X		X	X		
Intrusion	X	X	X			
Publicity				X	X	
Trespass		X			X	
Confidence	X			X		X
Defamation				X	X	
IIED			X	X		

[Key: Publicity = Right of Publicity; Confidence = Breach of Confidence; IIED = Intentional Infliction of Emotional Distress]
a See Restatement (Second) of Torts § 652D (1977) (disclosure); § 652E (false light); § 652C (appropriation); § 652B (intrusion); § 158 (trespass); § 757 (breach of confidence); § 558 (defamation); § 46 (intentional infliction of emotional distress); Restatement (Third) of Unfair Competition § 46 (2006) (right of publicity)

But think about the more common example of "revenge porn," the increasingly common disclosure of homemade nude pictures or sex videos after a breakup. Regrettably, websites cater to this kind of video, allowing uploaded sex videos of ordinary people to be accessible from any computer or phone in the world.[8] What remedies would someone who willingly made home sex videos have against the ex-lover who shared the images, or the website that distributed them? The disclosure tort might work, but as we have seen, even when the free speech critique doesn't apply, disclosure can be an ineffective and hard-to-prove cause of action. Intrusion, also, would be inapplicable—if the images were recorded consensually, then there could be no invasion of privacy or intrusion into seclusion. But thinking more broadly about the information torts could be helpful. If someone intentionally shares sex videos in order to embarrass a former lover, this would appear to be a classic case of intentional infliction of emotional distress. More creatively, breach of confidence law could be used to imply a confidential agreement into privately made sexy pictures. Under this theory, the creation of a sexy home movie as part of a romantic relationship could be seen as a confidence shared between two lovers. The disclosure of the video to others (even after the end of the romantic relationship) would seem to be a straightforward breach of confidence.[9]

I will not go further into the technical details of these torts. I want to conclude instead with a more important observation than whether trespass or the intentional infliction of emotional distress is the right tool for a particular kind of injury caused by the collection or disclosure of information. We have thought about the problems of privacy on Mabel Warren's terms for too long. If it was foolish to use her nineteenth-century understanding of privacy as a starting point in the twentieth century, it is even more so in the twenty-first. As we have seen repeatedly, the collection, use, and disclosure of information can cause serious problems. But when we imagine solutions to those problems, if we are thinking about tort law as a solution, there are many more options available than the old disclosure tort. If we want to craft useful solutions to privacy problems in the twenty-first century, we should, as Brandeis himself said in a different context, "let our minds be bold."[10] We should think much more broadly than the frequently ineffective or dangerous disclosure tort and look to different models of both injuries and remedies. We should realize that there is not one privacy tort, nor four, but at least *nine*, and we could look as well to other related legal theories. These could include the law of threats, harassment, or even stalking. In other words, if we want to understand and solve the problems we've used the privacy torts to deal with in the past, we need to move beyond disclosure.

Beyond Torts: Protecting Intellectual Privacy

But we must broaden our understanding of privacy even more. We must go beyond tort law. As personal information comes to define ever-larger parts of our society and economy, we must think even more creatively about how our information systems are built and regulated. Tort law alone is insufficient for this task, as are tort-focused notions of privacy that focus on harm to individuals that are large enough to warrant an expensive lawsuit. We must think more broadly about the kind of information society we want, how that society can be made more just and consistent with our commitments to civil liberties and equality, and exactly what "privacy" means and why it matters in these new contexts.

In part II, I identified intellectual privacy as one particularly important kind of privacy that deserves special protection through law. As we think more broadly about privacy law in the information age, our law should give greater attention to the protection and cultivation of expression through a more developed sense of intellectual privacy. In particular, more regulation of the collection, use, disclosure, and retention of information about intellectual activity is needed.

Records of intellectual activity are diverse. As we've seen, they can include ISP logs, search engine histories, book purchase records, e-reader data, and the contents of email, telephone calls, and other forms of communications like text messages. Protecting intellectual privacy will require detailed regulation, and in this as in other areas of law, the devil is in the details. But intellectual privacy is worth the effort. As I showed in part II, a meaningful guarantee of intellectual privacy against government and corporate actors is an essential civil liberty. If we lack intellectual privacy, we cannot say we are truly free. And the basic principles for the protection of intellectual privacy can be stated in a straightforward way. There are five of them.

Five Principles of Intellectual Privacy Protection

We should protect intellectual privacy through law by keeping five simple principles in mind. First, we need to remember that *intellectual privacy isn't just for intellectuals*. It's for anyone with an intellect, which is to say, it's for everyone. Second, *we mustn't forget the FIPs*, the Fair Information Principles that regulate how data is collected and used. Third, we must remember that *intellectual records are sensitive records* that demand higher protection than other kinds of data. In the consumer context, this means that notice about the creation and use of intellectual databases must be meaningful, and the choice to disclose our intellectual preferences must be conscious. Fourth, we must *reject the idea that privacy is binary*. Information invariably exists in a fluid state where some (but not all) people know it. And we should regulate information use by private actors as well as the government. Fifth, we must remember *the importance of confidentiality* as a way of protecting sensitive intellectual records.

1. Intellectual Privacy Isn't Just for Intellectuals

In the wrong light, an argument for intellectual privacy could seem elitist, a kind of special protection only for pointy-headed academics stroking their goatees in their ivory towers.[11] Nothing could be further from the truth.[12] Intellectual privacy isn't just for intellectuals. A free, democratic society rests on the idea that everyone should be free to think for themselves and believe what they want. Diversity in beliefs about politics, religion, sexuality, beauty, truth, and any other controversial topic is a strength rather than a weakness. And as we all use technology as aids to our thinking about and understanding of the world, we all need intellectual privacy. Intellectual privacy shouldn't extend only to academic libraries or the emails of scholars; it should also extend to any data that can reveal the wonderings of the human mind, the interests of individual readers, or the content of anyone's communications. Intellectual privacy protection need not be absolute (regulated wiretapping is appropriate in investigating crime, for example), but it should extend to everyone who thinks, reads, or communicates. Intellectual privacy is for anyone with an intellect. Intellectual privacy is for everyone.

2. We Mustn't Forget the FIPs

If we want to regulate government and corporate data processing to protect intellectual privacy, the best place to start is the Fair Information Principles. The tort model of privacy focuses on injuries from publication, like those suffered by Ryan Giggs and Mabel Warren. Even when it is applicable, it identifies serious emotional harm caused by publication, and tries to fix the harm through money damages. But this model of publication as the primary injury doesn't fit the nature of the modern information economy, in which small pieces of information are constantly being collected, combined, and analyzed, and in which massive individualized and quantifiable harm is rarely present. The idea of intellectual privacy suggests that the real danger of the data trade in intellectual data is small nudges away from thinking, reading, and talking about novel or dangerous ideas.

The FIPs are a much better model for remedying the effects of the intellectual data revolution. Rather than looking at the problem of information from the perspective of individuals wronged by massive harm, they look at the routine ways that data is collected, used, and disclosed. The FIPs look from the top down, whereas tort privacy looks from the bottom up. The FIPs try to prevent problems from happening before they occur, while tort privacy tries to fix harm that has already happened. The FIPs offer a holistic architectural solution, while tort privacy offers a piecemeal one. And the FIPs recognize that information use is social and contextual, rather than individual and isolated.

If we are concerned about the consequences of unregulated collection, use, and disclosure of information about our interests, fantasies, reading habits, or communications, the FIPs are a better fit. As we saw in chapter 5, the FIPs regulate data in a wide variety of ways, rather than just being a single kind of protection. They require notice about the kinds of data collection that is occurring and how it is being used. They prevent data that is collected for one purpose (for example, web browsing) from being used for another (for example, employment background checks or insurance eligibility). They allow individuals to view what data has been collected about them and to amend or correct data that is false. They are regulatory in a broad sense, rather than being remedial in a narrow one. Put simply, the FIPs regulate data in all of its complexity and offer nuanced solutions to nuanced problems.

3. Intellectual Records Are "Sensitive Records"

Applying the FIPs to records of our thinking, reading, and communications is only half of the answer. An equally important question is how much protection intellectual records should receive. The FIPs can help us to answer this question as well: intellectual records should be recognized as a new category of "sensitive data," defined as personal information that is particularly important, susceptible to abuse, or data of the kind that would cause people great harm if disclosed or misused.[13] We should treat intellectual records as "sensitive data" and erect meaningful legal requirements that limit its use and mandate its destruction after a reasonable (but finite) amount of time. In particular, we should protect ISP logs, search engine records, web-browsing habits, book and movie purchases, reading habits, and confidential communications against access by both the government and corporations.

As chapter 5 explained, when sensitive data is involved, stronger procedural protections are warranted as a matter of fair information practices. Although there is no single definition of sensitive data, the EU Data Protection Directive understands the term as including, for example, "personal data revealing racial or ethnic origin, political opinions, religious or philosophical beliefs, trade-union membership, and the processing of data concerning health or sex life."[14]

Internet, reading, or communications records are often related to politics, philosophy, health, or sex. We could squeeze them under this definition easily. But the cleanest way to treat intellectual records is to recognize them as a separate category of sensitive data, deserving separate and heightened protection on their own terms and for their own special reasons. This insight seems to be implicit in laws like the Video Privacy Protection Act—the idea that, because disclosure of reader records can be harmful, reading records deserve heightened procedural protection compared to other kinds of data. We should make this insight explicit and universal.

Reasonable minds can certainly disagree on how broadly we should define "reader records," but the idea of intellectual privacy helps us identify what matters and what doesn't. In fact, as long as we start taking intellectual privacy seriously and argue only about what records count and how much protection they receive, one of the goals I have in writing this book will have been achieved. But at a minimum, our definition of intellectual records should include Internet searches, ISP logs of websites visited, records of e-books and articles bought, rented, or read; films and videos watched; and the contents of communications. The key should be whether the records reveal the operation of our minds in thinking, reading, communicating, or otherwise trying to make sense of the world privately before we are ready to speak our ideas consciously and intentionally to the public.

Work would need to be done in defining the scope of any reader privacy bill, but there are effective models that currently exist: state and federal wiretapping laws, the California Reader Privacy Act, other state reader privacy acts, and library confidentiality laws. One could imagine a statute making Internet searches confidential by treating search engine data like library records, for instance. We often think of the Internet as a library; maybe we should start treating it like one.

From the idea that intellectual records are sensitive data, other conclusions follow for laws that regulate the collection of intellectual data on consumers. First, the creation and use of intellectual records warrant a *higher notice requirement* than we impose for other kinds of consumer data.

Consider the terms of service that govern things like website privacy policies or data collection by e-books. For most online contracts, the law requires merely *notice* of the proposed terms and the *choice* to reject them if they are unacceptable. As then-Judge Sonia Sotomayor put it in an influential case, the test is whether consumers "had reasonable notice of and manifested assent to" the collection of their information.[15] But what do these standards mean? For ordinary kinds of personal data, these standards might be relatively minimal—the fine print on a privacy policy link that is never read. Courts tend to uphold these sorts of terms most of the time, and that's probably the right conclusion.[16]

But when we are dealing with sensitive information, the balance changes. When we accept privacy terms for our intellectual records, we are entering into a contract for sensitive data, which requires a higher standard of notice. Constructive notice buried in a privacy policy might suffice, for example, when we are agreeing to let a shopping website place a cookie on our computer to identify us when we return, but if we are accepting the disclosure of our reading habits, actual notice should be required. Given the sensitivity of reader records and their importance to our intellectual freedom, holders of reader records should be required to let their clients actually know the terms on which reader records will be stored.

Scholars working at the intersection of law, computer science, and behavioral economics have suggested novel ways for how such notice can occur. Woodrow Hartzog has shown how the design of websites and other electronic interfaces affect the actual level of consumer notice.[17] Other scholars like Alessandro Acquisti and Ryan Calo have shown that certain design features and context affect our awareness that people are disclosing information about us, as well as the circumstances in which we are more likely to disclose.[18] Numerous studies have shown that software that creates the sense that another human being is present (for example, through the use of anthropomorphic avatars, human faces, or eyeballs) creates a medically measurable visceral response on the part of the user of being watched.[19] Such "visceral notice" could be used creatively to provide meaningful notice at a level warranted by the sensitivity of reader records. If you see the website watching you, you might realize that you're not alone and act accordingly.

Similarly, the sensitivity of reader records means that when consumers choose to disclose them, this *choice must be a conscious one*. As the theory of intellectual privacy explains, the risk of disclosure creates a "chilling effect," for example, when we read and research new things. We can protect these processes by giving readers the confidence that their reading patterns will only be disclosed when they choose to disclose them to others. We don't want readers to wonder whether their sensitive information will be disclosed inadvertently or because of poor privacy protections under a disclosure rule. We should give them meaningful guarantees that reader records will be confidential unless they consciously choose otherwise. We require what law professor William McGeveran has called "genuine consent,"[20] rather than the fiction imposed by the failure to object to or adjust hidden and constantly changing privacy settings. We should go beyond choice as meaning no more than a passive failure to object; we should instead embrace choice as a form of conscious control.

4. Rejecting Binary Privacy

Protecting intellectual privacy requires us to reject the idea of "privacy" as a binary concept that is either on or off. As we saw in chapter 1, this is one of the flaws at the center of the Warren and Brandeis tort privacy argument. It is a flaw that continues to shape how we think about privacy and information today. Privacy isn't binary; it isn't on or off, public or private; it's not known only in our heart of hearts or shouted by all from the rooftops.

Intellectual privacy in particular often deals with intermediate states of privateness and publicness. It also frequently involves intermediaries whose help we need to think, read, and communicate with intimates—Internet service providers, search engines, bookstores, librarians, telephone companies, and cloud storage providers, to name just a few. Understanding the problem of intellectual privacy requires us to recognize that information has always existed in intermediate states, and the emergence of digital technologies just makes this more obvious. Sharing information with a few other people doesn't make it public; it just makes it information. And any solution for the problems of intellectual privacy must take into account the fact that much information exists in this intermediate state, rather than at the extremes of "public" and "private."

There's another binary distinction between public and private that any intellectual privacy protection must deal with as well—the distinction between the "public sector" of government and the "private sector" of industry. Lawyers often try to keep our powerful government institutions analytically separate from powerful corporate institutions. We use the Constitution to regulate the government, but not private entities. And we regulate businesses and nonprofit private entities differently from the government. Often we do this for good reason.

Protecting intellectual privacy requires us to rethink the ways in which the First Amendment restricts the government's ability to acquire intellectual records, either on its own terms or by informing the protections of the Fourth Amendment's regulation of government searches and seizures. But constitutional law alone is insufficient to protect intellectual privacy. The constitutional values that intellectual privacy represents should inform the regulation of private institutions through the drafting of statutes and the interpretation of the common law as well. But information can flow easily in both directions between government and corporate databases, and "private" entities can menace our intellectual privacy as well. The problem of intellectual privacy transcends the public/private divide; we should be sure its solutions transcend simple binaries as well.

5. The Importance of Confidentiality

The fact that information exists in intermediate states leads to my final recommendation about how we should use law to protect intellectual privacy, which is to remember the importance of confidentiality. We need to recognize the importance of confidentiality as a value and as a solution to many problems of intellectual privacy. Our intellectual records are no longer held only by institutions like bookstores and libraries, protected by an overlapping matrix of professional ethics norms and legal duties of confidentiality. When video stores started to generate intellectual records in the 1980s, these new creatures sometimes lacked the ethical sense of librarians and independent bookstores. They also lacked the legal constraint of a confidentiality rule. This became obvious when the *Washington City Paper* obtained Robert Bork's records. The Video Privacy Protection Act mandating video records confidentiality was the product of this scandal. So we can understand the VPPA as the extension of a confidentiality rule to protect intellectual records in a new context.

Some of the advocates of information-sharing reject the idea that information is often in intermediate states. But I've tried to show how this position is a bit silly, and also inconsistent with how we've always lived, whether in the eighteenth century or the twenty-first. We have always shared information, and we've always recognized intermediate states of sharing, somewhere between things being known only to us and being known to the entire world. Sometimes the law or the rules of etiquette don't intervene to stop the spreading further. When the press is told newsworthy information, it can publish the information, privacy claims notwithstanding.[21]

But sometimes law or norms do intervene, depending upon the nature of the relationship and the sensitivity of the information. Many of these are professional relationships, such as those we have with our priests, accountants, lawyers, doctors, psychologists, or librarians. What these professional custodians of information have in common reveals the two sides of sharing. On the one hand, sometimes we need to share sensitive information with others so that they can help us, whether it's to lower our taxes, remove a nasty rash, find books on a particular topic, or stay out of prison. In order for us to have the benefit of their advice (more confidentially shared information), we need to be completely frank and open with them, so we put rules or norms in place that will keep our information confidential. This is what I have called the *information-sharing function of confidentiality*. We share a little, and we get something good in return, along with the promise that our sensitive information will go no further. Paradoxically, confidentiality can encourage sharing that is conscious *and* valuable.

There's no reason that these tested ideas of confidentiality and information-sharing cannot be adapted to the digital environment in the same way we adapted them to video stores twenty-five years ago. We still care about sensitive information, and we're creating a lot more of it every time we use our phones, tablets, or computers. This trend is only going to continue as the "Internet of things" networks the computers in our household appliances, cars, and the electrical "smart grid."[22] We might well conclude that much of this information should be shared freely. But we also need to remember that not all information is the same. There are certain categories of sensitive data that we should protect more than others, and these categories of data warrant confidentiality. Intellectual records are one such category. And confidentiality rules are a clear solution to many of the problems that changes in technology present to our intellectual privacy.

Just as we recognized in the past that certain professionals were fiduciaries of our information, so, too, in the Age of Information should we expand our definition of information fiduciaries to include bookstores, search engines, ISPs, email providers, cloud storage services, providers of physical and streamed video, and websites and social networks when they deal in our intellectual data. The duties of confidentiality we place on these fiduciaries need not be ironclad. Sometimes we want to share our views with the world, and intermediaries can help to do that, too. But that should be our choice, not theirs. We may also decide that there are times when the prevention of crime or terrorism might justify limited inroads into intellectual databases. But exceptions to our intellectual privacy should themselves be exceptional, rather than being commonplace. The importance of intellectual privacy demands no less.

II

Beyond Law

FREE SPEECH AND privacy are legal concepts, and we are used to thinking of them in legal terms, as rights guaranteed by the Constitution, statutes, or other kinds of legal rules. But often law is not enough. The law has limits, and law alone cannot solve all of the problems of privacy and free speech. If we care about these values as a society, we must protect them beyond the legal system, as part of our culture and social norms. These protections go beyond constitutional law regulating the government, and beyond private law regulating private entities. They are part of the culture we all share. Put simply, if we don't have a culture that is supportive of civil liberties, we cannot have civil liberties.

Putting privacy to one side for a moment, consider how the freedom of speech is protected in the United States. Certainly, there is legal doctrine like the First Amendment, but a constitutional guarantee alone cannot ensure meaningful exercise of free speech in practice. Most societies have some kind of formal law guaranteeing free speech, even those societies in which freedom of speech is rare in practice. Legal tools like the First Amendment are often just means to an end—in this case, a robust culture of public debate, self-governance, free thought, and artistic and creative freedom of expression. In addition to constitutional protections, free speech depends upon an inquiring press, universities, an educated and critical public, technological tools like printing or the Internet, and a social commitment to the idea that even the people we disagree with deserve the right to have their say. Without a culture of free speech to back its guarantees up, the Constitution's words become nothing more than empty promises. James Madison made this point during the Constitution's ratification debates when he argued that a Bill of Rights was not necessary, as it would provide only a "parchment barrier" against tyranny. Madison ultimately changed his mind about the Bill of Rights, but his broader concern remains vital: legal protections for civil liberties will only be parchment barriers without a culture of civil liberties backing them up.[1]

If we want to ensure that free speech and privacy (especially intellectual privacy) remain vital in the twenty-first century, legal rules like the ones I discussed in the previous chapter will not be enough. Those legal rules are necessary, and they are important, but they must be backed up by a culture of civil liberties. In this chapter, I will sketch out how I think culture can support digital civil liberties. While a full exploration of this issue could be a book of its own, the matter is important enough that it is worth some discussion before I conclude. My argument is a simple one. Legal rules in general, and constitutional rules in particular, will be increasingly insufficient to protect digital civil liberties in the twenty-first century. Our abilities to effectively exercise our civil liberties will depend substantially upon business and engineering decisions by software companies. If we want to have civil liberties, technologists and computer engineers will need to embrace free speech and intellectual privacy as a professional ethic, and build those values into the software and business systems they design. Users and activists must support these activities, but a substantial amount of moral responsibility for civil liberties must rest with technology companies.

Intermediaries and Free Speech

Think for a moment about what happens when you want to send a message. Maybe it's a phone call, a text to a lover, an email to a friend or colleague, a Facebook status update, a blog post intended for the world, or a letter to the editor of the *New York Times*. Each of these messages would be an exercise of your freedom of speech. But in order to send any of these messages, you'd need help. In each case you'd need help from at least one of the following: your ISP, email provider, telephone company, blogging platform, Facebook, or the *New York Times*. Scholars call these helpers *intermediaries*, because they occupy an intermediate step between speakers and audiences.[2] They are the companies and institutions we use, among other things, to speak. They stand in between us and our audience, and mediate our communications. Speakers don't have to use intermediaries. They can always utilize their free speech rights to hand out leaflets or put up signs on their property.[3] But digital intermediaries from phone companies to social networks to blogging platforms allow a much greater reach for those rights, often for a seemingly nominal price.

But just as these intermediaries have the capacity to expand our ability to express ourselves and communicate, they also *mediate* those communications. Intermediaries shape the ways we speak. Engineers and executives make decisions about what kinds of speech they will permit on their systems, and in the United States, the First Amendment doesn't apply to these "private" decisions. But these decisions shape, for better or worse, our practical ability to speak freely. In the twenty-first century, when it comes to free expression, engineering will be as important as law.[4]

The business and design decisions of intermediaries can shape speech without much intent to do so. Twitter's 140-character limit on tweets is one example of this. But services can shape speech in more conscious ways. Take, for example, Facebook's system of "status updates." Facebook users can post almost any photos or text they want through Facebook's system—all they need to do is enter it in the status update window, hit <enter>, and it is shared with their friends. But all user-generated content on Facebook is regulated by a legal document called the Terms of Service. Facebook's Terms of Service prevent a user from posting several categories of illegal or offensive material, including material that is "hate speech, threatening, or pornographic; incites violence; or contains nudity or graphic or gratuitous violence."[5] These are, of course, terms borrowed from First Amendment law, but unlike in the offline world, where free speech is protected by the courts, Facebook is its own court, free to interpret the meaning of "hate speech" or "nudity" for itself. Users who object to content on Facebook can flag it as offensive, which sets into motion a system of review. Facebook censors applying written guidelines decide whether the allegedly offensive speech remains or is deleted. Sometimes this can lead to odd results. Facebook recently courted controversy when its interpretations of nudity allegedly led to the removal of many photographs of breastfeeding mothers.[6] (Under pressure, Facebook relented and allowed the pictures.[7]) On the other hand, under pressure from anti-hate groups, Facebook has permitted the removal of several kinds of hateful speech that were protected by the First Amendment.[8] Facebook could remove the images from its site voluntarily, even though the First Amendment would prevent a government from censoring them.

I don't mean to pick on Facebook's decisions here, but rather to illustrate a couple of very important points about digital intermediaries and free speech. The first point is, of course, that decisions by intermediaries have a huge effect on the practical exercise of free speech. If Facebook won't let you share your hateful views or your breastfeeding photos, it becomes much harder to do so, especially if Facebook is where your friends spend their time online. And this effect doesn't just apply in the United States, where many of these companies are headquartered; it applies throughout the world. Facebook, Twitter, and Google, to pick three of the most important companies for free speech, operate globally.

A second insight that these examples suggest is that intermediaries have a choice. They can increase the ability to speak, they can decrease it, and they can discriminate against (or aid) certain kinds of speech. But while this is of tremendous practical importance to civil liberties, we lack the vocabulary to talk about it. Anglo-American law has spent much of the past millennium developing tools to restrain the power of the nation-state, from the Magna Carta to the First Amendment to the English Human Rights Act of 1998.[9] But we lack the words and the tools to think about similar powers exercised by corporations.[10] Is it "censorship" when Facebook eliminates nude pictures from its site? Have users validly consented to Facebook's actions by agreeing to the Terms of Service (a document read only by lawyers, the bored, and the paranoid)? Or is Facebook itself exercising some kind of corporate free speech right?[11] Put simply, we don't know.

Let me suggest a few basic principles that can guide our search for answers. The body of First Amendment law in the United States (and its analogs in other countries) contains a great deal of wisdom about the values of free speech, as well as the dangers of regulating expression for democracy. Intermediaries exercise something akin to the government power of censorship, a power that centuries of experience have shown to be a very dangerous one. A free speech rule might not bind Facebook or Twitter the way it would bind a government agency, but the wisdom of that rule should still be persuasive to an intermediary. Intermediaries, in other words, should act like they are bound by free speech law even when they are not.

This is not as outlandish a claim as it might appear to be at first. Private universities (like the one where I work) aren't bound by the First Amendment either, but they are often mindful of their responsibilities as institutions where debate and discussion happen. Expressive freedom for students (and academic freedom for faculty) are ingrained into not just the culture of universities but also their policies and procedures. For example, the first provision of the student judicial code at my own university reads: "Freedom of thought and expression is essential to the University's academic mission. Nothing in this code should be construed to limit the free and open exchange of ideas and viewpoints, even if that exchange proves to be offensive, distasteful, disturbing, or denigrating to some."[12]

Intermediaries like Facebook, YouTube, Twitter, WordPress, and others that provide tools for users to express themselves should take a page from universities and build protections for free speech into their culture. To be sure, intermediaries are diverse. It's easy to imagine special-purpose intermediaries (for children or political affinity groups) in which moderated discussions rather than free-flowing debate are a better fit for their missions. But the closer an intermediary comes to being a general purpose intermediary (especially near-monopolists like Facebook or Google search), the more important it becomes for that intermediary to embrace the kind of free speech self-restraint that democratic governments impose on themselves through constitutional law.

If intermediaries should be guided by free speech principles, which ones are the most important? Let me suggest a few. The first is that *ideas and opinions should be completely protected*. As Justice Lewis Powell put it aptly in the case of *Gertz v. Welch*, "there is no such thing as a false idea. However pernicious an opinion may seem, we depend for its correction not on the conscience of judges and juries but on the competition of other ideas."[13] (The idea that bad speech should be corrected by more speech, is, of course, Justice Brandeis's counter-speech theory from *Whitney*.) Second, *viewpoint-based discrimination is really dangerous*. Intermediaries should almost never restrict expression because they dislike its political or artistic viewpoint on an issue. Third, *even content-based restrictions are dangerous*. Content-based restrictions are ones that censor speech because of its topic. By cutting off an entire topic of discussion, they stifle debate and prevent discussions on topics that might matter.[14] Fourth, *restricting speech solely because it causes offense or hurts feelings is also dangerous*. As we saw earlier, a cornerstone of modern free speech law is the idea that emotional dislike of the speech by a listener is an insufficient reason to censor. Public debate, as Justice Brennan once memorably argued, needs to be "uninhibited, robust, and wide-open," and feelings naturally get hurt as part of such debate—a price we have to pay for the benefits the democratic process gives us.[15] Fifth, First Amendment law gives *special protection for political speech*, which is frequently speech critical of the government. By the same token, intermediaries should promote political discussion—both discussions of state politics and discussions of the intermediary itself. The best place for a robust discussion of Facebook's privacy policies, after all, is probably Facebook.

Even when they embrace the core principles of free speech, intermediaries will retain the discretion to remove many categories of speech that are inappropriate. Many kinds of speech can be regulated by the government consistent with the First Amendment. Speech that falls within the "unprotected" categories of threats, incitement to lawbreaking, obscenity, and child pornography can be removed. So, too, can speech obtained by invasions of privacy, breach of confidences, or violations of intellectual property rights that don't fall in the broad category of "fair uses." And because the First Amendment principles I have identified are merely advisory ones, intermediaries should have the flexibility to experiment with technological and legal means to mediate speech consistent with their purposes. A site that is a support group for battered women should not be forced to admit abusers. A social network for children could certainly regulate sex or violence more thoroughly. Or sites could experiment with anonymous, pseudonymous, or real-name identification of speakers for different kinds of purposes.

But the important point is this: intermediaries need to recognize that they have a special responsibility in the twenty-first century to safeguard expression, and they should not be able to dodge these responsibilities merely because they are not the government. In many ways, the fact that intermediaries are not publicly accountable like an elected official makes them even more threatening to civil liberties than the state. There is some evidence that intermediaries have started to recognize these responsibilities, developing codes of conduct and free speech policies.[16] But as the influence of intermediaries over free speech in practice grows, their importance is not going to wane. Intermediaries, especially the powerful ones, must be mindful of their power to censor.

Intermediaries and Intellectual Privacy

A similar conclusion follows for intellectual privacy. Throughout this book, when we've seen instances of intellectual privacy under threat, intermediaries have been intimately involved. Google's search records were at the center of the Search Subpoena, Amazon's data collection created the e-reader paradox of the Naughty Book, and ISP email records were the source of the dispute in the case of the Snake Oil Salesman. Even the *Olmstead* case, decided almost a century ago, involved the new technology of telephone wires that carried voice messages long distances. Each of these cases suggests that intellectual privacy in the future will also depend upon the actions of intermediaries—the companies and institutions we use to think, read, communicate, and otherwise make sense of the world. Gradually, over the decades, technologies have come to mediate our thinking, reading, and communications. The change has been so gradual that we have perhaps not really noticed that it is occurring. But ask yourself to what extent your intellectual activities are even possible without the assistance of intermediaries, trusted or otherwise. In the digital age, our thoughts may still be our own, but increasing amounts of our searching, reading, and communications are only possible with the help of these intermediaries, be they Internet and telecom companies, bookstores, or others.

On the whole, these developments have been tremendously positive. As long as we have a computer and network service, we can do amazing things. We can send emails across the country and the world, instantaneously and freely. We can use free videoconferencing software like Skype to turn our computers or tablets into the videophones we may have dreamed of as children. We can use computers to search the Internet for answers on Google.com, to read newspapers in any language we know, and to translate those in languages we don't. We can use bookstores like Amazon.com to order books on any subject imaginable, no matter where we live. And we can use electronic readers like the Nook or Kindle to download those books almost instantaneously if we would rather not wait, or if we would rather read the digital format. Cloud storage companies like Dropbox let us access all of our documents wherever we might be, and social network companies like Facebook connect us to friends old and new, wherever they might be.

The digital revolution has unleashed a transformative power upon the way we think, read, and communicate. The power of this transformation—as great as the Industrial Revolution—has made equally vast fortunes for the architects of the Information Revolution. But as the old saying goes, with great power comes great responsibility. As intermediaries have made our intellectual lives richer, as we have come to depend upon them, the decisions they make about their services have come to affect and even to shape our lives. Some of these decisions are business strategies; others are unanticipated consequences of design decisions made by software engineers. But the decisions matter, and they are shaping our society and the way it makes choices. As intellectual privacy has become a digital issue, it increasingly is dependent upon our intermediaries.

This is a recent development, but it isn't unprecedented. Humans have depended upon other people for millennia. More recently, we have depended upon professionals to help us make sound decisions. Our relationships with these professionals have occurred against the backdrop of legal rules, but also in the context of professional ethics. As digital intermediaries come to play an equally important role in our lives as our doctors and lawyers, perhaps it is time to think about their professional ethics, and the duties they owe as information professionals to protect the civil liberties of their users.

Law and medicine are old professions, which have had a long time to develop nuanced codes of professional ethics and the duties they owe to their patients and clients. The emergence of information professionals is somewhat newer, and we may justifiably wonder what the content of their information ethics should be. I would suggest that it includes the obligation to be responsible stewards of personal information, and to help users make reasoned and responsible choices about how their personal information is used. This question is a much broader one than intellectual privacy, but since this is a book about intellectual privacy, rather than privacy more generally, I will focus on this narrower issue. In determining the content of their ethical rules, information professionals in the digital age should also look to older kinds of professionals—doctors and lawyers, but most importantly to librarians.

Librarians and Information Ethics

It might seem odd at first to seek answers to questions of intellectual freedom for a digital age from librarians. After all, librarians aren't often thought of as particularly imaginative or innovative. But this stereotype is wrong. Librarians are our first and oldest information professionals, with special expertise in the issues intellectual records raise. Librarians have been struggling with the problems of reading records for centuries, as custodians of books and the records of those reading them.[17] And librarians have been very thoughtful about the duties they owe to their patrons, and the consequences of their ethics for civil liberties in the larger society.

One of the most important ethical duties of librarians along these lines is the professional duty of confidentiality. Article 11 of the 1939 Code of Ethics for Librarians maintained that "[i]t is the librarian's obligation to treat as confidential any private information obtained through contact with library patrons."[18] The current version of the Code states that "[w]e protect each library user's right to privacy and confidentiality with respect to information sought or received and resources consulted, borrowed, acquired or transmitted."[19]

Modern American librarians have enshrined their ethical views about intellectual freedom and intellectual privacy in the American Library Association's (ALA) 1948 Library Bill of Rights[20] and in a series of official interpretations of that document spanning the period from World War II to the Patriot Act.[21] The Library Bill of Rights itself was the culmination of decades of work by librarians as they attempted to understand the purpose of their profession and the duties of information stewardship that came along with it.[22] Earlier American librarians frequently thought of themselves as moral guardians of society with a special responsibility to "elevate" the morality of lower classes and immigrants.[23] But the Library Bill of Rights represents a very different understanding of the relationship between librarian and patron. The original 1948 Library Bill of Rights and its subsequent amended versions conceive of the library as a means of fostering the intellectual freedom of library patrons.[24] Affirming that "all libraries are forums for information and ideas," the Library Bill of Rights consists of six principles to guide the provision of library services:

I. Books and other library resources should be provided for the interest, information, and enlightenment of all people of the community the library serves. Materials should not be excluded because of the origin, background, or views of those contributing to their creation.

II. Libraries should provide materials and information presenting all points of view on current and historical issues. Materials should not be proscribed or removed because of partisan or doctrinal disapproval.

III. Libraries should challenge censorship in the fulfillment of their responsibility to provide information and enlightenment.

IV. Libraries should cooperate with all persons and groups concerned with resisting abridgment of free expression and free access to ideas.

V. A person's right to use a library should not be denied or abridged because of origin, age, background, or views.

VI. Libraries that make exhibit spaces and meeting rooms available to the public they serve should make such facilities available on an equitable basis, regardless of the beliefs or affiliations of individuals or groups requesting their use.[25]

Recognizing that the Library Bill of Rights is a living document, the ALA and its Office of Intellectual Freedom (OIF) have clarified its meaning over the years through a series of interpretations. These interpretations and other guidelines explain the application of the ALA's commitment to intellectual freedom, the right to read, and free access to ideas in particular contexts, such as library usage, censorship, governmental intimidation, and equality of access.[26]

Most important for present purposes are a series of ALA policies on the privacy and confidentiality of library records. The distinction between the two is significant. Patron "privacy," in the words of several influential librarians, "is the right to engage in open inquiry without having the subject of one's interest examined or scrutinized by others."[27] But recognizing that an important part of the librarian's professional mission is to help patrons find information, the policies also recognize the value of "confidentiality," the keeping of such information private on the patron's behalf.[28] In 1971 the ALA adopted its Policy on Confidentiality of Library Records.[29] As amended today, it "strongly recommends" that libraries adopt a policy of confidentiality regarding circulation records identifying patrons by name, advise all librarians that records shall only be released pursuant to a valid court order, and resist all such court orders up to the limits of the law.[30]

The ALA's fullest exploration of reader privacy and its relationship to intellectual freedom is its 2002 document, *Privacy: An Interpretation of the Library Bill of Rights*.[31] Recognizing at the outset that "[p]rivacy is essential to the exercise of free speech, free thought, and free association,"[32] it makes two separate commitments to user privacy and confidentiality. The first commitment deals with the rights of library users. This interprets Article IV of the Library Bill of Rights' commitment to free access as giving library users as much control as possible to select, access, and use library material. It asserts that "[l]ack of privacy and confidentiality has a chilling effect on users' choices. All users have a right to be free from any unreasonable intrusion into or surveillance of their lawful library use."[33] Moreover, the policy maintains that patrons have the right to use a library without any inferences made between their reading habits and their behavior.[34]

The policy's second commitment deals with the responsibilities of librarians and library users to each other. It declares that because "[t]he library profession has a long-standing commitment to an ethic of facilitating, not monitoring, access to information," libraries must take care to only collect personal information that is necessary to provide mission-critical library services.[35] Moreover, the commitment to intellectual freedom means that everyone in a library, whether librarian or fellow user, "has a responsibility to maintain an environment respectful and protective of the privacy of all users."[36]

Beyond the Library Bill of Rights, the ALA has engaged in advocacy to protect reader privacy. A 2009 position paper declares that "the impulse to be curious, to read, and to learn is essential for the health of our democracy and our economy."[37] The paper also recognizes the critical relationship between intellectual privacy and political freedom. It explains that "[t]he freedom to read and receive ideas anonymously is at the heart of individual liberty in a democracy. It ensures a person's right to gain knowledge and form opinions according to his or her own conscience. It is the foundation for self-determination and meaningful participation in the political process."[38] Crucially, the OIF also articulates the importance of privacy to avoid the "chilling effect" on reading caused by surveillance:

> When the right to privacy is eroded or stripped away, people are more likely to abandon or curtail their exploration of unpopular and unorthodox points of view. This chilling effect puts the intellectual development of our citizenry at risk. The very character of the American mind, which is premised on open inquiry, is thereby robbed of the free flow of ideas that makes innovation possible.[39]

The ALA has made this argument through more direct advocacy activities as well. In response to section 215 of the Patriot Act, which allows secret access to library records,[40] the ALA worked with the American Booksellers' Association and other groups to found the Campaign for Reader Privacy and try to overturn the law.[41] More recently, the OIF has sponsored "Choose Privacy Week," an initiative designed to give "citizens the resources to think critically and make more informed decisions about their privacy."[42]

Intellectual privacy theory and library ethics reveal the values behind confidentiality rules for intellectual records. They illuminate the reasons why confidentiality should be treated specially and some of the dangers of disclosure. They also reveal a central paradox of intellectual privacy: we need intellectual privacy to make up our minds, but we often need the assistance and recommendations of others as part of this process, be they librarians, search engines, or other intermediaries. The norms of librarians suggest one successful and proven solution to this paradox.

Toward an Information Ethics

An important part of any solution to intellectual privacy is the development of a professional ethics for information professionals, as is building those ethics into the institutional norms of intermediary companies. What would this look like in practice? At bottom, this would mean companies, government entities, and other intermediaries should adhere to the FIPs, mindful of the special importance of intellectual privacy. Many companies have already taken steps along these lines. Today, numerous businesses have a chief privacy officer, and other businesses have gone further. Engineers are good at solving problems, and an important part of protecting intellectual privacy is to get privacy protection into the design specification for any problems that engineers are trying to solve.

One way to do this is to use the idea of Privacy by Design, a set of privacy principles suggested in the 1990s by Dr. Ann Cavoukian, the information and privacy commissioner of Ontario. Privacy by Design recognizes that privacy protection in general cannot be ensured solely by legal rules, and that effective privacy protection requires companies to make privacy protection an ordinary but integral part of the way that they do business. It encourages businesses to see privacy as a business opportunity, to protect personal information throughout its life cycle, and to ensure that privacy-protective elements of the business are transparent, so that they work as intended.[43] In this last respect, Privacy by Design embraces Louis Brandeis's paradoxical idea that privacy is important, but sunlight is also the best disinfectant. The key, of course, is in identifying what activities should be kept private and what activities should be disinfected by the purifying light of transparency.

Privacy by Design is not perfect. It illustrates principles that can be useful in protecting intellectual privacy (and other kinds of personal information), but it is important that companies who adopt the Privacy by Design principles do so substantively, rather than as some kind of minimal compliance or public relations stunt. Meaningful protection of intellectual privacy depends upon substantive cultural norms, after all, rather than mere parchment barriers.

Some companies have gone further by trying to compete in the marketplace on the basis of privacy. A leader in these efforts is the nonprofit Mozilla Corporation, which produces the Firefox browser. Because it is a nonprofit, Mozilla has greater latitude to develop policies that promote values other than "shareholder value," the main goal of publicly traded corporations. Mozilla's corporate mission is laid out in a document called the "Mozilla Manifesto," which includes a commitment to an open and accessible Internet, the ability of individuals "to shape their own experiences on the Internet," and the ideas that "transparent community-based processes promote participation, accountability, and trust."[44] With respect to privacy, Mozilla tries to develop its products around six privacy principles, which are as follows:

1. No Surprises. Only use and share information about our users for their benefit and as spelled out in our notices.

2. Real Choices. Educate users whenever we collect any personal information and give them a choice whenever possible.

3. Sensible Settings. Establish default settings that balance safety and user experience appropriately.

4. Limited Data. Collect and retain the least amount of user information necessary. Try to share anonymous aggregate data whenever possible, and then only when it benefits the web, users or developers.

5. User Control. Do not disclose personal user experience without the user's consent. Innovate, develop and advocate for privacy enhancements that put users in control of their online experiences.

6. Trusted Third Parties. Make privacy a factor in selecting and interacting with partners.

There are several interesting features of the Mozilla principles. They resemble the FIPs, but are stronger in several ways, talking about *real* choices and *sensible* default settings, which appear to be a departure from the thin version of privacy as nothing more than hidden notice and limited choice that many websites adhere to. The Mozilla principles also embody the insight that users should be in meaningful control of how their personal information is used and the old Brandeis idea that transparency by commercial actors promotes accountability and deters wrongdoing.

Another company competing not just on privacy but intellectual privacy is the search engine DuckDuckGo.com, which competes with Google. Both Google and DuckDuckGo offer a search engine that is "free" to users but which serves them advertisements in addition to their search results. But the way the two companies have engineered their servers to provide ads is very different. DuckDuckGo serves ads based solely upon what someone searches for. Google uses so-called "behavioral advertisements," which are targeted to users based not only upon what they enter into the search box but also upon a profile of the user depending upon their web-browsing history. It thus utilizes a profile of an Internet user's intellectual and other interests to provide both "personalized" search and advertisements.[45]

The Search Subpoena case suggests that Google protects the confidentiality of search records when it can, but the fact that browsing profiles exist is a threat to intellectual privacy. Google may have no plans to sell or disclose your browsing history, but as we saw in the case of the search subpoena (and also learned from Edward Snowden), such records are particularly attractive to government agencies interested in preventing child pornography, terrorism, or other perceived threats. The fact that the profile is created in the first place is itself a potential problem for intellectual privacy. By contrast, the DuckDuckGo approach builds intellectual privacy protection into the design of the search algorithm in order to both protect the intellectual privacy of its users and to compete in the marketplace on that basis.

My goal here has not been to demonize Internet companies, but rather to encourage the development of an ethic of civil liberties in the ways that they build their business models and products. These companies were rarely started to advance civil liberties, and their success has been sudden and often unexpected. But with their success comes a responsibility to promote digital civil liberties. As we have seen, in the twenty-first century, the values that underlie the First Amendment will remain vitally important—the ability to express ideas, create art, develop beliefs about the world, and collaborate with confidants about all of these values. But if we care about free thought and expression in the digital age, constitutional law will not be enough. Legal scholar Jack Balkin puts the point very clearly: in the future, "the most important decisions affecting the future of freedom of speech will not occur in constitutional law; they will be decisions about technological design, legislative and administrative regulations, the formation of new business models, and the collective activities of end-users."[46] This insight is as true for free speech as it is for intellectual privacy. Intermediaries have started to take this insight into account, but they can do better. Developing a commitment to civil liberties and ethical, responsible stewardship of intellectual records at a minimum is a necessary next step.

But the responsibility for civil liberties in the digital age cannot rest with just the government and intermediaries. It lies with Internet users as well. Brandeis reminded us long ago in his eloquent *Whitney* opinion that civil liberties are an active process on the part of citizens. As we use digital platforms to think, read, communicate, and live our lives more generally, we must all be mindful of the importance of privacy and free speech in a democratic society. We must choose products that promote these liberties and reject ones that do not. If we are locked into using a company because the costs of switching are too high (for example, if all of our friends are on the same privacy-unfriendly social network), we must demand that the company change its ways. After all, if we do not demand civil liberties as individuals, we may not deserve them as a society.

Conclusion

AS THIS BOOK was being completed in 2013 and 2014, revelations about the National Security Agency's surveillance practices dominated headlines around the globe. Thanks to Edward Snowden's leaks and to courageous journalists at *The Guardian* and the *Washington Post*, we now know that the National Security Agency had been accessing vast amounts of personal information from telephone and Internet companies using a number of secret legal methods.[1] Coupled with earlier allegations that the NSA had been building a huge computing and Internet monitoring station in the Utah desert,[2] the disclosures began an international debate about privacy and security from terrorism. Although many people were outraged by the monitoring or found it "creepy," they lacked a language with which to justify their outrage and explain it to others. They frequently lacked an effective response to the argument made by supporters of these government programs that privacy is dead, or that law-abiding people should have nothing to fear from government monitoring.

The themes of this book are broader than the debates about privacy versus security, but they provide both a language with which to understand surveillance, as well as a response to the "privacy is dead" and the "nothing to hide" arguments.

Surveillance isn't dangerous because it's creepy. It's dangerous because it gives the watcher power over the watched, and it's dangerous because it menaces our intellectual privacy. In a free society, we have to care about the processes by which we all learn about and develop our beliefs regarding the world. If we know we are being watched, we are likely to think, read, and communicate differently—we are less likely to engage with dangerous or deviant ideas. But many of the ideas that we cherish the most today were once thought dangerous—ideas like gender and racial equality, or the idea that the government should work for the people and not the other way around. Meiklejohn was entirely correct when he argued that to be afraid of ideas was to be unfit for self-government. We should erect meaningful guarantees of intellectual privacy so that we can confront ideas on our own terms.

Intellectual privacy also provides a novel answer to the "nothing to hide argument." Intellectual privacy isn't about hiding our flaws or character defects from the world. It's about creating a space in which we can think, read, and communicate freely and fearlessly. A common response to the "nothing to hide" argument is that people with nothing to hide aren't very interesting.[3] Intellectual privacy suggests further that people asserting nothing to hide haven't been thinking for themselves.

Finally, what about the idea that privacy is dead? People have been bemoaning the death of privacy since before Warren and Brandeis. If privacy is dying a death, it is an absurdly melodramatic, drawn-out theatrical death. Of course privacy isn't dead, or even dying. Our conversations about the "death of privacy" are just a way of managing the boundaries among ourselves, each other, companies, and the government in a time of rapid technological change. Notions of privacy change over time and space. Certain conceptions of privacy might become less important— I have suggested that Mabel Warren and Ryan Giggs have advanced conceptions of privacy that we should do without.

But privacy will remain important, if for no other reason than it is often about information, and we are living in the information age, witnessing a revolution in technologies that run on information. And as ordinary people become accustomed to those new technologies—whether CCTV, social media, or Internet trackers—they can better imagine and insist on new rules for it. To make those legal, social, and technological rules, citizens need to understand the nature and scope of the problem. Intellectual privacy is one way of understanding a particular set of social problems having to do with information, and how those problems are becoming more severe during our information revolution.

But perhaps the clearest sign that privacy isn't dead is that the government agencies who would deny us intellectual privacy insist on privacy for their own secret surveillance. This is a reminder of Brandeis's insight that privacy matters in its proper time, but so, too, does publicity. The difficulty is in figuring out how much of each is needed and when. This balance depends upon the values at stake, and in this book, I have tried to make the case for the importance of intellectual privacy, to show its connection to the vital civil liberties of freedom of speech. When governments or corporations watch our mental and intellectual activities, the injury is not the tort harm of embarrassment, but a more vital one that cuts to the very core of what it means to live in a free, self-governing society.

We are not seeing the death of privacy, or needless fussing about an irrelevant concept. What we're seeing is the continuation of a global conversation about how to manage our information as technology marches on. And this is a good thing. As we build a digital tomorrow, the choices we make today—about the boundaries between our individual and social selves, between consumers and companies, and between citizens and the state—matter. They will have important consequences for the societies our children and grandchildren will inherit.

The theory of intellectual privacy I describe in this book will not solve all problems of privacy or information. It's not intended to. Instead, the idea of intellectual privacy is intended to identify a particularly important subset of privacy problems and show why they are an essential part of any protection of our most important civil and political liberties. Intellectual privacy matters because it protects our ability to think for ourselves and develop our beliefs. Without this ability, we cannot say that we are a free society.

Protecting intellectual privacy will not be costless in money or safety. By definition, intellectual privacy makes it easier for people to engage with radical and unpopular ideas. Some of those ideas will certainly be dangerous. But in a free society, we have to trust ourselves and each other with dangerous ideas. Alexander Meiklejohn reminds us that we must not be afraid of ideas if we want to govern ourselves.[4] And Brandeis's opinion in *Whitney* is a ringing declaration that we must confront dangerous ideas and have courage in our political institutions so that freedom of speech and thought can be an end as well as a means.[5] As we enter an uncertain digital future, when so much seems to be up for grabs, we should hold on to the important wisdom of the past, and adapt our most important civil liberties for the new electronic environments. Intellectual privacy should be an essential part of that future.

NOTES

Introduction

1. Spencer Ackerman & James Ball, *Optic Nerve: Millions of Yahoo Webcam Images Intercepted by GCHQ*, THE GUARDIAN, Feb. 27, 2014.
2. *Id.*
3. David Kravets, *School District Allegedly Snapped Thousands of Student Webcam Spy Pics*, WIRED.COM (April 16, 2010), available at http://www.wired.com/threatlevel/2010/04/webcamscanda/.
4. Kim Zetter, *School Spy Program Used on Students Contains Hacker-Friendly Security Hole*, WIRED.COM (May 20, 2010), available at http://www.wired.com/threatlevel/2010/05/lanrev/.
5. John P. Martin. *Lower Merion district's laptop saga ends with $610,000 settlement*, THE PHILADELPHIA INQUIRER, October 12, 2010.
6. Nate Anderson, *Meet the Men Who Spy on Women Through Their Webcams*, ARS TECHNICA, March 10, 2013, available at http://arstechnica.com/tech-policy/2013/03/rat-breeders-meet-the-men-who-spy-on-women-through-their-webcams/.
7. Zadie Smith, *Generation Why?*, THE NEW YORK REVIEW OF BOOKS, Dec. 23, 2010.
8. RAY KURZWEIL, THE SINGULARITY IS NEAR (2006).
9. LOUIS D. BRANDEIS, OTHER PEOPLE'S MONEY—AND HOW THE BANKERS USE IT 92 (1914).
10. United States v. Katz, 271 U.S. 354 (1926).
11. Griswold v. Connecticut, 381 U.S. 479 (1965); Roe v. Wade, 410 U.S. 113 (1973).
12. Michael D. Birnhack, *A Quest for a Theory of Privacy: Context and Control*, 51 JURIMETRICS J. 447 (2011); Paul M. Schwartz, *Privacy and Democracy in*

Cyberspace, 52 VAND. L. REV. 1609 (1999); ALAN F. WESTIN, PRIVACY AND FREEDOM (1967).

13. Gary T. Marx & Glenn W. Muschert, *Personal Information, Borders, and the New Surveillance Studies*, ANN. REV. L. & SOC. SCIENCE, Dec. 2007, at 375.

14. HELEN NISSENBAUM, PRIVACY IN CONTEXT (2009).

15. Neil M. Richards, *Reconciling Data Privacy and the First Amendment*, 52 UCLA L. REV. 1149, 1181–82 (2005).

16. Daniel J. Solove, *A Taxonomy of Privacy*, 154 U. PA. L. REV. 477 (2006). A more developed version of the taxonomy can be found in DANIEL J. SOLOVE, UNDERSTANDING PRIVACY 10 (2008).

17. SOLOVE, UNDERSTANDING PRIVACY, *supra*, at 10.

18. *See* James Madison, *The Virginia Report of 1799–1800, Touching the Alien and Sedition Laws; Together with the Virginia Resolutions* 227 (J. W. Randolph ed., 1850); ALEXANDER MEIKLEJOHN, FREE SPEECH AND ITS RELATION TO SELF-GOVERNMENT 26–27 (1948); Whitney v. California, 274 U.S. 357, 375 (1927) (Brandeis, J., concurring).

19. *See* JOHN MILTON, AREOPAGITICA (1644); Abrams v. United States, 250 U.S. 616, 630 (1919) (Holmes, J., dissenting).

20. *E.g.*, C. Edwin Baker, *Scope of the First Amendment Freedom of Speech*, 25 UCLA L. REV. 964, 991 (1978); Martin H. Redish, *The Value of Free Speech*, 130 U. PA. L. REV. 591, 594 (1982); David A. J. Richards, *Free Speech and Obscenity Law: Toward a Moral Theory of the First Amendment*, 123 U. PA. L. REV. 45, 62 (1974); Thomas Scanlon, *A Theory of Freedom of Expression*, 1 PHILA. & PUB. AFF. 204, 210–19 (1972).

Chapter 1

1. *Quoted in* MELVIN I. UROFSKY, LOUIS D. BRANDEIS: A LIFE (Pantheon 2009).

2. MARTIN GREEN, THE MOUNT VERNON STREET WARRENS: A BOSTON STORY, 1860–1910, at 104 (1989).

3. My discussion of the Warrens and Bayards draws on UROFSKY, A LIFE, *supra*; CHARLES CALLAN TANSILL, THE CONGRESSIONAL CAREER OF THOMAS F. BAYARD (1961); EDWARD SPENCER, THE PUBLIC LIFE AND SERVICES OF T. F. BAYARD (1880); and Amy Gajda, *What if Samuel D. Warren Hadn't Married a Senator's Daughter? Uncovering the Press Coverage that Led to the Right to Privacy*, 2008 MICH. ST. L. REV. 35, 44–57 (2008).

4. ALPHEUS THOMAS MASON, BRANDEIS: A FREE MAN'S LIFE 68 (1946); James H. Barron, *Warren and Brandeis, The Right to Privacy, 4 Harv. L. Rev. 193 (1890): Demystifying a Landmark Citation*, 13 SUFFOLK U. L. REV. 875, 908–09 (1979).

5. For press coverage of the wedding, see *The Washington Society World: Marriage of Senator Bayard's Daughter*, N.Y. TIMES, Jan. 26, 1883; *A Brilliant Bridal*, WASH. POST, Jan. 26, 1883. See generally Gajda, *supra*.

6. MASON, *supra*, at 47; UROFSKY, A LIFE, *supra*, at 30–31.

7.   UROFSKY, A LIFE, at 97.

8.   Gajda, *supra.*

9.   *Manola Gets an Injunction,* N.Y. TIMES, June 18, 1890, at 2; *Photographed in Tights,* N.Y. TIMES, June 15, 1890, at 2; see also DON R. PEMBER, PRIVACY AND THE PRESS 56 (1972).

10. E. L. Godkin, *The Rights of the Citizen: IV. To His Own Reputation,* 8 SCRIBNER'S MAG. 58, 65 (1890).

11. LAWRENCE M. FRIEDMAN, GUARDING LIFE'S DARK SECRETS (2007).

12. Barron, *supra,* at 891–907; Gajda, *supra,* at 44–57; Neil M. Richards, *The Puzzle of Brandeis, Privacy, and Speech,* 63 VAND. L. REV. 1295, 1302 (2010) [hereinafter Richards, Brandeis].

13. See 1 LETTERS OF LOUIS D. BRANDEIS 303 (David W. Levy & Melvin I. Urofsky eds., 1971).

14. Erwin N. Griswold, *The Harvard Law Review—Glimpses of Its History as Seen by an Aficionado, in* HARVARD LAW REVIEW: CENTENNIAL ALBUM 1 (1987).

15. Samuel D. Warren & Louis D. Brandeis, *The Right to Privacy,* 4 HARV. L. REV. 193 (1890).

16. Neil M. Richards & Daniel J. Solove, *Privacy's Other Path: Recovering the Law of Confidentiality,* 96 GEO. L.J. 123, 129–31 (2007).

17. G. EDWARD WHITE, TORT LAW IN AMERICA: AN INTELLECTUAL HISTORY 102–03 (expanded ed. 2003).

18. Warren & Brandeis, *supra,* at 195.

19. *Id.*

20. *Id.* at 196.

21. Barron, *supra,* at 884–87; James Q. Whitman, *The Two Western Cultures of Privacy: Dignity Versus Liberty,* 113 YALE L.J. 1151, 1205 (2004).

22. FRIEDMAN, *supra,* at 4.

23. *Id.* at 214–15.

24. Warren & Brandeis, *supra,* at 196.

25. *Id.*

26. *Id.*

27. *Id.* at 216.

28. *Id.* at 214.

29. *Id.* at 216.

30. *Id.*

31. *Id.*

32. *Id.*

33. *See* Anita L. Allen & Erin Mack, *How Privacy Got Its Gender,* 10 N. ILL. U. L. REV. 441, 441 (1990).

34. Warren & Brandeis, *supra,* at 195.

35. *Id.* at 214.

36. *Id.* at 216.

37. Richards & Solove, *Privacy's Other Path, supra,* at 1892–93. The California law was on the books from 1899 to 1905. It forbade the publication of "the portrait of

any living person a resident of California, other than that of a person holding a public office in this state" without their consent. 1899 Cal. Stat. 28, codified as Cal. Penal Code § 258 (1899), as repealed by 1915 Cal. Stat. 761.

38. Roberson v. Rochester Folding Box Co., 64 N.E. 442 (N.Y. 1902).

39. *Id.* at 447–48.

40. N.Y. CIV. RIGHTS LAW §§ 50–51 (McKinney 1903).

41. Pavesich v. New England Life Ins. Co., 50 S.E. 68 (Ga. 1905).

42. *Id.* at 74.

43. Neil M. Richards & Daniel J. Solove, *Prosser's Privacy Law: A Mixed Legacy*, 98 Calif. L. Rev. 1887, 1893–94 (2011).

44. William Prosser, *Privacy*, 48 CALIF. L. REV. 383, 406–07 (1960).

45. *Id.* at 389–92 (collecting cases).

46. Gajda, *supra*, at 43–44.

47. 299 S.W. 967, 968 (Ky. 1927).

48. *E.g.*, Leon Green, *The Right of Privacy*, 27 ILL. L. REV. 237 (1932); Rufus Lisle, *The Right of Privacy (A Contra View)*, 19 KY. L.J. 137 (1931); Roy Moreland, *The Right of Privacy Today*, 19 KY. L.J. 101 (1931); George Ragland Jr., *The Right of Privacy*, 17 KY. L.J. 85 (1929). Many of these articles were cited a few years later by Brandeis himself in a Supreme Court case that raised a similar fact pattern but was decided differently. Senn v. Tile Layers Protective Union, 301 U.S. 468, 482 n.5 (1937). See generally Neil M. Richards, *The Puzzle of Brandeis, Privacy, and Speech*, 63 VAND. L. REV. 1295 (2010) (explaining how Brandeis's views on privacy evolved over time).

49. 297 P. 91 (Cal. 1931).

50. *E.g.*, Green, *supra* note 48; Lisle, *supra*; Moreland, *supra*; Roscoe Pound, *The Fourteenth Amendment and the Right of Privacy*, 13 W. Res. L. Rev. 34 (1961).

51. WHITE, *supra*, at 174.

52. WHITE, *supra*, at 173–74.

53. Richards & Solove, *Prosser, supra*.

54. Prosser, *Privacy, supra*, at 388.

55. Richards & Solove, *Prosser, supra*, at 1895–1903.

56. Prosser, *Privacy, supra* note 44, at 389.

57. *Id.*

58. Richards & Solove, *Privacy's Other Path, supra*, at 1907–08.

59. *Id.*

60. Richards & Solove, *Prosser's Privacy Law, supra*.

61. Lake v. Wal-Mart Stores, Inc., 582 N.W.2d 231, 235 (Minn. 1998).

62. *Id.* at 232.

63. *Id.* at 235.

Chapter 2

1. My treatment of the life of Anita Whitney draws heavily on Ashutosh A. Bhagwat, The Story of Whitney v. California: *The Power of Ideas*, in CONSTITUTIONAL LAW STORIES (M. Dorf ed., 2004), and Vincent Blasi,

The First Amendment and the Ideal of Civic Courage: The Brandeis Opinion in Whitney v. California, 29 WM. & MARY L. REV. 653 (1988).

2. Clare Shipman, *The Conviction of Anita Whitney*, THE NATION, Mar. 20, 1920, at 365.

3. 1919 Cal. Stat. 281, 2 Hennings Gen. Laws, p. 3281, § 1, *cited in* Comment, *Criminal Law: Criminal Syndicalist Act: Constitutional Law, Validity of the Act Under the Free Speech Clause*, 10 CALIF. L. REV. 512, 512 n.1 (1922).

4. Blasi, *supra* note 1, at 656.

5. Whitney v. California, 274 U.S. 357 (1927); see also MELVIN I. UROFSKY, LOUIS D. BRANDEIS: A LIFE, 635 (2009) [hereinafter UROFSKY, A LIFE].

6. Lisa Rubens, *The Patrician Radical: Charlotte Anita Whitney*, 65 CAL. HISTORY, No. 3, at 158–71 (1986).

7. *Whitney*, 274 U.S. at 375–76 (Brandeis, J., concurring).

8. Letter from Louis D. Brandeis to Alice Goldmark (Nov. 29, 1890), *in* 1 LETTERS OF LOUIS D. BRANDEIS 94–95 (David W. Levy & Melvin I. Urofsky eds., 1971) [hereinafter LETTERS].

9. Letter from Louis D. Brandeis to Alice Goldmark (Feb. 26, 1891), *in* 1 LETTERS, *id.*, at 100.

10. LOUIS D. BRANDEIS, OTHER PEOPLE'S MONEY—AND HOW THE BANKERS USE IT, 62–63 (1914).

11. *Id.* at 94–97.

12. *Id.* at 101–04.

13. BRANDEIS, OTHER PEOPLE'S MONEY, *supra*, at 92.

14. MELVIN I. UROFSKY, LOUIS D. BRANDEIS AND THE PROGRESSIVE TRADITION 50 (1981) [hereinafter UROFSKY, PROGRESSIVE TRADITION].

15. Ken I. Kersch, *The Reconstruction of Constitutional Privacy Rights and the New American State*, 16 STUD. AM. POL. DEV. 61, 77 (2002).

16. Melvin I. Urofsky, *Louis D. Brandeis: Teacher*, 45 BRANDEIS L. J. 733, 733–34 (2007).

17. 208 U.S. 412 (1908).

18. UROFSKY, PROGRESSIVE TRADITION, *supra*, at 52–53; see also EDWARD A. PURCELL JR., BRANDEIS AND THE PROGRESSIVE CONSTITUTION 166 (2000).

19. DiSanto v. Commonwealth of Pa., 273 U.S. 34, 43 (1927) (Brandeis, J., dissenting).

20. 248 U.S. 215 (1918).

21. *Id.* at 263.

22. *Id.* at 262–63.

23. *E.g.,* Fox v. Washington, 236 U.S. 273 (1914); Patterson v. Colorado, 205 U.S. 454 (1906).

24. DAVID M. KENNEDY, OVER HERE: THE FIRST WORLD WAR AND AMERICAN SOCIETY 24–26 (1980).

25. DAVID M. RABBAN, FREE SPEECH IN ITS FORGOTTEN YEARS 256 (1999); RONALD SCHAFFER, AMERICA IN THE GREAT WAR: THE RISE OF THE

WELFARE STATE 15 (1991); Phillippa Strum, *Brandeis: The Public Activist and Freedom of Speech*, 45 BRANDEIS L. J. 659, 668 (2007).

26. 249 U.S. 185 (1919).
27. *Id.* at 183–85.
28. 249 U.S. 47 (1919).
29. *Id.* at 50–51.
30. *Id.* at 52.
31. MARK A. GRABER, TRANSFORMING FREE SPEECH: THE AMBIGUOUS LEGACY OF CIVIL LIBERTARIANISM 106–08 (1992); Rabban, *supra*, at 282; G. Edward White, *The First Amendment Comes of Age: The Emergence of Free Speech in Twentieth Century America*, 95 MICH. L. REV. 299, 318 (1996).
32. Frohwerk v. United States, 249 U.S. 204 (1919); Debs v. United States, 249 U.S. 211 (1919).
33. Robert M. Cover, *The Left, the Right, and the First Amendment: 1918–1928*, 40 MD. L. REV. 349, 374 (1981).
34. UROFSKY, A LIFE, *supra*, at 533–54.
35. GERALD GUNTHER, LEARNED HAND: THE MAN AND THE JUDGE 161–67 (1994); Gerald Gunther, *Learned Hand and the Origins of Modern First Amendment Doctrine: Some Fragments of History*, 27 STAN. L. REV. 719, 732 (1975).
36. *See* Bradley C. Bobertz, *The Brandeis Gambit: The Making of America's First Freedom, 1909–1931*, 40 WM. & MARY L. REV. 557, 607–11 (1999) (discussing *Danger Ahead*, 108 NATION 186 (1919); *Freedom of Speech: Whose Concern?*, 18 NEW REPUBLIC 102 (1919); *The Call to Toleration*, 20 NEW REPUBLIC 360 (1919)); see also Strum, *supra*, at 675.
37. Zechariah Chafee Jr., *Freedom of Speech in War Times*, 32 HARV. L. REV. 932 (1919).
38. Strum, *supra*, at 675–76; UROFSKY, A LIFE, *supra*, at 553.
39. UROFSKY, A LIFE, *supra*, at 555–56.
40. *Id.*
41. Abrams v. United States, 250 U.S. 616, 630 (1919) (Holmes, J., dissenting).
42. UROFSKY, A LIFE, *supra*, at 553.
43. Cover, *supra*, at 381.
44. 251 U.S. 467, 482 (1920) (Brandeis, J., dissenting).
45. 252 U.S. 239, 253 (1920) (Brandeis, J., dissenting).
46. 254 U.S. 325 (1920) (Brandeis, J., dissenting).
47. United States *ex rel.* Milwaukee Soc. Democratic Publ'g Co. v. Burleson, 255 U.S. 407, 417–36 (Brandeis, J., dissenting).
48. 274 U.S. 357, 372 (1927) (Brandeis, J., concurring).
49. 268 U.S. 652 (1925) (Holmes, J., dissenting).
50. 279 U.S. 644 (1929) (Holmes, J., dissenting).
51. LOUIS MENAND, THE METAPHYSICAL CLUB 4 (2001); Vincent Blasi, *Holmes and the Marketplace of Ideas*, 2004 SUP. CT. REV. 1, 2; Thomas C. Grey, *Holmes, Pragmatism, and Democracy*, 71 OR. L. REV. 521, 523 (1992).

52. White, *supra*, at 325.

53. 252 U.S. 239, at 251–52 (1920).

54. *Id.* at 267, 269–70 (Brandeis, J., dissenting).

55. *Id.* at 269 (Brandeis, J., dissenting).

56. *Id.* at 269 (Brandeis, J., dissenting).

57. Whitney, 274 U.S. at 377 (Brandeis, J., concurring).

58. Whitney, 274 U.S. at 375 (Brandeis, J., concurring).

59. Letter from Louis D. Brandeis to Alice Goldmark (Oct. 27, 1890), *in* 1 LETTERS, *supra*, at 94.

60. Letter from Louis D. Brandeis to Robert W. Bruere (Feb. 25, 1922), *quoted in* ALPHEUS THOMAS MASON, BRANDEIS: A FREE MAN'S LIFE 585 (1946).

61. Whitney, 274 U.S. at 375 (Brandeis, J., concurring).

62. Blasi, *supra*, at 674.

63. *Id.* at 674–75.

64. Whitney, 274 U.S. at 378 (Brandeis, J., concurring).

65. 274 U.S. 380, 387 (1927).

66. 301 U.S. 242 (1937).

67. 299 U.S. 353 (1937).

68. *DeJonge*, 299 U.S. at 365; *Herndon*, 301 U.S. at 247.

69. 376 U.S. 254, 272 (1964); see also NAACP v. Button, 371 U.S. 415, 433 (1963) (first using the "breathing space" analogy).

70. 418 U.S. 323, 339 (1974); *accord* Kingsley Int'l Pictures Corp. v. Regents of the Univ. of N.Y., 360 U.S. 684, 688–89 (1959).

71. Daniel J. Solove & Neil M. Richards, *Rethinking Free Speech and Civil Liability*, 109 COLUM. L. REV. 1650, 1657–58 (2009).

72. Sullivan, 376 U.S. at 270 (quoting Whitney v. California, 274 U.S 357, 375–76 (1927) (Brandeis, J., concurring)).

73. Solove & Richards, *supra*, at 1657.

74. Blasi, *supra*, at 692–95 (collecting examples).

75. 403 U.S. 15, 24 (1971).

76. *Id.* (citing Whitney, 274 U.S. at 375–77 (Brandeis, J., concurring)).

Chapter 3

1. Gordon Rayner & Steven Swinford, *Ryan Giggs unmasked as gagging order footballer*, THE TELEGRAPH, May 23, 2011; Daniel Taylor, *Manchester United's marathon man: Ryan Giggs reaches a thousand games*, THE GUARDIAN, Mar. 1, 2013; *Ryan Giggs: "sex addict" Manchester United star "had third affair,"* THE TELEGRAPH, Jun. 8, 2011; CTB v. News Group Newspapers Ltd & Anor, [2011] EWHC 1232 (QB).

2. James E. Stanley, *Max Mosley and the English Right to Privacy*, 10 WASH. U. GLOBAL STUD. L. REV. 641 (2011); Douglas v. Hello! Ltd, [2006] QB 125; Mosley v. News Group Newspapers Ltd [2008] EMLR 679.

3. Human Rights Act, 1998, c.42.

4. European Convention on Human Rights, § 1, art. 8, Nov. 4, 1950.

5. Rayner & Swinford, *supra*.

6. Martin Evans, David Cameron: Twitter gossip makes super-injunctions unsustainable and unfair, THE TELEGRAPH, May 23, 2011.

7. Kevin McCarra, *Barcelona turn Manchester United into a mere irrelevance*, THE GUARDIAN, May 29, 2011.

8. AMY WALLACE, THE PRODIGY (1986); *Harvard's Child Prodigy: All Amazed at Mathematical Grasp of Youngest Matriculate, Aged 13 Years*, N.Y. TIMES (Oct. 10, 1909), at A1.

9. Sidis v. F-R Publishing Group, 113 F.2d 806, 809 (2d Cir. 1940).

10. Samantha Barbas, *The Death of the Public Disclosure Tort: A Historical Perspective*, 22 YALE J. L. & HUMAN. 171, 212–13 (2010).

11. RESTATEMENT (SECOND) OF TORTS § 652D (1977).

12. *Id.* cmt. a.

13. *Id.*

14. *See, e.g.*, Miller v. Motorola, 560 N.E.2d 900 (Il. App. Ct. 1990); *see also* Beaumont v. Brown, 257 N.W.2d 522 (Mich. 1977); *see generally* DANIEL J. SOLOVE & PAUL SCHWARTZ, INFORMATION PRIVACY LAW 116 (3d ed. 2006) (collecting cases).

15. Robert C. Post, *The Social Foundations of Privacy: Community and Self in the Common Law Tort*, 77 CAL. L. REV. 957, 992 (1989); *see also* Jonathan B. Mintz, *The Remains of Privacy's Disclosure Tort: An Exploration of the Private Domain*, 55 MD. L. REV. 425, 438 (1996).

16. Lior J. Strahilevitz, *A Social Networks Theory of Privacy*, 72 U. CHI. L. REV. 919, 921 (2005).

17. Neil M. Richards, *The Puzzle of Brandeis, Privacy and Speech*, 63 VAND. L. REV. 1295, 1308 (2010).

18. 248 U.S. 215, 262 (1918).

19. Richards, *The Puzzle of Brandeis, supra*, at 1330–35.

20. Barbas, *supra*, at 173.

21. Time v. Hill, 385 U.S. 374 (1967) (citing N.Y. Times v. Sullivan, 376 U.S. 254 (1964)).

22. 385 U.S. at 385.

23. Barbas, *supra*, at 214.

24. Snyder v. Phelps, 131 S. Ct. 1207, 1216 (2011).

25. Richards, *The Puzzle of Brandeis, supra*, at 1323–34.

26. 310 U.S. 296, 311 (1940).

27. Harry Kalven Jr., *The* New York Times *Case: A Note on "The Central Meaning of the First Amendment,"* 1964 SUP. CT. REV. 191, 208.

28. 376 U.S. 254, 270 (1964).

29. Firestone v. Time, 424 U.S. 448, 475 n.3 (1976); Gertz v. Welch, 418 U.S. 323, 349 (1974).

30. *See, e.g.*, Bartnicki v. Vopper, 532 U.S. 514, 526–28 (2001); Fla. Star v. B.J.F., 491 U.S. 524, 526 (1989); Smith v. Daily Mail Publ'g Co., 443 U.S. 97 (1979);

Okla. Publ'g Corp. v. Okla. Cnty. Dist. Court, 430 U.S. 308 (1977); Cox Broad. Corp. v. Cohn, 420 U.S. 469 (1975).

31.　*Fla. Star*, 491 U.S. at 524 (quoting *Smith*, 443 U.S. at 103).

32.　*See* Whalen v. Roe, 429 U.S. 589 (1977); Carter v. Broadlawns Med. Ctr., 667 F. Supp. 1269 (S.D. Iowa 1987); Doe v. Borough of Barrington, 729 F. Supp. 376 (D.N.J. 1990), Doe v. S.E. Pa. Transp. Auth., 72 F.3d 1133 (3d Cir. 1995).

33.　485 U.S. 46 (1988).

34.　*Id.* at 55.

35.　*Id.*

36.　Snyder v. Phelps, 131 S. Ct. 1207, 1219 (2011) (quoting Boos v. Barry, 485 U.S. 312, 322 (1988)).

37.　*See, e.g.*, THOMAS I. EMERSON, THE SYSTEM OF FREEDOM OF EXPRESSION 556 (1970); DANIEL J. SOLOVE, THE FUTURE OF REPUTATION (2008); Edward J. Bloustein, *Privacy, Tort Law, and the Constitution: Is Warren and Brandeis's Tort Petty and Unconstitutional as Well?*, 46 TEX. L. REV. 611 (1968); Harry Kalven Jr., *Privacy in Tort Law—Were Warren & Brandeis Wrong?*, 31 LAW & CONTEMP. PROBS. 326, 327 (1966); Julie E. Cohen, *Examined Lives: Informational Privacy and the Subject as Object*, 52 STAN. L. REV. 1373 (2000); Peter B. Edelman, *Free Press v. Privacy: Haunted by the Ghost of Justice Black*, 68 TEX. L. REV. 1195 (1990); Marc. A. Franklin, *A Constitutional Problem in Privacy Protection: Legal Inhibitions on Reporting of Fact*, 16 STAN. L. REV. 107 (1963); Amy Gajda, *Judging Journalism: The Turn Toward Privacy and Judicial Regulation of the Press*, 97 CAL. L. REV. 1039 (2009); Ruth Gavison, *Too Early for a Requiem: Warren and Brandeis Were Right on Privacy vs. Free Speech*, 43 S.C. L. REV. 437 (1992); Paul Gewirtz, *Privacy and Speech*, 2001 SUP. CT. REV. 139 (2001); Robert C. Post, *The Social Foundations of Privacy: Community and Self in the Common Law Tort*, 77 CAL. L. REV. 957 (1989); Roscoe Pound, *The Fourteenth Amendment and the Right of Privacy*, 13 W. RES. L. REV. 34 (1961); William Prosser, *Privacy*, 48 CAL. L. REV. 383 (1960); Neil M. Richards, *Reconciling Data Privacy and the First Amendment*, 52 UCLA L. REV. 1149 (2005); Frederick Schauer, *Free Speech and the Social Construction of Privacy*, 68 SOC. RES. 221 (2001); Eugene Volokh, *Freedom of Speech and Information Privacy: The Troubling Implications of a Right to Stop People from Speaking About You*, 52 STAN. L. REV. 1049 (2000).

38.　Kalven, *supra*, at 328.

39.　Zimmerman, *supra*, at 293.

40.　Post, *supra*, at 1007–08. Post goes on to assert that "[c]ommon law courts, like the rest of us are searching for ways to mediate between these two necessary and yet conflicting regimes. We can understand the public disclosure tort, then, as holding a flickering candle to what Max Weber called in 1918 the 'fate of our times,' which is of course the 'rationalization and intellectualization, and above all, … the 'disenchantment of the world.'" *Id.* at 1008.

41.　SOLOVE, FUTURE OF REPUTATION, *supra*, at 129, 160.

42. Zimmerman, *supra*; Volokh, *supra*.

43. *See, e.g.*, Michaels v. Internet Entertainment Grp., Inc., 5 F. Supp. 2d 823 (C.D. Cal. 1998).

44. *Id.* at 44.

45. Richards, *The Puzzle of Brandeis, supra*, at 1323–24.

46. Both Article 8(2) and Article 11(2), for instance, contain an exception for the right that it may be limited when "necessary in a democratic society" for "the protection of the rights and freedoms of others." Mosley v. News Group Newspapers Ltd. [2008] EMLR 679; Gavin Philipson, *Transforming Breach of Confidence? Towards a Common Law Right of Privacy under the Human Rights Act*, 66 MOD. L. REV. 726 (2003).

47. Whitney v. California, 274 U.S. 357, 375–76 (1927) (Brandeis, J., concurring).

Chapter 4

1. Lisa W. Foderaro, *Private Moment Made Public, Then a Fatal Jump*, N.Y. TIMES, Sept. 29, 2010.

2. Ian Parker, *The Story of a Suicide*, THE NEW YORKER, Feb. 6, 2012.

3. *Id.*

4. The "It Gets Better Project" was launched a day before Tyler Clementi's suicide, but the public debate the suicide generated undoubtedly aided the project in its mission. See http://www.itgetsbetter.org/pages/about-it-gets-better-project/.

5. *E.g.*, Kelly Heyboer, *Rutgers Freshman Is Presumed Dead in Suicide after Roommate Broadcast Gay Sexual Encounter Online*, THE STAR-LEDGER, Sept. 29, 2010.

6. Bartnicki v. Vopper, 200 F.3d 109, 116 (3d. Cir. 1999) (quoting Smith v. Daily Mail Publ'g Co. 443 U.S. 97, 103 (1979), *aff'd*, 532 U.S. 514 (2001)).

7. LEE BOLLINGER, UNINHIBITED, ROBUST, AND WIDE-OPEN 18 (2010).

8. DANIEL J. SOLOVE, THE FUTURE OF REPUTATION 129 (2007).

9. Bartnicki, *supra*, at 127.

10. *See, e.g.*, Michaels v. Internet Entm't Grp., Inc., 5 F. Supp. 2d 823 (C.D. Cal. 1998).

11. Snyder v. Phelps, 131 S. Ct. 1207, 1211 (2011).

12. Bartnicki v. Vopper, 532 U.S. 514, 532 n.19 (2001).

13. Smith v. Daily Mail Publ'g Co., 443 U.S. 97, 103 (1979).

14. ERWIN CHEMERINSKY, CONSTITUTIONAL LAW: PRINCIPLES AND POLICIES 687 (4th ed. 2011).

15. *E.g.*, N.Y. Times v. United States 403 U.S. 713, 726 (1971) (Brennan, J., concurring) (quoting Near v. Minn, 283 U.S. 697, 716 (1931)).

16. *N.Y. Times*, 403 *U.S.* at 730–40 (White, J., concurring).

17. 18 U.S.C. § 793(e).

18. Landmark Commc'ns v. Va., 435 U.S. 829 (1978).

19. Neb. Press Ass'n v. Stuart, 427 U.S. 539 (1976).

20. *See* Gavin J. Phillipson, *Trial By Media: The Betrayal of the First Amendment's Purpose*, 71 L. & CONTEMP. PROBS. 15, 16–17 (2008).

21. Nick Bravin, *See You in Court Mr. Assange*, SLATE, Dec. 10, 2010, available at http://www.slate.com/id/2276592.

22. 4 WILLIAM BLACKSTONE, COMMENTARIES ON THE LAWS OF ENGLAND 169 (1769).

23. RESTATEMENT (SECOND) OF TORTS § 652B (2011).

24. This point is also made clear by the RESTATEMENT (SECOND) OF TORTS § 652B, cmts. a–b (1977).

25. Hamberger v. Eastman, 206 A.2d 239 (N.H. 1964).

26. *Id.* at 242.

27. *Id.*

28. Dietemann v. Time, Inc., 449 F.2d 245, 245 (9th Cir. 1971).

29. *Id.* at 249.

30. *Id.*

31. *See, e.g.*, Desnick v. Am. Broad. Co., 44 F.3d 1345 (7th Cir. 1995) (finding no intrusion on facts similar to those in Dietemann, except that the intrusion took place in a medical office building rather than a home).

32. Shulman v. Grp. W Prods., Inc., 955 P.2d 469, 493–94 (Cal. 1998).

33. *See, e.g.*, 720 ILL. COMP. STAT. ANN. 5/14–2 (West 2006) (eavesdropping); 18 U.S.C. § 2518 (2012) (wiretapping); LA. REV. STAT. ANN. § 14:283 (video voyeurism); CAL. CIV. CODE § 1708.8 (West 2011) (paparazzi).

34. N.J. STAT. ANN. § 2C:14–9 (West 2004).

35. Food Lion, Inc. v. Capital Cities/ABC, Inc., 194 F.3d 505(4th Cir. 1999); Desnick v. Am. Broad. Cos., 44 F.3d 1345 (7th Cir. 1995); Dietemann v. Time, 449 F.2d 245 (9th Cir. 1971); Rodney A. Smolla, *Information as Contraband: The First Amendment and Liability for Trafficking in Speech*, 96 NW. U. L. REV. 1099 (2002).

36. Seth Kreimer makes a creative argument to this effect. Seth F. Kreimer, *Pervasive Image Capture and the First Amendment: Memory, Discourse, and the Right to Record*, 159 U. PENN. L. REV. 335 (2011).

37. This is the fact pattern of the famous intrusion case of *Hamberger v. Eastman*, 206 A.2d 239 (N.H. 1964), in which a landlord had installed a secret listening device in the bedroom of his tenants, a married couple. But intrusion can also remedy invasions of private spaces that do not collect information—for example, a pattern of harassing phone calls that invade the tranquility of a victim's home.

38. Daniel J. Solove & Neil M. Richards, *Rethinking Free Speech and Civil Liability*, 109 COLUM. L. REV. 1650 (2009).

39. *See* VIDEO VOYEURISM PREVENTION ACT OF 2004, 18 U.S.C. § 1801 (West 2004); DANIEL J. SOLOVE & PAUL M. SCHWARTZ, PRIVACY LAW FUNDAMENTALS 22 (2011) (collecting state laws).

40. ACLU v. Alvarez, 679 F.3d 583 (2012).

Chapter 5

1. U.S. Dep't of Health, Educ. & Welfare, *Records, Computers, and the Rights of Citizens: Report of the Secretary's Advisory Comm. On Automated Personal Data Systems* (1973).

2. Marc Rotenberg, *Fair Information Practices and the Architecture of Privacy*, 2001 STAN. TECH. L. REV. 1 (2001).

3. DANIEL J. SOLOVE AND PAUL M. SCHWARTZ, INFORMATION PRIVACY LAW 37–40 (4th ed. 2011).

4. Joel R. Reidenberg, *Setting Standards for Fair Information Practice in the U.S. Private Sector*, 80 IOWA L. REV. 497, 514–15 (1995).

5. European Commission, *Commission Proposes a Comprehensive Reform of the Data Protection Rules* (Jan. 25, 2012), http://ec.europa.eu/justice/newsroom/data-protection/news/120125_en.htm.

6. VIKTOR MAYER-SCHÖNBERGER, DELETE: THE VIRTUE OF FORGETTING IN THE DIGITAL AGE (2009).

7. 18 U.S.C. § 2710(e); 15 U.S.C. § 1681(w).

8. Center for Democracy and Technology, *On the "Right To Be Forgotten": Challenges and Suggested Changes to the Data Protection Regulation*, May 2, 2013, available at https://www.cdt.org/files/pdfs/CDT-Free-Expression-and-the-RTBF.pdf.

9. Paul M. Schwartz, *Free Speech vs. Information Privacy: Eugene Volokh's First Amendment Jurisprudence*, 52 STAN. L. REV. 1559, 1561–62 (2000).

10. Neil M. Richards, *Reconciling Data Privacy and the First Amendment*, 52 UCLA L. REV. 1149, 1167–68 (2005).

11. 20 U.S.C. § 1232g.

12. *See, e.g.*, MO. REV. STAT. § 182.817 (2000); (representative state library privacy statute); Health Insurance Portability and Accountability Act Regulations (HIPAA), 45 C.F.R §§ 160–164 (2002) (health privacy); Fair Credit Reporting Act, 15 U.S.C. § 1681 (1970) (consumer financial information).

13. Richards, *Reconciling Data Privacy, supra*, at 1194–1207.

14. Daniel J. Solove & Neil M. Richards, *Rethinking Free Speech and Civil Liability*, 109 COLUM. L. REV. 1650 (2009).

15. Eugene Volokh, *Freedom of Speech and Information Privacy: The Troubling Implications of a Right to Stop People from Speaking About You*, 52 STAN. L. REV. 1049, 1050–51 (2000).

16. FRED H. CATE, PRIVACY IN THE INFORMATION AGE 68–71 (1997).

17. Jeffrey Rosen, *The Right to Be Forgotten*, 64 STAN. L. REV. ONLINE 88 (2013).

18. Bartnicki v. Vopper, 532 U.S. 514, 527–28 (2001); Fla. Star v. B.J.F., 491 U.S. 524, 526 (1989); Smith v. Daily Mail Publ'g Co., 443 U.S. 97 (1979); Okla. Publ'g Corp. v. Okla. Cnty. Dist. Court, 430 U.S. 308 (1977); Cox Broad. Corp. v. Cohn, 420 U.S. 469 (1975).

19. *Bartnicki*, 532 U.S. at 529 (quoting *Florida Star*, 491 U.S. at 532–33).

20. *See generally* Richards, *Reconciling Data Privacy, supra*, at 1182–83 (collecting examples).

21. Solove & Richards, *supra*.
22. Cohen v. Cowles Media Co., 501 U.S. 663, 670 (1991).
23. Individual Reference Servs. Group v. FTC, 145 F. Supp. 2d 6 (D.D.C. 2001), *aff'd sub nom.* Trans Union LLC v. FTC, 295 F.3d 42 (D.C. Cir. 2002). *See also* Trans Union Corp. v. FTC, 245 F.3d 809, 818–19 (D.C. Cir. 2001), *cert. denied sub nom.* Trans Union LLC v. FTC, 536 U.S. 915 (2002), Justice Kennedy dissenting from denial of certiorari, 536 U.S. 915, 916 (2002).
24. On its website, IMS declares itself as "a leading provider of information, services and technology for the healthcare industry," and as a provider of "analytics and services: Integrated solutions across healthcare to optimize commercial effectiveness, clinical decisions and care delivery." See www.imshealth.com.
25. *Id.*
26. Christopher R. Smith, *Somebody's Watching Me: Protecting Patient Privacy in Prescription Health Information*, 36 VT. L. REV. 931 (2012).
27. VT. STAT. ANN. tit. 18, § 4631 (Supp. 2010).
28. IMS Health, Inc. v. Ayotte, 550 F.3d 42, 91 (1st Cir. 2008), *rev'd sub nom.* Sorrell v. IMS Health Inc., 131 S. Ct. 2653 (2011).
29. Sorrell v. IMS Health Inc., 131 S. Ct. 2653 (2011).
30. *Id.* at 2672.
31. *Id.* at 2663.
32. 505 U.S. 377 (1992).
33. *Id.* at 391.
34. *Sorrell,* 131 S. Ct. at 2657 (citing *R.A.V. supra*).
35. *Id.* at 2663.
36. *Id.* at 2667 (citations omitted).
37. *Id.*
38. *Id.* at 2763 (Breyer, J., dissenting).
39. Ashutosh Bhagwat, *Sorrell v. IMS Health: Details, Detailing, and the Death of Privacy*, 36 VT. L. REV. 855, 856 (2012).
40. Jane Bambauer, *Is Data Speech?* 66 STAN. L. REV. 57, 63 (2014).
41. Volokh, *supra*, at 1051.
42. 42 U.S.C. § 1320d-2; 45 CFR pts. 160 and 164 (2010).
43. Sorrell, 131 S. Ct at 2668.
44. Sorrell, 131 S. Ct. at 2672.
45. See ERWIN CHEMERINSKY, CONSTITUTIONAL LAW 474, 529–30 (2001).
46. See Richards, *Reconciling Data Privacy, supra*, at 1168–1181; Frederick Schauer, *The Boundaries of the First Amendment: A Preliminary Exploration of Constitutional Salience*, 117 HARV. L. REV. 1765 (2004).
47. See Schauer, *supra*, at 1805 (providing examples).
48. See Schauer, *supra*, at 1768.
49. *See, e.g.,* GEOFFREY R. STONE ET AL., THE FIRST AMENDMENT 3 (4th ed. 2012).
50. *See, e.g.,* RONALD KROTOSZYNSKI, THE FIRST AMENDMENT IN CROSS-CULTURAL PERSPECTIVE 12–25 (2006).

51. For political expression, see, e.g., *New York Times v. Sullivan,* 376 U.S. 254 (1964); *Cohen v. California,* 403 U.S. 15 (1971). For artistic expression, see, e.g., *Burstyn v. Wilson,* 343 U.S. 495 (1952); *Brown v. Entertainment Merchants Association,* 131 S. Ct. 2729 (2011). For advertising, see, e.g., *Central Hudson Gas & Electric Corp. v. Public Service Commission of New York,* 447 U.S. 557 (1980); *Lorillard Tobacco Co. v. Reilly,* 533 U.S. 525 (2001).

52. *See, e.g.,* R.A.V. v. City of St. Paul, 505 U.S. 377 (1992) (cross burning); *Cohen, supra* note 51, (swearing); Barnes v. Glen Theatre, Inc., 501 U.S. 560 (1991); Schad v. Borough of Mt. Ephraim, 452 U.S. 61 (1981) (nude dancing); Ashcroft v. ACLU, 535 U.S. 564 (2002) (virtual child pornography); Bridges v. California, 314 U.S. 252 (1941) (threats); United States v. Alvarez, 132 S. Ct. 2537 (2012) (lies); Snyder v. Phelps, 131 S. Ct. 1207 (2011) (hate speech); Boy Scouts of America v. Dale, 530 U.S. 620 (2000) (discrimination).

53. ALEXANDER BICKEL, THE LEAST DANGEROUS BRANCH 16 (1962).

54. *See* Barry Friedman, *The History of the Countermajoritarian Difficulty, Part Three: The Lesson of Lochner,* 76 N.Y.U. L. REV. 1383, 1392 (2001).

55. G. EDWARD WHITE, THE CONSTITUTION AND THE NEW DEAL 241–42 (2000).

56. 198 U.S. 45 (1905).

57. BARRY CUSHMAN, RETHINKING THE NEW DEAL COURT 54–56 (1998).

58. Jack M. Balkin, *"Wrong the Day It Was Decided":* Lochner *and Constitutional Historicism,* 85 B.U. L. REV. 677 (2005).

59. *Id.*

60. Richards, *Reconciling Data Privacy, supra,* at 1210–21. I should disclose that I gave pro bono counsel to the state of Vermont during the *Sorrell* litigation.

61. Sorrell, 131 S. Ct at 2685 (Breyer, J., dissenting).

62. 15 U.S.C. § 16781c(b).

63. European Commission, *supra.*

64. Center for Democracy and Technology, *supra.*

Chapter 6

1. HENRY DAVID THOREAU, WALDEN 61 (1992) (1854).

2. TIMOTHY MACKLEM, INDEPENDENCE OF MIND 56 (2006).

3. Jessica Litman, *The Public Domain,* 39 EMORY L.J. 965, 965–66 (1990) (internal citations omitted). *See also* JAMES BOYLE, SHAMANS, SOFTWARE, AND SPLEENS: LAW AND THE CONSTRUCTION OF THE INFORMATION ECONOMY ch. 6 (1997); JAMES BOYLE, THE PUBLIC DOMAIN: ENCLOSING THE COMMONS OF THE MIND (Yale 2008); LAWRENCE LESSIG, FREE CULTURE (2004).

4. Whitney v. California, 274 U.S. 357, 375 (Brandeis, J., concurring).

5. For classic examples of the search for truth rationale, see JOHN STUART MILL, ON LIBERTY 53 (Stefan Colli ed. 1989) (1859); Abrams v. United States, 250 U.S. 616, 624–31 (1919) (Holmes, J., dissenting); for the democratic self-governance rationale, see ALEXANDER MEIKLEJOHN, FREE

SPEECH AND ITS RELATION TO SELF-GOVERNMENT 93–94 (1948) and Whitney v. California, 274 U.S. 357, 376 (1927) (Brandeis, J., concurring); and for individual autonomy-promoting theories, see C. Edwin Baker, *Scope of the First Amendment Freedom of Speech*, 25 UCLA L. REV. 964, 991 (1978); Martin H. Redish, *The Value of Free Speech*, 130 U. PA. L. REV. 591, 594 (1982); David A. J. Richards, *Free Speech and Obscenity Law: Toward a Moral Theory of the First Amendment*, 123 U. PA. L. REV. 45, 62 (1974); and Thomas Scanlon, *A Theory of Freedom of Expression*, 1 PHIL. & PUB. AFF. 204, 210–19 (1972).

6. Meiklejohn, *supra*, at 27.
7. Abrams, 250 U.S. at 630.
8. *Id.*
9. *See, e.g.*, LEE C. BOLLINGER, UNINHIBITED, ROBUST, AND WIDE-OPEN: A FREE PRESS FOR A NEW CENTURY 46–47 (2010).
10. Snyder v. Phelps, 131 S. Ct. 1207 (2011).
11. *See, e.g.*, IVAN HARE & JAMES WEINSTEIN, EDS., EXTREME SPEECH AND DEMOCRACY (Oxford 2009); RONALD J. KROTOSZYNSKI JR., THE FIRST AMENDMENT IN CROSS-CULTURAL PERSPECTIVE: A COMPARATIVE LEGAL ANALYSIS OF THE FREEDOM OF SPEECH (2009).
12. *See, e.g.*, Danielle Keats Citron, *Cyber Civil Rights*, 89 B.U. L. REV. 61 (2009).
13. United States Senate, *Final Report of the Select Committee to Study Governmental Operations with Respect to Intelligence Activities*, Vol. 3 (1976).
14. Neil M. Richards, *The Dangers of Surveillance*, 126 HARV. L. REV. 1934, 1954 (2013).
15. Electronic Communications Privacy Act, 18 U.S.C. §§ 2510–2522 (2006).
16. Virtually all Western countries include a protection for freedom of speech. *See, e.g.*, U.S. CONST. AMEND. I; EUROPEAN CONVENTION ON HUMAN RIGHTS Art. 11 (1950); UK Human Rights Act of 1998 (incorporating the ECHR including Art. 11 into English law). For an overview of which national constitutions protect free speech and press, see David S. Law & Mila Versteeg, *The Evolution and Ideology of Global Constitutionalism*, 99 CALIF. L. REV. 1163 (2011).
17. Jeremy Bentham, Letter V, in THE PANOPTICON WRITINGS 43 (Verso 1995) (1787).
18. MICHEL FOUCAULT, DISCIPLINE AND PUNISH 200 (1975).
19. Bentham, *supra*.
20. GEORGE ORWELL, NINETEEN EIGHTY-FOUR (Penguin 1983) (1949).
21. *Id.* at 2–3.
22. *See generally* DAVID LYON, SURVEILLANCE STUDIES: AN OVERVIEW (Polity 2007).
23. *E.g.*, Brandon Welsh & David P. Farrington, *Effects of Closed-Circuit Television on Crime*, 587 ANNALS AM ACAD. POL. & SOC. SCI. 110 (May, 2003); Kevin Walby, *Police Surveillance of Male-with-Male Public Sex in Ontario, 1983–94*, in SURVEILLANCE: POWER, PROBLEMS, POLITICS (Sean

P. Hier & Josh Greenberg eds., 2010); GARY MARX, UNDERCOVER: POLICE SURVEILLANCE IN AMERICA (1988); JOHN GILLIOM, OVERSEERS OF THE POOR (2001); MIKE MCCAHILL, THE SURVEILLANCE WEB (2002); TIM NEWBURN & STEPHANIE HAYMAN, POLICING, SURVEILLANCE, AND SOCIAL CONTROL (2002); KENT UNNELL, PISSING ON DEMAND (2004).

24. *See, e.g.*, KEVIN D. HAGGERTY & MINAS SAMATAS, EDS., SURVEILLANCE AND DEMOCRACY (2010); Kevin Haggerty & Amber Gaszo, *Seeing Beyond the Ruins: Surveillance as a Response to Terrorist Threats*, 30 CANADIAN J. SOC. 169 (2005); DAVID LYON, THE ELECTRONIC EYE: THE RISE OF SURVEILLANCE SOCIETY (1994); OSCAR GANDY, THE PANOPTIC SORT (1993); JAMES B. RULE, PRIVATE LIVES AND PUBLIC SURVEILLANCE (1974); ALAN F. WESTIN, PRIVACY AND FREEDOM (1967).

25. Melissa Bateson et al., *Cues of Being Watched Enhance Cooperation in a Real-World Setting*, 2 BIOLOGY LETTERS 412, 412–14 (2006).

26. LYON, THE ELECTRONIC EYE, *supra*, at 5.

27. TIM NEWBURN & STEPHANIE HAYMAN, POLICING, SURVEILLANCE, AND SOCIAL CONTROL (2002).

28. Hustler Magazine v. Falwell, 485 U.S. 46, 52 (1988).

29. *Id.*

30. For example, in *Laird v. Tatum*, 408 U.S. 1 (1972), the Supreme Court accepted the idea that surveillance of political activities can violate the First Amendment, but declined to find a violation under the facts of that case. *In Tattered Cover v. City of Thornton*, 44 P.3d 1044 (Colo. 2002), the Colorado Supreme Court held that the free speech provision of the Colorado Constitution included a right to read anonymously that was chilled by government seizure of bookstore records.

31. MACKLEM, *supra*, at 36.

Chapter 7

1. Notice of Motion and Motion to Compel Compliance with Subpoena Duces Tecum at 4, Gonzales v. Google, Inc., No. CV 06–8006 MISC JW, 2006 WL 778720, at *679 (N.D. Cal. Mar. 17, 2006).

2. Gonzales v. Google, Inc., 234 F.R.D. 674, 679 (N.D.Cal. 2006).

3. Order Granting in Part and Denying in Part Motion to Compel Compliance with Subpoena Duces Tecum at 3, 16, Gonzales v. Google, Inc., 234 F.R.D. 674 (2006).

4. Communications Decency Act of 1996, 47 U.S.C. § 230 (2006).

5. Peter H. Lewis, *Protest, Cyberspace-Style, for New Law*, N.Y. TIMES, Feb. 8, 1996.

6. Reno v. ACLU, 521 U.S. 844 (1997).

7. *Reno*, 521 U.S. at 870.

8. Before it was struck down, COPA was codified at 47 U.S.C. § 231.

9. Ashcroft v. ACLU, 542 U.S. 656 (2004).

10. *Id.* at 668.

11. *Gonzales*, Notice of Motion, *supra*, at 3.

12. Gonzales v. Google, Inc., 234 F.R.D. 674, 677 (N.D.Cal. 2006).

13. *Id.* at 688.

14. *Id.* at 686–87.

15. Michael Barbaro & Tom Zeller, Jr., *A Face is Exposed for AOL Searcher No. 4417749*, N.Y. TIMES, Aug. 9, 2006.

16. Paul Ohm, *Broken Promises of Privacy: Responding to the Surprising Failure of Anonymization*, 57 UCLA L. REV. 1701 (2010).

17. J. B. BURY, A HISTORY OF FREEDOM OF THOUGHT 14 (1913).

18. RENÉ DESCARTES, DISCOURSE ON THE METHOD (1637).

19. JOHN MILTON, AREOPAGITICA (1644).

20. JOHN STUART MILL, ON LIBERTY 9 (Stefan Colli ed. 1989) (1859).

21. *Id.* at 8.

22. The Treason Act of 1351, 25 Edw. 3, Stat. 5, c.2.; see also William O. Douglas, *The Right of Association*, 63 COLUM. L. REV. 1361, 1364 (1963).

23. Instructions by the Virginia Convention to Their Delegates in Congress, 1774, in 1 JEFFERSON, PAPERS 141, 143 (Boyd ed., 1950).

24. Douglas, *supra*, at 1365.

25. 4 WILLIAM BLACKSTONE, COMMENTARIES *151–52.

26. JONATHAN SWIFT, GULLIVER'S TRAVELS 124 (Herbert Davis ed., 1977) (1726).

27. *See* 3 JOSEPH STORY, COMMENTARIES ON THE CONSTITUTION OF THE UNITED STATES 705–07 (Carolina Academic Press 1987) (1833). *See also id.* at 727.

28. *See* An Act for Establishing Religious Freedom, 12 HENINGS STATUTES AT LARGE 84 (facsimile reprint 1969) (1823).

29. James Madison, *Memorial and Remonstrance Against Religious Assessments* (1785), in 2 THE WRITINGS OF JAMES MADISON 183, 184 (Gaillard Hunt ed., 1901).

30. U.S. CONST. art. VI.

31. U.S. CONST. art. III, § 3.

32. LEONARD LEVY, ORIGINS OF THE FIFTH AMENDMENT (1968).

33. LEVY, *id.* at 245 (quoting Jenner's Case, Stowe MS. 424, fols. 159b–160a (1611)).

34. William J. Stuntz, *The Substantive Origins of Criminal Procedure*, 105 YALE L.J. 393, 415–16 (1995).

35. U.S. CONST. amend. V.

36. Nita Farahy, *Incriminating Thoughts*, 64 STAN. L. REV. 351, 361–64 (2012).

37. Stuntz, *supra*, at 413–14.

38. *Id.* at 418.

39. U.S. CONST. amend. IV.

40. Ken I. Kersch, *The Reconstruction of Constitutional Privacy Rights and the New American State*, 16 STUD. AM. POL. DEV. 61, 76 (2002).

41. See Stuntz, *supra*.

42. LEONARD W. LEVY, ORIGINS OF THE BILL OF RIGHTS 159–63 (1999).

43. For more on Wilkes's colorful life, see ARTHUR CASH, JOHN WILKES: THE SCANDALOUS FATHER OF CIVIL LIBERTY (2007).

44. *Id.*

45. Stuntz, *supra.*

46. Stuntz, *supra*, at 403.

47. 98 U.S. 145 (1878).

48. *Id.* at 166.

49. 279 U.S. 644, 654–55 (1929) (Holmes, J., dissenting).

50. Olmstead v. United States, 277 U.S. 438, 478 (1928) (Brandeis, J., dissenting).

51. Palko v. Connecticut, 302 U.S. 319, 327 (1937).

52. G. Edward White, *The First Amendment Comes of Age: The Emergence of Free Speech in Twentieth-Century America*, 95 MICH. L. REV. 299, 330–42 (1996); Neil M. Richards, *The "Good War," the Jehovah's Witnesses, and the First Amendment*, 87 VA. L. REV. 781, 781–82 (2001) (book review).

53. See Neil M. Richards, *Intellectual Privacy*, 87 TEX. L. REV. 387, 411 n.141 (2008) (collecting cases).

54. 319 U.S. 624 (1943).

55. *Id.* at 642.

56. See Richards, *Intellectual Privacy, supra*, at 412 n.144 (collecting cases).

57. Stanley v. Georgia, 394 U.S. 557, 568 (1969).

58. ALEXANDER MEIKLEJOHN, FREE SPEECH AND ITS RELATION TO SELF-GOVERNMENT, 24–27 (1948).

59. JONATHAN ZITTRAIN, THE FUTURE OF THE INTERNET (AND HOW TO STOP IT) (2009).

60. John Perry Barlow, *A Declaration of the Independence of Cyberspace*, Feb. 8, 1996, available at https://projects.eff.org/~barlow/Declaration-Final.html.

61. *Id.*

62. *Id.*

63. J. C. R. Licklider, *Man-Computer Symbiosis,* IRE TRANSACTIONS ON HUMAN FACTORS IN ECONOMICS HFE-1, at 4 (1960).

64. TIM BERNERS-LEE, WEAVING THE WEB 2 (1999).

65. Digital Millennium Copyright Act, 17 U.S.C. §§ 512, 1201–1205, 1301–1332; 28 U.S.C. § 4001 (2006).

66. Council Directive 2006/24/EC, on the Retention of Data Generated or Processed in Connection with the Provision of Publicly Available Electronic Communications Services or of Public Communications Networks and Amending Directive 2002/58/EC, 2006 O.J. (L 105/54).

67. NICHOLAS CARR, THE BIG SWITCH: REWIRING THE WORLD, FROM EDISON TO GOOGLE 110 (2008).

68. TIM WU, THE MASTER SWITCH 172 (2010).

69. VIKTOR MAYER-SCHÖNBERGER, DELETE: THE VIRTUE OF FORGETTING IN THE DIGITAL AGE 52 (2009).

70. *E.g.,* http://www.amazon.com/Kindle-Paperwhite-Resolution-Display-Built-/dp/B007OZNZG0/ref=r_kdia_h_i_gl.

71. JOHN BATTELLE, THE SEARCH (2006).

Chapter 8

1. Chris Irvine, *Sir Salman Rushdie: 'Fifty Shades of Grey makes Twilight look like War and Peace'*, THE GUARDIAN, Oct. 9, 2012.

2. Julie Bosman, *Discreetly Digital, Erotic Novel Sets American Women Abuzz*, N.Y. TIMES, Mar. 9, 2012.

3. Barbara W. Tuchman, *The Book*, 34(2) BULL. AM. ACAD. ARTS & SCI. (Nov. 1980).

4. MARYANNE WOLF, PROUST AND THE SQUID: THE STORY AND SCIENCE OF THE READING BRAIN (2007).

5. NICHOLAS CARR, THE SHALLOWS: WHAT THE INTERNET IS DOING TO OUR BRAINS 60 (2010).

6. ST. AUGUSTINE, CONFESSIONS 114 (Penguin 1961).

7. CARR, THE SHALLOWS, *supra*, at 74.

8. Jacobellis v. Ohio, 378 U.S. 184, 197 (1964) (Stewart, J., concurring).

9. Miller v. California, 413 U.S. 15, 24 (1973).

10. Kathleen M. Sullivan, *The First Amendment Wars*, THE NEW REPUBLIC, Sept. 28, 1992, at 37.

11. Stanley v. Georgia, 394 U.S. 557 (1969).

12. The facts of the case can be found in *Home Movies*, TIME, Apr. 18, 1969, at 78; in the U.S. Supreme Court's opinion, 394 U.S. 557 (1969); and at the transcript of oral argument before the Supreme Court, available at http://law2.umkc.edu/faculty/projects/ftrials/conlaw/Stanleyoral.html, and the earlier opinion of the Supreme Court of Georgia upholding Stanley's conviction. Stanley v. State, 224 Ga. 259 (1968). Georgia charged Stanley under Ga. Code Ann. § 26-6301 (Supp. 1968).

13. *Stanley*, 394 U.S. at 559.

14. *Id*. at 568.

15. Id. at 564.

16. *Id*. at 565.

17. *See* Osborne v. Ohio, 495 U.S. 103 (1990).

18. Ashcroft v. Free Speech Coalition, 535 U.S. 234 (2002).

19. *See, e.g.*, Rebekah Denn, *Is It Creepy That Amazon is Tracking Most-Highlighted Kindle Passages?*, CHRISTIAN SCI. MONITOR, May 3, 2010.

20. *Amazon.com Privacy Notice*, AMAZON.COM, http://www.amazon.com/gp/help/customer/display.html?nodeId=468496 (last updated Mar. 3, 2014).

21. *Cf.* Alexandra Alter, *Your E-Book Is Reading You*, WALL ST. J., http://online.wsj.com/article/SB10001424052702304870304577490950051438304.html (last updated July 19, 2012).

22. ELI PARISER, THE FILTER BUBBLE 44 (2011).

23. Riva Richmond, *As "Like" Buttons Spread, So Do Facebook's Tentacles*, N.Y. TIMES BITS BLOG (Sept. 27, 2011, 3:51 PM), http://bits.blogs.nytimes.com/2011/09/27/as-like-buttons-spread-so-do-facebooks-tentacles/.

24. *Id*.

25. See *Statement of Rights and Responsibilities*, FACEBOOK, https://www.facebook.com/legal/terms (last modified Nov. 1, 2013).

26. Somini Sengupta, *Rushdie Runs Afoul of Web's Real-Name Police*, N.Y. TIMES, Nov. 14, 2011. After Rushdie criticized Facebook (ironically enough) on Twitter, Facebook restored his account under the "Salman Rushdie" name. *Id.*

27. Neil M. Richards, *The Perils of Social Reading*, 101 GEO. L.J. 689 (2013).

28. David Streitfeld & Bill Miller, *Quest for Book Buys Faces High Bar*, WASH. POST, Apr. 10, 1998, at B01.

29. *See* KENNETH W. STARR, COMMUNICATION FROM KENNETH W. STARR, INDEPENDENT COUNSEL, H.R. DOC. NO. 105–310, at 19, 20 & n.61 (2d Sess. 1998).

30. Richards, *The Perils of Social Reading, supra*, at 698.

31. Digital Millennium Copyright Act, 17 U.S.C. §§ 512, 1201–1205, 1301–1332; 28 U.S.C. § 4001 (2006).

32. See Neil M. Richards & Daniel J. Solove, *Privacy's Other Path: Recovering the Law of Confidentiality*, 96 GEO. L.J. 123, 174–75 (2007).

33. See AM. MED. ASS'N, CODE OF MEDICAL ETHICS: FUNDAMENTAL ELEMENTS OF THE PATIENT-PHYSICIAN RELATIONSHIP, Opinion 10.01(4) (1992) (doctors); MODEL RULES OF PROF'L CONDUCT R. 1.6 (1983) (lawyers); AM. INST. OF CPAS, CODE OF PROF'L CONDUCT R. 301 (2011) (accountants); THE NAT'L CATHOLIC RISK RETENTION GRP., INC., MODEL CODE OF PASTORAL CONDUCT 3 (2004) (priests).

34. The *spousal communications privilege* prevents communications from a person to their spouse being introduced against them at trial. The distinct *marital privilege* allows a person to prevent their current spouse being called as a witness against them. The theory behind both privileges is that the damage that would occur to marital relationships in the absence of the privileges is greater than the harm to the truth-seeking process that the privileges cause. *See* Wolfle v. United States, 291 U.S. 7, 14 (1934).

35. Video Privacy Protection Act, 18 U.S.C. § 2710(b)(1) (1988).

36. Michael Dolan, *The Bork Tapes Saga*, THE AMERICAN PORCH: AN INFORMAL HISTORY OF AN INFORMAL PLACE, http://theamericanporch.com/bork2.htm.

37. Dolan, *The Bork Tapes Saga, supra,* at 56.

38. 134 CONG. REC. S5398–5401 (daily ed. May 10, 1988).

39. 18 U.S.C. § 2710(a)–(b).

40. 18 U.S.C. § 2710(b)–(c).

41. Amazon.com LLC v. Lay, 758 F. Supp. 2d 1154, 1158–59 (W.D. Wash. 2010) (citation omitted).

42. Dirkes v. Runnemede, 936 F. Supp. 235, 236 (D.N.J. 1996); *but see* Daniel v. Cantrell, 375 F.3d 377, 380–84 (6th Cir. 2004) (holding that law enforcement officials investigating a case are not "video tape service providers" under the VPPA).

43. *In re* Hulu Privacy Litig., No. 11–03764, 2012 WL 3282960, at *4–6 (N.D. Cal. Aug. 10, 2012).

44. See Video Privacy Protection Act, ELEC. PRIVACY INFO. CTR., http://epic. org/privacy/vppa/ (codified at 18 U.S.C. § 2710 (2002)).

45. CONN. GEN. STAT. § 53–450 (2003); MD. CODE ANN., CRIM. LAW § 3–907 (LexisNexis 2002).

46. See CAL. CIV. CODE § 1799.3 (Deering Supp. 2012); DEL. CODE ANN. tit. 11, § 925 (2007); IOWA CODE § 727.11 (2012); LA. REV. STAT. ANN. § 37:1748 (2007); N.Y. GEN. BUS. LAW § 670 (McKinney 2012); R.I. GEN. LAWS § 11–18–32 (2012).

47. MICH. COMP. LAWS § 445.1711–1715 (West 1988).

48. See Tattered Cover, Inc. v. City of Thornton, 44 P.3d 1044, 1051–53 (Colo. 2002) (en banc).

49. CAL. CIV. CODE § 1798.90 (Deering Supp. 2012).

50. Id. § 1798.90(b)(1).

51. Id. § 1798.90(c)(3).

52. Library records confidentiality is protected in at least forty-eight states and the District of Columbia. Anne Klinefelter, *Library Standards for Privacy: A Model for the Digital World?*, 11 N.C. J.L. & TECH. 553, 557 (2010). For a catalogue of such statutes, see *id.* at 562.

53. MO. REV. STAT. § 182.817 (2000).

54. Id. § 182.815 (2000).

55. For more on this development, see Richards *The Perils of, Social Reading*, *supra*; Neil M. Richards, *Keep Your Update to Yourself*, WIRED MAGAZINE: THE WIRED WORLD IN 2013 (UK Edition 2012).

Chapter 9

1. The Enzyte Commercial is *available at* http://www.youtube.com/ watch?v=ghrWz7cVXv8.

2. The facts in this paragraph can be found in Judge Boggs's opinion in United States v. Warshak, 631 F.3d 266 (6th Cir. 2010).

3. 631 F.3d at 314.

4. United States v. White, 401 U.S. 745, 746–47 (1971).

5. United States v. Miller, 425 U.S. 435 (1976).

6. Smith v. Maryland, 442 U.S. 735 (1979).

7. Id. at 745–46.

8. Olmstead v. United States, 277 U.S. 438, 466 (1928).

9. Id. at 465 (Brandeis, J., dissenting).

10. Id. at 464–66 (Brandeis, J., dissenting).

11. 277 U.S. 438, 471 (1928) (Brandeis, J., dissenting).

12. Id. at 471–72 (Brandeis, J., dissenting).

13. Id. at 473 (Brandeis, J., dissenting) (quoting *Boyd v. United States*, 116 U.S. 616, 630 (1886).)

14. Id. at 473 (Brandeis, J., dissenting).

15. Id. at 474 (Brandeis, J., dissenting).

16. Id. at 478 (Brandeis, J., dissenting).

17. *Id.* (Brandeis, J., dissenting).

18. Id. (Brandeis, J., dissenting).

19. Id. at 478–79 (Brandeis, J., dissenting).

20. *Id.* at 474 (Brandeis, J., dissenting).

21. 254 U.S. 325, 334 (1920) (Brandeis, J., dissenting).

22. *Id.* at 337–38 (Brandeis, J., dissenting) (emphasis added).

23. *Id.* at 335 (Brandeis, J., dissenting).

24. *Id.* at 335–36 (Brandeis, J., dissenting) (emphasis added).

25. Louis D. Brandeis, *Hours of Labor,* Address to the Civic Federation of New England (1906) *reprinted in* VINCENT BLASI, IDEAS OF THE FIRST AMENDMENT 702 (2d ed. 2012).

26. Robert M. Cover, *The Left, the Right, and the First Amendment: 1918–1928,* 40 MD. L. REV. 349, 377 (1981).

27. Schaefer v. United States, 251 U.S. 466, 495 (1920) (Brandeis, J., dissenting).

28. United States *ex rel.* Milwaukee Soc. Democratic Publ'g Co. v. Burleson, 255 U.S. 407, 417–36 (Brandeis, J., dissenting).

29. *Id.* at 431.

30. *See* Vincent Blasi, *The First Amendment and the Ideal of Civic Courage: The Brandeis Opinion in* Whitney v. California, 29 WM. & MARY L. REV. 653, 673–77 (1988) (providing examples).

31. *See* Melvin I. Urofsky, *The Brandeis-Frankfurter Conversations,* 1985 SUP. CT. REV. 299, 320 (1985) (published and edited version of Frankfurter's notes).

32. 262 U.S. 390 (1923).

33. MELVIN I. UROFSKY, LOUIS D. BRANDEIS: A LIFE 619 (2009).

34. Katz v. United States, 389 U.S. 347 (1967).

35. *Id.* at 360–61 (Harlan, J., concurring).

36. Omnibus Crime Control and Safe Streets Act of 1968, Pub. L. 90-351, 82 Stat. 197, enacted June 19, 1968 (codified at 42 U.S.C. § 3711).

37. Electronic Communications Privacy Act, 18 U.S.C. §§ 2510–2522 (2006).

38. United States v. United States Dist. Court, 407 U.S. 297 (1972). The case is known as the *Keith* case after Judge Damon Keith, who issued the order in the lower court.

39. *Id.* at 302.

40. Bruce Schneier, *The Eternal Value of Privacy,* WIRED MAGAZINE, May 18, 2006.

41. Neil M. Richards & Daniel J. Solove, *Privacy's Other Path: Recovering the Law of Confidentiality,* 96 GEO. L. J. 123, 133–34 (2007).

42. Anuj C. Desai, *Wiretapping Before the Wires: The Post Office and the Birth of Communications Privacy,* 60 STAN. L. REV. 553 (2007); RICHARD JOHN, SPREADING THE NEWS: THE AMERICAN POSTAL SYSTEM FROM FRANKLIN TO MORSE (1998).

43. *Ex parte* Jackson, 96 U.S. 727, 733 (1877); *see also* Desai, *supra,* at 574–75.

44. Richards & Solove, *supra,* at 142; Note, *The Right to Privacy in the Nineteenth Century,* 94 HARV. L. REV. 1892, 1899 (1981).

45. Note, *supra,* at 1899 (quoting J. HOLBROOK, TEN YEARS AMONG THE MAIL BAGS, at xviii (1855)).

46. *Cf.* Paul Gewirtz, *Privacy and Speech*, 2001 SUP. CT. REV. 139, 165 (arguing that people are best able to express themselves when they do not fear public exposure or being made the subject of gossip).

47. Neil M. Richards, *The Dangers of Surveillance*, 126 HARV. L. REV. 1934 (2013).

48. Omnibus Crime Control and Safe Streets Act of 1968, Pub. L. No. 90–351, tit. III, 82 Stat. 197, 211–23 (codified as amended in scattered sections of 18, 42, and 47 U.S.C.).

49. PRESIDENT'S COMM'N ON LAW ENFORCEMENT & ADMIN. OF JUSTICE, THE CHALLENGE OF CRIME IN A FREE SOCIETY 202 (1967).

Chapter 10

1. Neil M. Richards & Daniel J. Solove, *Prosser's Privacy Law: A Mixed Legacy*, 98 CALIF. L. REV. 1887 (2011).

2. *See* RESTATEMENT (SECOND) OF TORTS § 46 (1977).

3. Neil M. Richards & Daniel J. Solove, *Privacy's Other Path: Recovering the Law of Confidentiality*, 96 GEO. L. J. 123, 156–57 (2007).

4. RESTATEMENT (SECOND) OF TORTS § 757 (1979); *see also* Alan B. Vickery, Note, *Breach of Confidence: An Emerging Tort*, 82 COLUM. L. REV. 1426 (1982); Susan M. Gilles, *Promises Betrayed: Breach of Confidence as a Remedy for Invasion of Privacy*, 43 BUFF. L. REV. 1 (1995); Neil M. Richards & Daniel J. Solove, *Privacy's Other Path: Recovering the Law of Confidentiality*, 96 GEO. L.J. 123 (2007).

5. Daniel J. Solove & Neil M. Richards, *Rethinking Free Speech and Civil Liability*, 109 COLUM. L. REV. 1650 (2009).

6. *Id.*

7. William L. Prosser, *Privacy*, 48 CALIF. L. REV. 383, 389 (1960).

8. Meredith Bennett-Smith, *Hollie Toups Leads Women in Revenge Porn Class Action Lawsuit Against Texxxan.com, GoDaddy*, HUFFINGTON POST (Jan. 25, 2013), http://www.huffingtonpost.com/2013/01/25/hollie-toups-leads-women-suing-revenge-porn-site-texxan-go-daddy_n_2546066.html.

9. A similar argument is made by law professor Woodrow Hartzog. *See* Woodrow Hartzog, *How to Fight Revenge Porn*, THE ATLANTIC (May 10, 2013), *available at* http://www.theatlantic.com/technology/archive/2013/05/how-to-fight-revenge-porn/275759/.

10. New State Ice Co. v. Liebmann, 285 U.S. 262, 311 (1932) (Brandeis, J., dissenting).

11. *See, e.g.*, Danielle Keats Citron & David Gray, *Total Surveillance's Privacy Harms: A Reply To Professor Neil Richards*, 126 HARV. L. REV. F. 262 (2013), responding to Neil M. Richards, *The Dangers of Surveillance*, 126 HARV. L. REV. 1934 (2013).

12. For starters, I have a round head and no goatee.

13. Joel R. Reidenberg, *Setting Standards for Fair Information Practice in the U.S. Private Sector*, 80 IOWA L. REV. 497, 514–15 (1995).

14. Council Directive 95/46, art. 8, 1995 O.J. (L 281) 38 (EC).

15. Specht v. Netscape Commc'ns Corp., 306 F.3d 17, 28 (2d Cir. 2002). For purposes of full disclosure, the author represented Netscape in this case.

16. Woodrow Hartzog, *Website Design as Contract*, 60 AM. U. L. REV. 1635, 1642–45 (2011) (collecting cases).

17. *Id.* at 1650–70.

18. *See* Leslie K. John, Alessandro Acquisti & George Loewenstein, *Strangers on a Plane: Context-Dependent Willingness to Divulge Sensitive Information*, 37 J. CONSUMER RES. 858, 868 (2011); M. Ryan Calo, *Against Notice Skepticism in Privacy (And Elsewhere)*, 87 NOTRE DAME L. REV. 1027 (2012).

19. M. Ryan Calo, *People Can Be So Fake: A New Dimension to Privacy and Technology Scholarship*, 114 PENN ST. L. REV. 809, 849 (2010).

20. William McGeveran, *Disclosure, Endorsement, and Identity in Social Marketing*, 2009 U. ILL. L. REV. 1105, 1158–59.

21. Neil M. Richards, *The Limits of Tort Privacy*, 9 J. ON TELECOMM. & HIGH TECH. L. 357, 359 (2011).

22. Scott R. Peppet, *Unraveling Privacy: The Personal Prospectus and the Threat of a Full-Disclosure Future*, 105 NW. U. L. REV. 1153, 1167 (2012).

Chapter 11

1. JACK N. RAKOVE, JAMES MADISON AND THE CREATION OF THE AMERICAN REPUBLIC 97 (3rd ed. 2006). The importance Madison placed on the role of public opinion in maintaining a republican form of government is evident in James Madison, *British Government*, THE NATIONAL GAZETTE, Jan. 30, 1792, *available at* http://oll.libertyfund.org/?option=com_staticxt&staticfile=show.php%3Ftitle=1941&chapter=124395&layout=html&Itemid=27.

2. Danielle Keats Citron & Helen L. Norton, *Intermediaries and Hate Speech: Fostering Digital Citizenship for Our Information Age*, 91 B.U. L. REV. 1435 (2011).

3. *See, e.g.*, Schneider v. State, 308 U.S. 147 (1939) (leaflets); City of Ladue v. Gilleo, 512 U.S. 43 (1994) (signs).

4. Jack M. Balkin, *The Future of Free Expression in a Digital Age*, 36 PEPPERDINE L. REV. 101 (2008).

5. *See Facebook Terms of Service*, *available at* https://www.facebook.com/legal/terms.

6. *Facebook Nurse-In: 60 Breastfeeding Moms Protest at Facebook Headquarters*, HUFFINGTON POST, Feb. 8, 2012, http://www.huffingtonpost.com/2012/02/08/facebook-nurse-in-60-brea_n_1263532.html; Kristy Kemp, *Breastfeeding Advocate, Outraged When Nursing Photos Were Removed From Facebook*, HUFFINGTON POST, Apr. 4, 2013, http://www.huffingtonpost.com/2013/04/05/kristy-kemp-breastfeeding-photos_n_3021288.html.

7. D. L. Cade, *Facebook Apologizes after Banning Mom Over Breastfeeding Photo*, PETAPIXEL, Apr. 8, 2013, http://petapixel.com/2013/04/08/facebook-apologizes-after-banning-mom-over-breastfeeding-photo/.

8. Doug Gross, *Under Pressure, Facebook Targets Sexist Hate Speech*, CNN, May 30, 2013, http://www.cnn.com/2013/05/29/tech/social-media/

facebook-hate-speech-women. Larry Magrid, *Facebook Grapples with Hate Speech*, HUFFINGTON POST, June 6, 2013, http://www.huffingtonpost.com/larry-magid/facebook-hate-speech_b_3385647.html.

9. Magna Carta (1215); U.S. CONST. AMEND. I; HUMAN RIGHTS ACT OF 1998, c.42.

10. REBECCA MACKINNON, CONSENT OF THE NETWORKED, 243–48 (2012).

11. *Cf.* Citizens United v. FEC, 558 U.S. 310 (2010).

12. Washington University Student Judicial Code, art. I.A, *available at* http://wustl.edu/policies/judicial.html.

13. Gertz v. Robert Welch, Inc., 418 U.S. 323, 339–40 (1973).

14. Geoffrey Stone, *Content Regulation and the First Amendment*, 25 WM. & MARY L. REV. 189 (1983).

15. N.Y. Times Co. v. Sullivan, 376 U.S. 254, 270 (1964).

16. Jeffrey Rosen, *The Delete Squad: Google, Twitter, Facebook and the New Global Battle over the Future of Free Speech*, THE NEW REPUBLIC, Apr. 29, 2013, *available at* http://www.newrepublic.com/article/113045/free-speech-internet-silicon-valley-making-rules#; Adam Thierer, Op-Ed., *Speech Policies for Information Platforms Are Hard*, Sept. 16, 2012, FORBES, http://www.forbes.com/sites/adamthierer/2012/09/16/speech-policies-for-information-platforms-are-hard/.

17. *See* Marc Jonathan Blitz, *Constitutional Safeguards for Silent Experiments in Living*, 74 UMKC L. REV. 799, 808, 836–38 (2006).

18. CODE OF ETHICS FOR LIBRARIANS, art. 11 (1939), *quoted in* American Library Ass'n, *Privacy: An Interpretation of the* Library Bill of Rights, *in* AMERICAN LIBRARY ASS'N, INTELLECTUAL FREEDOM MANUAL 192 (7th ed. 2002) [hereinafter INTELLECTUAL FREEDOM MANUAL].

19. CODE OF ETHICS FOR LIBRARIANS, art. 3 (1995), *available at* http://www.ala.org/advocacy/proethics/codeofethics/codeofethics.

20. *Library Bill of Rights*, AM. LIBRARY ASS'N, http://www.ala.org/advocacy/intfreedom/librarybill (adopted June 19, 1939, by the ALA Council; amended October 14, 1944; June 18, 1948; February 2, 1961; June 27, 1967; January 23, 1980; inclusion of "age" reaffirmed January 23, 1996) [hereinafter *Library Bill of Rights*].

21. *See* Judith F. Krug, *ALA and Intellectual Freedom: An Historical Overview*, *in* INTELLECTUAL FREEDOM MANUAL, *supra*, at 18–20.

22. *Id.*

23. EVELYN GELLER, FORBIDDEN BOOKS IN AMERICAN PUBLIC LIBRARIES, 1876–1939: A STUDY IN CULTURAL CHANGE, at xv (1984); WAYNE A. WIEGAND, THE POLITICS OF AN EMERGING PROFESSION: THE AMERICAN LIBRARY ASSOCIATION, 1876–1917, at 9–10 (1986).

24. INTELLECTUAL FREEDOM MANUAL, *supra*, at 25–27.

25. *Library Bill of Rights, supra*.

26. INTELLECTUAL FREEDOM MANUAL, *supra*, at iv–vii.

27. Candace Morgan, Deborah Caldwell-Stone & Daniel Mach, *Privacy and Confidentiality in Libraries, in* INTELLECTUAL FREEDOM MANUAL, *supra*, at 402.

28. *Id.*

29. *Policy on Confidentiality of Library Records*, AM. LIBRARY ASS'N, http://www.ala.org/advocacy/privacyconfidentiality/privacy/privacyconfidentiality (adopted Jan. 20, 1971).

30. *Id.* (as amended July 2, 1986).

31. *Privacy: An Interpretation of the Library Bill of Rights*, AM. LIBRARY ASS'N, *in* INTELLECTUAL FREEDOM MANUAL, *supra*, at 190.

32. *Id.*

33. *Id.* at 192–93.

34. *Id.* at 193.

35. *Id.*

36. *Id.*

37. AM. LIBRARY ASS'N, RALLYING AMERICANS TO DEFEND THEIR RIGHTS IN A DIGITAL AGE: A POSITION PAPER ON INFORMATION PRIVACY 1.

38. *Id.*

39. *Id.*

40. See USA PATRIOT Act of 2001 § 215, 50 U.S.C. §§ 1861–1862 (West Supp. 2002).

41. CAMPAIGN FOR READER PRIVACY, http://www.readerprivacy.org/.

42. *Choose Privacy Week*, CHOOSEPRIVACYWEEK.ORG, http://www.chooseprivacyweek.org.

43. Ann Cavoukian, *Privacy By Design: The Seven Foundational Principles* (2011), *available at* http://www.privacybydesign.ca/content/uploads/2009/08/7foundationalprinciples.pdf.

44. THE MOZILLA MANIFESTO, *available at* http://www.mozilla.org/en-US/about/manifesto/.

45. STEPHEN LEVY, IN THE PLEX: HOW GOOGLE THINKS, WORKS, AND SHAPES OUR LIVES (2011).

46. Balkin, *supra*, at 101.

Chapter 12

1. *E.g.*, Glenn Greenwald & Ewen MacAskill, *NSA PRISM Program Taps into User Data of Apple, Google, and Others*, THE GUARDIAN, June 6, 2013.

2. James Bamford, *The Black Box*, WIRED, Apr. 2012, at 78, 80.

3. DANIEL J. SOLOVE, NOTHING TO HIDE (2011).

4. ALEXANDER MEIKLEJOHN, FREE SPEECH AND ITS RELATION TO SELF-GOVERNMENT 27 (1948).

5. Whitney v. California, 274 U.S. 357, 375–76 (1927) (Brandeis, J., concurring).

INDEX

215